Micro-Entrepreneurship

FOR

DUMMIES

A Wiley Brand

by Paul Mladjenovic
Author of *Stock Investing For Dummies*, 4th Edition

FOR

DUMMIES
A Wiley Brand

Micro-Entrepreneurship For Dummies®

Published by
John Wiley & Sons, Inc.
111 River St.
Hoboken, NJ 07030-5774
www.wiley.com

About the Author

Paul Mladjenovic, CFP is a nationally sought after micro-entrepreneur, consultant, speaker, and author. His companies, PM Financial and Prosperity Network, help companies achieve higher levels of success and profitability and individuals with financial matters, especially to launch their own home-based business. In 1985 he achieved his Certified Financial Planner practitioner (CFP) designation. He leads national seminars on business start-up topics, including: the "Home Business Goldmine" and "How to Start a Zero-Cost Internet Business" (found at www.ravingcapitalist.com).

In 2012 he published the fifth edition of his book *Zero-Cost Marketing* (www.zerocostmarketing.net), helping businesses both small and large to achieve unprecedented success with minimal cost. Additionally, Paul's video program "Tax Winner" (www.taxwinner.com) offers home-based businesses tax education.

Paul has written *Stock Investing For Dummies,* 4th Edition, *Precious Metals Investing For Dummies* (both by John Wiley & Sons, Inc.), and the *Job Hunter's Encyclopedia* (Prosperity Network). The Kindle edition of *Stock Investing For Dummies* was ranked No. 1 in the stock investing category on Amazon in 2012. In recent years, Paul's economic forecasts and commentaries have been featured in business and financial media such as MarketWatch, FinancialSense.com, Kitco.com, and numerous other media. You can find his economic, business, and financial video commentaries at www.youtube.com/paulmlad. He edits the free financial and business ezine, "Prosperity Alert," available at www.ravingcapitalist.com where you can also find his downloadable audio seminars and ebooks.

Dedication

I thank God for blessing me with a fantastic and supportive family! I dedicate this book to my wife Fran and our sons Adam and Joshua. You are always in my heart and I am grateful for you.

I also dedicate this book to the millions of good people that could better their lives and personal prosperity if they turn their talents and passions into a micro-entrepreneurial enterprise of their own.

Author's Acknowledgments

First and foremost, I offer my appreciation and gratitude to the wonderful people at Wiley. It has been a pleasure to work with such a top-notch team that works so hard to create products that offer readers tremendous value and information. I wish all of you continued success! Wiley has some notables whom I want to single out.

The first person is Chad Sievers (my project editor and copy editor). From day one he has given me and this book his tremendous guidance, and I am grateful to have worked with him. His patience, professionalism, and editing talents have kept me focused and productive.

The technical editor, William B. Donato, is a great micro-entrepreneur whose efforts and feedback I appreciate very much. He made sure that my facts and strategies were sound and up-to-date.

My gratitude again goes out to my fantastic acquisitions editor, Stacy Kennedy, for taking this first edition from a great idea to a great book! *For Dummies* books don't magically appear at the bookstore or some website; they happen because of true professionals like Stacy. Wiley is fortunate to have her (and so many other Wiley stars involved) . . . I am grateful to her!

Fran, Lipa Zyenska, I appreciate your great support and humor during the writing and updating of this book. It's not always easy dealing with the world, but with you by my side, I know that God has indeed blessed me. Te amo!

Lastly, I want to acknowledge you, the reader. Over the years, you've made the *For Dummies* books what they are today. Your devotion to these wonderful books helped build a foundation that played a big part in the creation of this book and other works yet to come. Thank you!

Publisher's Acknowledgments

We're proud of this book; please send us your comments at http://dummies.custhelp.com. For other comments, please contact our Customer Care Department within the U.S. at 877-762-2974, outside the U.S. at 317-572-3993, or fax 317-572-4002.

Some of the people who helped bring this book to market include the following:

Acquisitions, Editorial, and Vertical Websites

Project Editor: Chad R. Sievers

Acquisitions Editor: Stacy Kennedy

Copy Editor: Chad R. Sievers

Assistant Editor: David Lutton

Editorial Program Coordinator: Joe Niesen

Technical Editor: William B. Donato

Editorial Manager: Carmen Krikorian

Editorial Assistant: Alexa Koschier

Art Coordinator: Alicia B. South

Cover Photos: © malerapaso / iStockphoto.com

Composition Services

Project Coordinator: Sheree Montgomery

Layout and Graphics: Joyce Haughey

Proofreaders: Melissa Cossell, ConText Editorial Services, Inc.

Indexer: BIM Indexing & Proofreading Services

Publishing and Editorial for Consumer Dummies

    Kathleen Nebenhaus, Vice President and Executive Publisher

    David Palmer, Associate Publisher

    Kristin Ferguson-Wagstaffe, Product Development Director

Publishing for Technology Dummies

    Andy Cummings, Vice President and Publisher

Composition Services

    Debbie Stailey, Director of Composition Services

Contents at a Glance

Table of Contents

Introduction

If you want more income in your life and are willing to try a self-employed route, you've come to the right place. *Micro-Entrepreneurship For Dummies* is the perfect place to explore the idea of creating your own home-based business and create a viable source of income.

I have taught literally thousands of people about how to get into either a part-time or full-time business (since 1987), and the unstable economic environment during the past few years has been the worst I have seen. However, these times also tell me that everyone needs to take greater personal responsibility and control over their personal prosperity. The best ways to do so is to start a business (no matter how small or "micro") in your spare time.

Whether you have dreams of building a large successful business (every big business started as a micro-entrepreneurial enterprise), you're unemployed and want to start your own small business, or you just need some supplemental income on the side, micro-entrepreneurship is your best bet. This book can arm you with ideas, strategies, and lots of resources to help you kick-start your venture!

About This Book

Micro-Entrepreneurship For Dummies has been an honor for me to write. I'm grateful that I can share my thoughts, information, and experience of more than 30 years with such a large and devoted group of readers.

The timing of this book couldn't be better. I warned my readers in my book *Stock Investing For Dummies*, 2nd Edition (John Wiley & Sons, Inc.) that the economy is very unstable and difficult. Prosperity is something that is managed regularly as a two-pronged approach:

- **You build wealth in passive ways.** In passive wealth-building, you make your money work for you in passive ways (such as stocks, bonds, mutual funds, and so on).

- **You build wealth in active ways.** In active wealth-building, you turn your spare time into business pursuits so that you can make wealth with your time, talent, and efforts. In today's economy, a business is a financial necessity that belongs in your money-making arsenal.

In this book, I show you that you have what it takes to create a business that can provide you with income that either supplements your income or can provide you with full-time income.

For years in my business and financial seminars, when I introduce myself, I call myself a "raving capitalist" (I even have a website called `raving capitalist.com`). I say that because I came from a communist country (the former Yugoslavia) — and that's how you become a raving capitalist! But I take it a step farther. I think that everyone has a capitalist inside, and you should take that spirit and build wealth by serving others. The whole point is making money by providing goods and services that others want or need — a win-win situation.

This book is all about creating win-win situations for you — you serve others and you prosper as a micro-entrepreneur!

Conventions Used in This Book

To make navigating through this book easier, I've established the following conventions:

- **Boldface** text points out keywords or the main parts of bulleted items.
- *Italics* highlight new terms that are defined.
- `Monofont` is used for web addresses. URLs also appear as hyperlinks to the respective websites in the ebook versions of *Micro-Entrepreneurship For Dummies*.

When this book was printed, some Web addresses may have needed to break across two lines of text. If that happened, rest assured that I haven't put in any extra characters (such as hyphens) to indicate the break. So when using one of these Web addresses, just type in exactly what you see in this book, pretending the line break doesn't exist.

What You're Not to Read

Sidebars (gray boxes of text) in this book give you a more in-depth look at a certain topic. Although they further illuminate a particular point, these sidebars aren't crucial to your understanding of the rest of the book. Feel free to read them or skip them. Of course, I'd love for you to read them all, but my feelings won't be hurt if you decide to skip over them.

Foolish Assumptions

I figure you've picked up this book for one or more of the following reasons:

- ✔ You want to add financial security to your current situation either full-time or part-time.
- ✔ You want to take control over your financial situation.
- ✔ You're unemployed and you want to explore the possibilities of self-employment.
- ✔ You need a great gift! When Uncle Mo expressed an interest in becoming a micro-entrepreneur, you thought that this book was the perfect gift!

How This Book Is Organized

The information is laid out in a straightforward format. The sections are in order of what you will deal with as a micro-entrepreneur running a business (no matter how big or small).

Part I: Getting Started with Micro-Entrepreneurship

Understanding the essentials of starting a business (no matter how small) is important. I hope you take some time to re-assess yourself and consider a business. Here you find out the best path toward being a micro-entrepreneur and what type of business is suitable for you. Businesses are as varied as the people that run them, and you'll have an easier time succeeding when you choose a business that mirrors your interest and ability.

Chapter 2 goes into how to do a business plan so that you know the step-by-step approach to launching your business. Chapter 3 covers the most important part of the business — you and how you tick. Chapter 4 talks about your presence on the Internet and how to create it (such as with a website or blog). Chapter 5 is about finding opportunities in the marketplace.

Part II: Finding Great Micro-Entrepreneurship Ideas

When you're ready to take the plunge into your own business, you're better off doing something that is well-suited to who you are and what you are best at.

The great success is when the right business matches the right micro-entrepreneur. In this part, I discuss this "soup-to-nuts" approach, and you explore the possibilities. It covers everything from creating products and services to auctions, writing, self-publishing, affiliate marketing, and advertising. The great strength in this part (actually in the entire book) is the wealth of sites and resources that help you accomplish a successful business.

Part III: Marketing and Selling Your Micro-Business

Part III is about marketing, pure and simple. This phase stymies most business folks. Having products and services is fine, but you need customers if you're going to make a profit. Marketing is all about finding people who are willing and able to pay you for your products and services.

Given that, the chapters in this part provide assistance, ranging from how to find your best customers (market research) to all the steps in the marketing process, including selling and persuasion. This part also covers the various ways to market, ranging from publicity and guest blogging to ezine and blog marketing.

Part IV: Considering Taxes and Legal Issues

This part is not only about growing your enterprise but it's also about keeping more of the fruits of your labor. This part includes chapters on how to get help with managing and running your business through outsourcing, how to take your business from the micro to the macro level (including franchising), and how to keep more of the fruits of your labor by finding tax benefits and minimizing the impact of taxes.

Part V: The Part of Tens

I wrap up the book with a hallmark of *For Dummies* books — the Part of Tens. These chapters give you a mini crash course in how to avoid the pitfalls of being in business (see Chapter 22) and ten ways to make money in a business (check out Chapter 23).

Icons Used in This Book

Like every *For Dummies* book, I have included small icons in the margins to direct you to important paragraphs of text. Here are the icons that I use:

When you see this icon, I'm reminding you about some information that you should always keep stashed in your memory, whether you're new to the world of micro-entrepreneurship or an old pro.

This icon flags a particular bit of advice that just may give you an edge over other entrepreneurs.

Pay special attention to this icon because the advice can prevent headaches, heartaches, and . . . uh . . . business aches.

Where to Go from Here

You may not need to read every chapter to make you more confident as a micro-entrepreneur, so feel free to jump around to suit your personal needs. Because every chapter is designed to be as self-contained as possible, you can cherry-pick what you really want to read. For instance, scan the table of contents or the index, find a topic that interests you, and flip to that chapter.

However if you're like me, you may want to start at Chapter 1 and check out every chapter because you never know when you may come across a new tip or resource that can make a profitable difference in your business. I want you to be successful so that I can brag about you in the second edition!

Part I

getting started with Micro-Entrepreneurship

In this part . . .

- Get an overview of what a micro-entrepreneur is.

- Discover how to start your micro-business the right way to position it for long-term success.

- Get the lowdown on business plans (and find out whether you really need one as a micro-entrepreneur).

- Understand yourself and your abilities better so you can choose the right type of niche and path for you.

- Create a web presence with a website, blog, and social media for your start-up enterprise.

- Find worthwhile business opportunities and get them off the ground with confidence.

Chapter 1

Micro-Entrepreneurship 101: Just the Basics, Please

As the economy continues to struggle, and enterprises both big and small need to become leaner and meaner, an environment has emerged for the micro-entrepreneur. Micro-entrepreneurships are smaller and more nimble and come in a variety of enterprises, ranging from a single person working from home to a few people working out of an office. When large companies need work done and they don't have the wherewithal to hire a conventional employee, they're more likely to work with a micro-entrepreneur.

From 2008 to 2012, a major structural change occurred with the US economy. Standard full-time employment is no longer a given; millions of jobs were wiped out due to a variety of developments, ranging from the popping of the housing bubble (which wiped out hundreds of thousands of construction and real estate-related jobs), to financial firm bankruptcies (Bear Stearns, Lehman Brothers, and so on), to thousands of companies going out of business or drastically cutting back. Millions lost jobs — jobs that could take decades to regain. In the meanwhile, businesses across the economic landscape have been forced to be more efficient and more austere. Consumers also pulled back on spending, and frugality became the rule and not the exception.

Fortunately, adversity can bring opportunity. Many companies (and consumers) that needed products and services (but couldn't afford the typical vendors and employees to provide these wants and needs) turned to micro-entrepreneurs. Having a service done by a single mom from home, for example, was more cost-effective than hiring an employee, especially if it was a relatively small assignment. In this arrangement, the company saved money, and the micro-entrepreneur working from home received a nice paycheck. Similar conditions paved the way for innovative, small firms (whether they were a single person working from home or a firm of several employees that were home-based); the micro-entrepreneurship arrived.

This chapter serves as your steppingstone into the world of micro-entrepreneurship. Here I explain the ins and outs of what being a micro-entrepreneur really means, the different types of business you may want to pursue as a micro-entrepreneur, and my suggestions for making your business noticed (and successful). I also point out a few tax and legal issues you need to know. After reading this chapter, you'll have a basic understanding and can delve deeper into this book for whatever specific topic interests you.

Understanding What Being a Micro-Entrepreneur Means

Being a micro-entrepreneur may mean different things to different people; however, the concept of what one is and what one does really isn't that difficult. A *micro-entrepreneur* is someone who has launched and managed a small business (typically at home, but could also be at a formal business location) and is seeking to expand its profitability. Some define a micro-entrepreneurship as a small enterprise that ranges from a one-person, home-based operation to one that has up to five employees. I specifically define a micro-entrepreneurship as one that starts initially as a one-person operation that may expand with the use of contractors (outsourcing) and potentially future employees. The employees (if they're hired) are primarily home-based to save on the need to obtain office space. I take the "micro" part seriously (especially in a difficult economy where saving on expenses is vital).

Before you tackle any type of business, including a micro-business, you need to do certain things, so that when you do tackle it, you succeed. In these sections, I make sure you know what you're getting involved with so you know which business path you need to take.

Following your path to be a micro-entrepreneur

When you're ready to embark on your ambitious path to be a successful businessperson, you do the same thing a soon-to-be traveler does. You get a map and chart your course to your destination — okay, well, sort of.

As a micro-entrepreneur, your map and travel instructions are actually laid out in this book. I provide all of the major considerations for a successful small business from start-up considerations to marketing and other growth issues. When I first started my micro-enterprise in 1981, I could have used a road map like this book to help me plot my path forward. I could have avoided some pitfalls along the way and also taken advantage of opportunities much sooner.

In order to be successful, micro-entrepreneurs create a business plan so they can think through what they will do to ensure greater success with their venture. Chapter 2 helps you put together your business plan and much more. Don't just sit there . . . it's time to plan for your success.

Figuring out whether you have what it takes to be a micro-entrepreneur

Because you're reading this book, you have what it takes to be a micro-entrepreneur. You have the desire, which is the first criterion for being a micro-entrepreneur. You want to succeed, right? In addition to desire, initially look at these four *E*s and the related questions to see if you have what it takes:

- ✔ **Enjoyment:** What do you really enjoy doing?
- ✔ **Experience:** What do you have plenty of experience in?
- ✔ **Education:** What have you learned extensively or proficiently during your years in school (including college)?
- ✔ **Expertise:** What are you really competent in? What are you the go-to person for?

These questions tap into just the top layer of traits you need to consider. Chapter 3 discusses many more questions to help you figure out what makes you (yes, you, the micro-entrepreneur) tick.

Recognizing potential opportunities

To identify opportunities for your micro-entrepreneur business, having a presence on the Internet is beyond a must. In fact, it should be considered mandatory for every micro-entrepreneur. The best (and most common) ways to have an online presence is with a website and/or a blog. Chapter 4 explains how you can create this presence (and do so inexpensively and even for free).

With the Internet's help, finding opportunities to make money in a topic or niche that you like is easy and even fun. I am not kidding about the fun; the niche you're in needs to be enjoyable so that you have what it takes to persevere in the area of your interest. Because hundreds of viable categories exist for you to profit from, you want to make sure you locate opportunities in the right way and then specialize in them so that you can stand out in your area of expertise. Chapter 5 shows you how to find these opportunities.

Deciding What Type of Business Works for You

If you think that there isn't a business or money-earning approach right for you, then you aren't really looking hard enough. There are plenty of ways you can succeed as a micro-entrepreneur. Just as there are different diets for different weight-conscious folks and different financial plans for budget-conscious folks, there are different businesses for people that want to earn money.

Here are the different areas that you can create your micro-business and sell the following:

- ✔ **Arts and crafts:** If you're the creative type who enjoys a peaceful weekend afternoon creating something of beauty (or something useful or functional), then you may want to consider an arts-and-crafts business. Chapter 6 takes a closer look at what goes into creating — don't look at it as creating an object of some kind — think of it as creating something of physical and financial value. If you did a good job creating something, someone would love to buy it from you. You make money in a win-win situation. Guess what? You can do it again and again.

- ✔ **Collectibles and other stuff:** You may have extra stuff taking up space and collecting dust in your garage or attic. You can sell some of that cool stuff on online auctions, such as eBay (and an array of other auction sites), and make lots of money. Even better, you're getting rid of stuff and decluttering your life while making some money at the same time. If you want to go bigger, you can purchase collectibles on the cheap at garage sales, estate sales, and auctions and then re-sell them online. Find out more about the auction business in Chapter 7.

- ✔ **Your services:** I don't think it's an odd thing to say that people are here in this world to serve someone. Whether you serve a boss, a customer, your country, or your family, the idea of service is (or should be) part of being human. For micro-entrepreneurs, service is at the heart to a win-win scenario. To get paid, give your customers value by giving them some type of service to earn that money. Therefore, no matter who you are, you can be of service to someone and make a profit doing it. Whether you're designing a nuclear power plant or simply cleaning someone's closet, you can make money. Chapter 8 explains how to do so.

✔ **Written word:** If you can draft clear ideas on paper, you can make some good money, part-time or full-time, writing for all sorts of organizations that need this type of content. Some of them are offline (like magazines) while many are online (gazillions of websites and blogs). Refer to Chapter 9 on how writing can be a great business for you.

✔ **Information products:** You can also produce your own information products, such as a book, report, newsletter, audio product (like a CD or podcast), or a video product. In today's world, anyone can become a self-publisher, which is very exciting.

When I first started in business (some time after the Cretaceous Period in 1981), self-publishing was difficult unless you paid good money to graphic artists, book printing firms, and so on. Thankfully, technology has changed for the better. If you have knowledge and information to share (or even something fictional like a short story or novel), you can easily become a self-publisher. Chapter 10 provides more detail.

✔ **Other people's products:** You don't have to make money by creating your own stuff. Being creative and making physical or information products may not be your idea of a fun time. Maybe you want to make money by selling someone else's stuff. Thousands of products are available for sale, and you can get a piece of that action by becoming an affiliate. An *affiliate* means that you make commissions or referral fees by helping established companies sell their products and services. In fact, being an affiliate is big business on the Internet! You can find out more in Chapter 11 about affiliate work.

✔ **Advertising:** You can make money from advertising. Tons of websites and blogs allow advertisers to put ads on their sites. In return, those advertisers pay money — even for actions as seemingly tiny as clicking a link. Take a look because it's all over the Internet. You may as well make money, too. Chapter 12 includes the details.

Making Your Micro-Business Noticeable

Operating all businesses (give or take) can be boiled down to two phases: the set-up phase (which I cover in Parts I and II) and the marketing phase. Marketing simply means how you find folks (your *target market*) who are willing and able to buy what you're offering so you can make money (of course, at a profit).

The following sections help you grapple with the single toughest topic for most businesses (but especially for small businesses and micro-entrepreneurs like you and me): marketing.

Advertising your services or products

Getting people to notice your business and the services and products you sell isn't always easy, but it's an important aspect of being a micro-entrepreneur, if you want your business to be successful. The second half of Chapter 12 gives you an in-depth taste of how to advertise your business so your customers know about you and where to find you.

Identifying your market

An essential aspect of marketing is knowing who your market is. In other words, you need to know who you're selling to and who your best customers are. You can then use this information to better offer your products and services. The more you know about which customers are your target market is and where they are, the more successful you'll be. The best way to discover this information is by conducting market research. I discuss how to perform market research and how to focus on your target market in Chapter 13.

Communicating with your clients

Selling to your customers boils down to persuasive communication. After all, if you want their money, you need to be able to persuade them that buying your stuff is one of the best things they could do. This persuasion can either be spoken (over the phone or in person) or written (such as in an email or sales letter). How you do it can increase your chance of success. Check out Chapter 14 for more specific how-to information to be more persuasive with your customers.

Marketing your business

Wouldn't it be great if customers just found you and bought your product or service? That would make life and running a business much easier. Business owners spend so much time looking for customers that it would be good for a change if they were looking for you. The way you market your business can take some of the pressure off you.

Here are some great ways you can market your business:

- **Search engines:** Fortunately, today is the age of search engines, such as Google, Bing, Yahoo!, and so on, that can help arrange just such a transaction. Find out how search engines tick so you can use them to your advantage. The more you know how they work and what strategies and resources to use, the closer you'll come to having your customers find you. Chapter 15 gives you the nitty gritty.

- **Ezines and blogs:** You can market your business by building a list of folks and keeping them informed through either an *ezine* (an online newsletter) or a blog. This tried-and-true method has worked well for many and can work for you. Check out Chapter 16 for more opportunities with these methods.

- **Social media:** Facebook and Twitter are just the tip of the social media iceberg. You can use them to strategize and make a profit and still have a piña colada (near your laptop or smartphone to monitor the situation). Chapter 17 has lots of resources and strategies to help you profit. With that, I think you will "like" this chapter.

- **Other avenues:** As the author of *Zero-Cost Marketing*, I love it when micro-entrepreneurs can boot-strap their way to financial success with marketing methods that cost nothing. Instead of expensive marketing and advertising, the nimble micro-entrepreneur can do methods that only require time, effort, and initiative. Chapter 18 covers some very effective marketing methods, such as article marketing, publicity, and forum marketing.

Being Aware of Taxes and Other Issues

Growing your income and your business to new levels means new things to deal with. Knowing how to handle these issues is important to protect your business interests. These sections can help you with your growing pains with tax and other legal issues that may pop up.

Getting others to help you in your business

You can't grow to the next level with your business if you're doing everything. Fortunately, in today's economy, many helping hands are waiting for you and at pretty reasonable rates.

Outsourcing (using outside contractors to perform non-core business activities to save the company time and/or money or to add efficiency or take advantage of technical knowledge) used to be something that only big companies were involved with. Small or home-based businesses were small enough that hired help either wasn't necessary or was too costly to consider. Today is a different world.

Outsourcing is available even to you, toiling away in the dead of night. You can get help with many tasks — even from experts in their field for a fraction of the cost (or at least, less than you think). Check out outsourcing in Chapter 19 (you can thank me later).

Growing your business

If you want to go from being a micro-entrepreneur to being a macro-entrepreneur (you know, hit it big), where you have franchises or dealerships that you can sell across the country or globe, you want to be able to take advantage of things that many entrepreneurs aren't even aware of. A good example is using service marks to add more profit to your bottom line. In addition, imagine making a six- or seven-figure profit when you sell your micro-entrepreneurship business (how cool would that be?).

Chapter 20 has more about service marks. A *service mark* is a word, phrase, name, or symbol that is legally registered to represent an exclusive service or service company and makes it so that others can't copy it without getting formal permission from the company. If these methods work out and you get the chance to rub elbows with Donald Trump, you can send me a case of lobster tails (Mrs. Mladjenovic loves seafood).

Tackling taxes (but fortunately no death)

Whether you're a small, one-person operation operating from home or a bigger business down at the corporate part of town, you have to deal with taxes, regulations, and other government creations that businesses (and their customers) have to deal with.

Whenever you're talking profit, you're also talking taxes. Each business's taxes are unique, including what you can deduct and can't deduct, so talk with an accountant who can help you deal with them.

You also have to figure out your business structure. Your choices include sole proprietor, LLC, or something else? For answers and resources on the issue of taxes (and related legal matters), go to Chapter 21.

Chapter 2

Knowing Your Path as a Micro-Entrepreneur

I'm the biggest advocate of folks starting their own business. No matter who you are or what your situation is, there is a business — some kind of business — that is personally right for you. In this chapter, I help you figure out a path for you and your business. I realize that everyone is different, and some of the information in this chapter may not apply to you, but it's still good to know what to do and what not to do.

Recognizing Whether You Need a Formal Business Plan

Every business in history started off as an idea. Think about what type of business you want to have. I assist you in finding ideas in many of the chapters in Part I and Part II. For example, Chapter 3 helps you figure out your idea by first understanding yourself better. This section assumes you already have an idea in hand. Now, you're ready to start your business, so you need a plan, and pronto.

A *business plan* is a detailed statement describing the business's operations and marketing along with goals to be attained and the strategies and methods to be used to reach those goals. As a micro-entrepreneur, you don't necessarily need a formal business plan. If, for example, you're selling trinkets and stuff from your attic and basement on eBay or Amazon to make a few extra bucks in your spare time, then you don't need a business plan, at least certainly not a formal or complex one. Think about it like this: Do you need a map when you're driving to your local store? Probably not. However, when you're driving to an attraction you've never been to, and it's located several hours in the part of the country where you've never been, then you do need a map (or your GPS). Many folks shy away from launching their business dreams (even modest ones) because some authority type in a pinstriped suit admonished them about not starting a business without a business plan.

However, on the other hand, when you have a serious desire to turn your business idea into a sustainable and ongoing business, then a business plan becomes more of a necessity. It's especially true if you're hoping to have the backing of potential business partners or financing from a financial source, such as a bank, credit union, venture capital firm, or a government agency (such as the Small Business Administration or your state's economic development authority).

When the moment comes that you need (or feel you need) a business plan, then this chapter is a good place to start (take it from an authority type who rarely wears a pin-striped suit)!

Eyeing What Your Business Plan Addresses

The over-arching point of your business plan is basically there to address what may be the five most important questions in your business venture. The following list breaks down these five questions in greater depth:

- ✓ **What do you plan to do?** A business plan helps you figure out your goals and mission statement. Here you explain your plans and what you're aiming to do. Set your focus regarding what your products and/or services are going to be and how you'll conduct your business. In addition, make sure you have clear financial goals, such as what you want to achieve during your first year in business, such as generating sales revenue of more than $50,000 or getting five major clients.

- ✓ **What are you able to do?** A business plan can spell out your business's capabilities (yours specifically if you're a one-person operation). It addresses your strengths and how you're able to carry out the functions of your business. You can specify activities, such as how you'll create the product or service and how daily operations will be. Here you can address your strengths and weaknesses.

  You can identify what you personally can do and which tasks you may need help with. Perhaps you'll need assistance with bookkeeping, taxes, and so on.

✔ **What is the reality of your marketplace?** A business plan identifies who your potential customers are and whether you're dealing with a large market or a small niche. You can also figure out who your customers are. Are they large companies with large advertising budgets or smaller companies that you compete with online?

✔ **How will you make money?** Your business plan helps you specify how you'll make your revenue — from making products or providing services. It helps clarify whether you'll sell online, have affiliates help you sell, or have joint ventures. You want to be as clear as possible how you'll make money.

✔ **How will you finance your business activities?** A business plan spells out how you'll pay for your operations and potential projects — from savings, a business loan, or other source of funds (or a combination of these). Your other options include doing your business on a shoestring budget or with working capital from a third party (such as a local bank, credit union, or an investor). Some micro-entrepreneurs have used funds from a credit card (which I don't recommend), whereas others have received financial assistance from family and friends (make sure you have very clear agreements and payment terms to avoid confusion and conflict). See the nearby sidebar for details about getting additional funding.

When your business needs funds: Where to get financial assistance

You should start your business, regardless of funding considerations. Why? First, if you're a micro-entrepreneur working from home, you probably don't have a large financial need for operating your business. Second, much of the assistance and/or business tools you may need can be acquired or used for free or at very low-cost.

Take websites and blogs, for instance. You can find plenty of good resources that help you set up a blog for free. You can also set up a fully functional website for an initial cost of under $10 (see Chapter 4 for details). The point is that micro-entrepreneurs don't need huge capital needs for their business activities, at least not initially.

However, if there is a need for expansion (going to macro-entrepreneur status), then financing will become an issue. (Chapter 20 addresses some ways.) Fortunately, these are creative times in the world of business financing. A new type of financing called *crowdfunding* is when a business receives financing from a group of individuals who participate in the funding for the business. (You can find out more about crowdfunding from websites such as www.crowdfunding.com, www.kickstarter.com, and www.indiegogo.com.)

Naming the Type of Business Plan You Have

When you choose to create a business plan, you have one of two models to choose from. These sections briefly explain them:

- ✔ **Action plan:** An *action plan* means that you're using the business plan in your day-to-day activities. In other words, you're actually using what you wrote to help you conduct your business activities; it acts like a tour guide, and you use it to stay focused on your business goals.

- ✔ Besides stating your goals, this approach means that you detail specifics on what you're doing and will be doing during the days and weeks when you're conducting business. An action-plan mode is particularly important for home-based businesses because many micro-entrepreneurs can easily get distracted. You want to avoid busy work in favor of work that keeps you moving forward to your sales and profit goals.

- ✔ **Static proposal:** A business plan that acts like a *static proposal* means that it doesn't change. In other words, it's not an action plan. It merely serves as a useful proposal to individuals outside your business for the purpose of convincing them to become partners or lenders. Some advisors call it a *presentation style plan.*

Some business plans can be a hybrid of these two modes, but the whole point of which type you use is who the audience is for your business plan. In other words, ask yourself who needs to be convinced, motivated, or guided by the business plan's contents. If the audience is a group of potential investors, you would present more of a static proposal, whereas if your audience is you and your staff, you'd use an action plan.

Investors (such as angel investors and venture capital firms) and those providing financing (bankers, loan companies, and so on) want to know that the business plan exudes and projects competence and experience from the entrepreneur (or business management team).

For example, investors and bankers want to know to what tangible extent you are committed to the business. Do you have personal assets tied to the enterprise or have you pledged personal money that shows a real commitment to its success? They also want to see that you have experience in this type of enterprise.

Looking Closer at a Business Plan and What It Constitutes

Your business map is like the road map that shows where you are and where you want to be. What goes into the business plan will vary based on what folks you are talking to. Here are the main general components of a typical business plan:

- **Section one:** This section is for the business itself. Here you discuss the industry, your business structure, your particular product or service, and how you plan to make your business a success.

- **Section two:** This section is for the market. Here is where you describe and analyze potential customers: who and where they are, what makes them buy, and so on. Here, you also describe the competition and how you'll position yourself to beat it.

- **Section three:** This section covers the financial information and contains important financial statements that I discuss in this section. This part may require help from your accountant and a good spreadsheet software program.

Breaking these main sections down further, I pinpoint the components that you should be aware of. Here is an extensive list of what is usually in a detailed business plan:

- **Table of contents:** Just like a book, a business plan can use a table of contents. Here you list the contents, their order, and maybe even page numbers. You may not need to create an extensive table of contents if your business plan is meant only for your eyes, but if others, particularly investors and lenders, are meant to see it, then use a table of contents.

- **Executive summary:** In a nutshell, the *executive summary* describes what your business is about. If outside parties want to get a quick and reliable snapshot of you and your enterprise, they should be able to get it in the executive summary.

- **Mission statement:** The *mission statement* is a brief description of a company's fundamental purpose. It answers the question, "Why do we exist?" The mission statement expresses the business's purpose both for you, your staff (if any), and for those in the marketplace. For help in drafting your mission statement, refer to the resources later in this chapter.

✔ **Company overview:** The *company overview* is a brief summary (one or two pages at most) of the company's history, its management, products, and position in the market. The overview may also mention things such as accomplishments made by the entrepreneur or company that were notable.

✔ **Business environment:** This section explains the kind of environment in which the business operates. Basically it gives an accurate picture of the economic environment, which can in return help you make better decisions. It also touches on the type of economy (slow or growing) and whether the market size has grown for what you offer, or not. It also looks at the bigger picture of the industry and its status. This section also reviews what your market research tells you about consumer trends and changing tastes.

✔ **Market analysis:** The more you know about you customer (your target market), the easier it will be to generate sales. This section describes who your customers are, what their buying habits are, and who your typical customer for your business is.

✔ **Competitor analysis:** The more you know about your competitors, the better you'll compete. This section identifies your customers and explains how you stack up to your competitors' strengths and weaknesses.

✔ **Company strategy:** This section is the general direction and scope of the way your business will have its various parts (production, marketing, customer service, and so on) working together to achieve objectives.

✔ **Company setup and description:** This section is an actual description of your company, including what it looks like and its composition (staff, assets, and so on). As a micro-entrepreneur, this section is more valuable the more complex your business is.

✔ **Marketing plan:** I include this section for completeness' sake because the marketing plan is an integral part of the business plan. For some points about the marketing plan, refer to the next section, "Updating Your Business Plan" in this chapter.

✔ **Financial statements:** *Financial statements* are documents that detail the financial condition of your business, such as its revenues and expenses, what it owns and what it owes, and other important financial details necessary for both the entrepreneur and any lenders or investors that may participate in funding the business. When you write a business plan, make sure you include the following statements:

  • **Balance sheet:** This statement is a list of the business assets you own and the business liabilities you owe. Your total assets minus your total liabilities equal your *net worth* (also referred to as your *net equity*). In other words, what does the business own and owe, and which is greater?

- **Profit and loss statement:** This statement shows the total revenue and total expenses (with the net gain or loss) for the business for a given period (such as a month, a quarter, or a year). This statement is also referred to as an *income statement* or a *P&L statement.* This statement shows how profitable (or not) the business is.

- **Cash flow statement:** This is similar to the profit and loss statement, but it's mostly intended to show the flow of money going through the business. It shows what money is flowing out (such as paying bills) and what money is flowing in (such as sales).

- **Use of funds statement:** Investors and lenders usually like to see this statement. It's intended to show them how you'll use the money that is provided to you (from either invested money or loaned money). They want to see that you'll efficiently and profitably use the money.

- **Pro-forma statements:** The previous statements reflect past moments or past periods, but this statement is intended to predict or forecast a reasonable estimate of future financial activity. Usually, these are done in several ways where the entrepreneur makes forecasts that are considered best case, worst case, and a reasonable estimate of future sales and profits.

A couple of good guides to help you understand financial statements are the latest editions of the following:

- *How to Read a Financial Report; Wringing Vital Signs out of the Numbers* by John A. Tracy, CPA (John Wiley & Sons, Inc.)

- *Reading Financial Reports* by Lita Epstein (John Wiley & Sons, Inc.)

✔ **Budget:** A *budget* may or may not be in a static proposal, but it's a good consideration in the action plan mode because you want to track the inflow and outflow of money. You want to stay within your means and conduct business to the extent that it won't put you in debt or otherwise weaken you financially.

A budget can also be a *pro-forma budget*, which means that you're projecting or estimating what you expect your expenses and financial needs to be in an upcoming financial period, such as the next month or the next quarter.

✔ **Action plan:** This portion of the business plan details the steps you'll take and the timeline over which you'll take the steps to achieve certain objectives in the business.

✔ **Appendix:** This section is usually the last portion of the business plan, and it may include corroborating data or reports that help to flesh out or back up assertions in your business plan. Maybe, for example, you plan to launch a new store in Cincinnati, so you include in the appendix a magazine article or a government report highlighting what a wonderful business environment that city would be for this new location.

Updating Your Business Plan

A business plan isn't a static document that you create and then put on a shelf to look at later when you feel nostalgic (especially if it's of the action plan variety). (Check out the earlier section, "Naming the Type of Business Plan You Have" for more information.) Here are four things to keep in mind when periodically updating your business plan. If your business plan is to be a guiding instrument in your business life, keep it updated.

- ✔ **Market changes:** When you're offering your products and services to the marketplace, you need to keep track of significant changes regarding your customers and your competitors. A good business tries to adapt to changes and new trends in its marketplace. Identify the changes that are occurring in your marketplace that translate into changes for your business and marketing approach. Refer to Chapters 5 and 13 for more guidance on markets and market research.

- ✔ **Financial changes:** As your business grows and changes, your finances will likely change, too. Focus on being able to take advantage of any changes or handle any new pitfalls.

   If your business is doing well, for example, and sales are up, then you should take advantage by either paying down debt or upgrading your business equipment. And if your business isn't doing well, you may want to sell some assets to gain some extra cash for the slow periods or refinance your debt to lower your monthly payments.

- ✔ **New developments:** Long after the ink is dry on your first business's plan, new developments may occur that will change your business plan as the business progresses. Maybe you're creating new products and services, hiring new staff, or forging new business alliances. Perhaps the best development of all is that you reached the milestones from the original business plan and now you're set to target and reach new milestones.

- ✔ **Your business plan versus your marketing plan:** For many self-employed folks (part-time or full-time), a complete business plan isn't the answer. Perhaps the issue is only a portion of the business plan — the marketing plan.

   The *marketing plan* encompasses only that activity that you're doing to ultimately make money. Marketing is all about learning about and finding your customers, publicity, advertising, and all approaches that can lead to the sale. Although I cover marketing throughout the book, here are some resources to help you understand and create a marketing plan for your business plan:

- American Marketing Association (www.marketingpower.com)
- The Direct Marketing Association (www.the-dma.org)
- Marketing Profs (www.marketingprofs.com)
- The National Mail Order Association (www.nmoa.org)

See the chapters in Part III for more specifics.

Creating Your Business Plan: Helpful Resources to Review

The great thing for you is that in today's information-rich environment, you needn't do a business plan all by yourself. You can find tons of resources for help. Check out this list for assistance.

✔ **Dummies.com:** I admit I may be biased as a *For Dummies* author, but this site (www.dummies.com) can help you with business plan guidance. Search for "business plan" and get some great articles. In addition, when I wrote this chapter, I looked up "business plan" (see that? I practice what I preach) and I found the newest edition for *Business Plans Kit For Dummies* by Steven D. Peterson, Peter E. Jaret, and Barbara Findlay Schenck (John Wiley & Sons, Inc.). I also found the Cheat Sheet from that book, which gives some great tips on creating a business plan.

Don't stop there, though. The site is good for useful articles and some nifty Cheat Sheets on a batch of topics scattered through this book.

✔ **Sample business plans:** Here are some places where you can find sample business plans:

- Bplans (www.bplans.com)
- Reference for Business (www.referenceforbusiness.com)
- Small Business Administration (www.sba.gov)

✔ **Business organizations:** Here are organizations that have plenty of guidance for small businesses and entrepreneurs. Do a search at their sites for "business plan" and other concerns that you can think of:

- Association of Small Business Development Centers (www.asbdc-us.org)
- National Federation of Independent Business (www.nfib.org)
- Service Corps of Retired Executives (www.score.org)

Making Other Stops on Your Path

The business plan is certainly the most important potential document in the early days of your business as it develops, but you also need to ponder some other important considerations as you create your business so they don't blindside you in your entrepreneurial pursuits. Keep these in mind:

✔ **Your business name:** Choosing a business name is like choosing a baby's name, only different. Your business name gives a constant reminder about the value of your company and for what you offer. Choose a name very carefully because it's a business asset.

 You can register your business name at the state or county level. Check out Chapter 21 for more information about registering your business name.

✔ **Your business structure:** I could easily write an entire book on the business structure you choose, whether it be sole proprietorship, partnership (if your business will be two or more owners or partners), corporation, or limited liability company (LLC). When working out your business plan, make sure you select the one right for you. Chapter 21 gives you some insight into which decision might be right for you.

✔ **Licenses and permits:** Check to see whether your business needs any type of license or permit to operate. At the very least, you may need a tax ID number (issued by the IRS). (See Chapter 21 for more about this number.)

 Although you probably don't need a license as a home-based business, you should probably check. The best place to explore this topic is at the local office of the Small Business Administration (www.sba.gov). Even though it's a federal agency, it usually has staff that is familiar with state and local requirements for businesses. If it doesn't, the SBA can usually refer to the state or local office that can let you know if you need a license or permit for your type of business.

✔ **Your accounting system:** When you're tracking all the numbers to tell you how your business is doing, it boils down to your accounting system. Your accounting system should be a software package that matches your needs. Some businesses are so simple that a spreadsheet program is sufficient (you can get free spreadsheet software through the Open Office productivity software suite found at www.openoffice.org). For most businesses, accounting software is a better choice. You can shop and compare various accounting software programs at sites such as Top Ten Review (www.toptenreviews.com), Accounting Software World (www.accountingsoftwareworld.com), and Find Accounting Software (www.findaccountingsoftware.com).

Whether you're using popular accounting and financial software such as Quickbooks, Quicken, Microsoft Money, or some other program, set up a system to help you easily see how well you're doing and aid you in the day-to-day financial transactions. Fortunately, today's accounting software is very powerful and gives you the ability to easily track every penny. Ask your business adviser or tax professional about accounting software suggestions if needed.

✔ **Your business location:** For micro-entrepreneurs, business location probably isn't a big concern unless you're agonizing over doing business in the spare bedroom or somewhere in the basement. When you create your business plan, determine exactly where your location will be.

✔ **Marketing and sales:** To me, the big hurdles for entrepreneurs are in the realm of sales and marketing. I won't spend a lot of time on this crucial topic in this chapter because I do cover it in greater detail in a variety of chapters. Here, though, are some places to go:

  • **Salesmanship:** As the head of your business, you're the lead salesperson. Of course, when you're a micro-entrepreneur, you are the entire sales force. Therefore, understanding the process of selling and building up your sales skills is very important. I cover this topic in greater detail in Chapter 14.

  • **Your customers:** Understanding those folks that will buy from you is critical information. Chapter 13 provides more information about what you can find out about your customers.

  • **Marketing:** To do a variety of marketing strategies ranging from utilizing search engines, social media marketing, and more, head over to Chapters 15 to 18 that go through the various marketing strategies that you can employ on the Internet.

Making Your Business Path Easier: Tools for the Road

When you're ready to roll up your sleeves and do the work, the good news is that plenty of tools and resources are available to help make your journey along your path of micro-entrepreneur smoother. When you're essentially by yourself, knowledge and productivity are important. Here are some considerations for your tool chest.

Going online for some education

One of the great trends in society right now is that education is migrating to the Internet. Factors such as cost, convenience, and competition have made taking classes over the Internet and from the comfort of home a reality.

For the micro-entrepreneur who needs to know more about a specific business topic or skill, gaining knowledge and training is easier than ever. In the past, people felt that to do well in business, they had to plow lots of time, money, and effort into getting an MBA or some advanced degree. But whether you're out to get an entire range of business skills and knowledge or just need a slice of knowledge, you can do it now with less time and less money (just don't skimp on the effort).

Besides using your favorite search engine, here are some places to check out:

✔ **Your local university:** Sooner or later, that traditional college or university will have online courses, if it doesn't already. Contact its business department for details or search on its website for details.

✔ **Educational firms:** Many firms now specialize in online education and training. Some examples are the University of Phoenix (www.phoenix.edu), Ed2go (www.ed2go.com), and Universal class (www.universialclass.com). More of these types of firms are coming. Choose the ones that have a long history and a good reputation.

✔ **Large companies:** Some companies also have strong educational programs. A good example is Hewlett-Packard. It has online classes ("HP Learning Center") on small business technology (you can find out more at https://h30440.www3.hp.com/learningcenter/Default.aspx.

✔ **Online tutorial sites:** Plenty of great sites provide video tutorials on various business, Internet, and technology topics. Some to consider are Eli the Computer Guy (www.elithecomputerguy.com), Webucator (www.webucator.com), and Eclasses.org (www.eclasses.org).

Teleconferencing or videoconferencing

With the rise of services such as Skype (www.skype.com) and similar services, now you can communicate cheaply with your contacts. With smartphone usage exploding, you can take advantage of cheap or free telecom services with services such as Fring (www.fring.com), FreeConference (www.freeconference.com), and Ring Central (www.ringcentral.com).

Teleconferencing and videoconferencing services and software can also help you communicate with your customers, vendors, and business partners easier than ever. A wealth of choices is available, and you can also go to sites such as Teleconferencing Directory (www.teleconferencingdirectory.net).

Using open-source software

Gone are the days when a small business had to buy expensive software suites from major companies. Now you can get great software suites from major companies (and small ones, too). A software suite is just a bundle of software that any business would need. A typical bundle has software that does word processing, spreadsheets, presentations, database or contact management, graphics, and so on. Much of this software is referred to as *open-source* software, which means that software developers can freely have access to the programming code for the software to modify or improve it as needed. This contrasts with software that is designed entirely by a company's programming staff and not amenable to change or modification by other independent programmers.

One of the most popular free software suites is Open Office by Oracle (www.openoffice.org). It competes with paid software packages, such as Microsoft's Office suite (www.microsoft.com). Either suite can help you tremendously, so do your comparison (of course, *free* has an edge over *paid* for the budding micro-entrepreneur).

Organizing and being more productive

Whether you're managing your time or finding ways to be more productive and organized, plenty of tools and tips can help you. Some good places to find them are at Online Organizing (www.onlineorganizing.com) and Get Organized Now (www.getorganizednow.com).

Relying on colleagues

You can reference a host of resources, tools, and strategies from people who have done what you're doing. You can find out what others in your niche or market are doing now to staying ahead of the pack. Refer to the following:

✔ **A professional association:** Virtually every business niche has an association that keeps track of the trends, news, opportunities, and so on. Find the right association with your search engine or at places such as the Encyclopedia of Associations (www.gale.cengage.com).

✔ **LinkedIn:** This great social media site (www.linkedin.com) has all sorts of great groups that professionals can tap into. You can get referred to great resources by pros in any of the various groups you find. For instance, several active groups specialize in business start-ups.

✔ **Technorati:** This site (www.technorati.com) has literally hundreds of great blogs for home businesses and small businesses that offer great tips and information for business start-ups.

✔ **Business.com:** This site (www.business.com) is one of my favorite search engines for all things business. Whether you're looking for business resources or need to do some vital research, this site should be part of your Internet tools.

Chapter 3

Understanding Yourself: What Makes You Tick

*O*wning a micro-business and being self-employed isn't as difficult as you think, or at least not as difficult as most people make it out to be. The first thing that you need to understand isn't the business — but to understand yourself. You want to start a business that fits you as a person and your passions. If not, you're setting yourself up for failure. Consider this chapter a mirror. You can look squarely into it and figure out who you are and what excites you, which can then help you determine what type of business is right for you.

Tapping Into the Process of Starting Your Business

The process of beginning your business is directly tied to you and what type of person you are, and what type of entrepreneur you are (in other words, what makes you tick) because the activity of being in business is an ongoing process that stretches across weeks, months, and years. Being clear about who you are and what you enjoy is important for long-term success; you want to choose an activity that you enjoy and one that is a fit to the real you.

In these sections, I help you conduct a self-examination where you can get a clearer idea of who you are and what your interests are. With this information, you can make a more-informed choice about the type of business you want to pursue.

Doing your 10-10 list to find your passion

The famed entrepreneur Richard Branson said that if you can indulge your passion, life will be far more interesting than if you're just working. He added that you'll work harder at it and you'll know more about it. So passion (or at least enjoyment is at the core of your success).

The great secret of success as a micro-entrepreneur is that you're truly happy doing what you do. You want to do something (sell a product or provide a service) that you're eager to do than to try to make money doing something that you would rather avoid doing.

One of the first things I tell folks in my home business start-up class to do is what I refer to as a 10-10 list. A *10-10 list* is one of my favorite ways to help hopeful or prospective entrepreneurs choose a suitable business. This short exercise can help match the right business idea to the right would-be entrepreneur. You may be a capable businessperson, but if you decide to do a business that you aren't well suited to, being successful will be more difficult. It's a wise idea to choose a business that is matched to your abilities, experience, and interests. The 10-10 list helps to reveal a lot about you, which is important in order to start and manage a business that fits you.

To create this list, follow these easy steps:

1. **Take a blank piece of paper (8.5 by 11 will do) and draw a line down the middle.**

2. **On the left side, start with the first "E" word, which is "Enjoyment" (you can also refer to it as Column A).**

3. **List ten things that you really enjoy doing (of course, if you have fewer than ten, that's okay).**

   When I say enjoy, I mean activities that interest you — to the point that you would do them even if you weren't getting paid to do so (digging ditches probably won't make this list).

   You may only have a handful of things that you enjoy doing or you may have 47 things that you really have fun doing, but do your best to write down the top ten things, no matter how frivolous they sound. I don't care if you put down taking naps on the couch, watching TV, or skiing.

4. **On the right side of the line (you can also call it Column B), focus on the following four areas and answer these questions.**

   Think of EEET as a shortcut for the following, which all refer to your competence:

   - **Experience:** What do you have plenty of experience in?

   - **Education:** What have you learned extensively or proficiently during your years in school (high school, college, or vocational)?

   - **Expertise:** What are you really competent in? What are you the "go to" person for?

   - **Talent:** What do you have natural ability in?

   Shoot for ten items if possible in this column, but if you can't, it's okay. Think of those things that really exhibit your competence, the stuff you're really good at. This list may even serve as a preliminary bio that you can develop later on when you want the world (or, at the very least, your prospective customers) to know why you're a great entrepreneur to do business with.

5. **Take a hard look at what you listed on both sides of the line.**

   Wherever the two lists intersect or have a commonality, you need to take a closer look at that intersection because it's probably an ideal business for you (or pretty darned close). Say that you love movies, and enjoy writing (this is on the left side of the 10-10 list). You also have experience in movies and professional writing, and you even have a degree in English. (These are listed on the right side.) When you combine them, you see that you have some business potential. Some examples of suitable businesses include blogging about movies, writing movie-oriented articles, joining an affiliate marketing program, and permitting advertising on your blog. You get the idea?

Figure 3-1 shows an example of what a 10-10 list may look like.

As you look at this figure, ask yourself some more in-depth questions to discover more. As there are all types of businesses, there are all types of people. What type of person are you? Are you analytical or outgoing? The type of person you are will dictate what type of entrepreneur you'll become.

For instance, if you're analytical and detail-oriented, a business that deals with complicated matters probably would suit you, such as tax preparation or consulting work in engineering. If you're outgoing and a good speaker or conversationalist, being in sales or marketing may better suit you.

Column A	Column B
Enjoyment	Experience, Education, Expertise, or Talent
1 I love movies.	Worked in movie industry for eight years
2 I enjoy vacationing.	BA in English
3 Skiing	Worked as a reporter for five years
4 Theater	I have a flair for writing.
5 Restaurants	I am very detailed-oriented.
6	
7	
8	
9	
10	

Where Column A intersects with Column B, investigate it as a good potential business.

Results/Comments:
Because I love movies and I have lots of education and experience with writing and the movie industry, I will make money writing articles and reviews on movies and make money from movie-related affiliate programs.

Figure 3-1:
A sample
10-10 list.

If you have a few ideas, you can then choose the one that is that has the larger market. Figuring out which has the greater market is easy in some cases. For example, if your interests are Cambodian rugs, elephant-foot umbrella stands, and smartphones, then choose the obvious (if it's not obvious, choose the smartphones). Now, if you aren't sure, do my ten-second test. Put each interest you have in a search engine and do the one with the most hits or results. Of course, if you choose the second one on your list, it's okay. Just choose the one closest to your passions. A successful business appeals to both your mind and your heart.

An offshoot of the 10-10 list is the grid of possibilities. The *grid of possibilities* is a tool to help you spur on your creativity for business success. You can use the grid for a variety of purposes, but its strength is marketing ideas. Refer to Chapter 13 for more on how you can use the grid to nail down your best business.

Focusing on where enjoyment meets competence

The ideal business for you typically lies at the intersection of enjoyment and competence. Most people understand the business value of competence.

After all, you should know what you're doing. Enjoyment is just as easily important. If you aren't enthused about what you offer in your enterprise, the value you offer and the fun of doing it, then don't bother doing it. Go get a job and then spend your spare time doing something else.

I have been in business (either part-time or full-time) since 1981. I thoroughly enjoy my business, and the enjoyment factor keeps me going day-in and day-out. Being in your business means that you need to have initiative and be a self-starter. If you don't enjoy the business, you'll find excuses not to do it and the business more than likely will fail.

Figuring out your personality and the type of entrepreneur you are

You've probably heard different strokes for different folks. The same goes for entrepreneurs — micro or otherwise. I have discovered long ago that certain types of businesses are good for certain types of people. Very often, failure or success is just finding the right match.

Many "experts" say that many (if not most) people aren't well suited at being an entrepreneur. I disagree very strongly. Everyone has something that he or she can do well in some type of entrepreneurial capacity. Many folks have the image of an entrepreneur as being a specific type of person. I actually have seen all types of people succeed as entrepreneurs, and some of them were as different as night and day to me.

Figuring out the best path to micro-entrepreneurship boils down to finding a fit. Personality is a big part of that fit. Spend some time on finding a fit, and your business future will be much brighter. To help you find the right fit, refer to the earlier section, "Doing your 10-10 list" for starters. After all, finding what you have passion for is a great place for your micro-entrepreneurship journey.

You can also turn to other places for help to find out what your personality type is. Do an assessment at www.theentrepreneurnextdoor.com. This website can assist you in figuring out how your personality has an impact on your entrepreneurial success.

Here are some other sites that have resources and information on how to choose a business based on what type of person you are or what type of personality you have:

- Entrepreneur Magazine (www.entrepreneurmag.com)
- Inc. Magazine (www.inc.com)
- Service Corps of Retired Executives (www.score.org)

 ✔ Small Business Administration (www.sba.gov)

 ✔ Small Business Advocate (www.smallbusinessadvocate.com)

Remembering your great moments

Everyone has fond memories, so why not tap into those memories? You can profit from them to help you determine what type of business is right for you. The best businesses spring up from passions you've embraced from an earlier time.

Take the time to write and list those fond memories that keep enduring. Odds are good that you have a business idea tucked away. Some people have even turned this nostalgic passion into a memorabilia business that is successfully sold on a website, a blog, or even as a thriving activity on eBay (more about auctions in Chapter 7). For instance, some people remember great pastimes, such as knitting or traveling, and have found profitable opportunities with them.

Recognizing the Qualities You Need to Be a Micro-Entrepreneur

Being a micro-entrepreneur and an employee is sometimes like the difference between night and day. Employees, no matter how good they are, show up and work partly due to the obligatory nature of the arrangement; they get paid to show up, do their work, and answer to the boss. That is the raw essence of the matter, whereas entrepreneurs have a different dynamic.

Micro-entrepreneurs know that the customer is the boss, but no one is forcing the entrepreneur to work. Micro-entrepreneurs have to be self-starters and to possess some qualities that aren't as necessary in an employee.

Too often, distractions can easily prevent the micro-entrepreneur from working, and she can find herself doing other things than what is truly necessary to make her businesses successful and profitable. You, the entrepreneur, need to have (or to cultivate) the following qualities so you can succeed in your business endeavors.

Having initiative

Being a self-starter means that you're in charge of your own efforts and you are your own motivator. Things don't just happen . . . customers don't come to you, and products and services don't start themselves. You need to have *initiative* because in your business, you're the leader (even if you're the only one in your business), and you have to make things happen if you intend to be successful and profitable in your business.

Having initiative may be the biggest difference between an entrepreneur and employee. The employee is frequently dependent on people and processes that are started by someone else. That's not the case for a micro-entrepreneur.

In my business, if I don't do something (or at least get it started), then it just doesn't get done. If it doesn't get done, then at the end of the day, I don't make money. Someday, you may have employees or other folks helping you (family or maybe some independent contractors), but when you're starting off as a home-based micro-entrepreneur, you need to take the initiative to do things; no one will push, guilt, or cajole you into doing what is needed.

Being able to prioritize

When you're the only one (at least initially) in your business, you know you need to do plenty of things to reach profitability with your business. You need to be able to *prioritize* and determine which tasks are more important and do them first. For example, do you call clients, create products, write an article, or file some documents that have been piling up lately?

List your priorities in your business. You'll have important things to do and urgent things to do — they're not always synonymous. Some things you *must* do in your business, and some things are nice to do but not immediately necessary. You need to figure out what they are in your business so you can focus on the must-do list first. Break it down the following way:

- ✔ **The A list:** This list is an immediate and essential concern, especially for the well-being and growth of your budding enterprise. This list may include servicing an important client or finalizing a marketing campaign to get new clients.

- ✔ **The B list:** This list includes important activities that can certainly benefit your business, but they aren't drop-dead urgent. This list may include talking to potential joint venture partners for future business plans or taking that business management class.

Work on your A list during the early part of the week and get to your B list in the evenings or later in the week. Keeping clients happy and have your marketing strategies actively working (to gain future clients) are of the utmost importance. Of course, everyone works a little differently. I like to do my A list projects early in the day when I have the most energy. Other activities that don't require great focus and energy (such as filing or discussing future projects with associates) can be done at other times. Everyone is a little different; make sure you match your greatest projects to when you feel you're at your peak performance.

As I write this book, I have several piles of paper that need attention (I say "several" because I am rounding down). These piles include everything from receipts that need filing, papers that need to be scanned, and other documents that need to be read and/or filed away. Those piles may be there a while, but writing this book is a more pressing matter — it's on my A list and a priority.

Managing your time

Working from home demands your attention in so many ways, including not only business but also personal. You certainly can't work 24 hours per day, but you also can't not give your business the time and work it needs for you to do well. As a result, being able to manage your time and divvy up your day between your personal and business activities is of utter importance.

Many software packages (and smartphone apps) are available to help you manage your time and activities. A few options that can help you keep track of your professional time and projects include

- ✔ Microsoft Outlook
- ✔ Google Calendar
- ✔ QuickBooks

Plenty of software packages have free trial periods, so you can use their software to see if it works for you. You can go to sites, such as www.download.com and www.filehippo.com, for free demos.

If you don't develop some time-management skills, your business (and you) won't prosper as you should. You can check out *Successful Time Management For Dummies* by Dirk Zeller (John Wiley & Sons, Inc.) for more specific advice.

Staying focused

The most successful entrepreneurs tend to be *focused*; in other words, they stick to the important task at hand until completion. To develop *focus,* create a to-do list and keep it in front of you and check off each completed task. Make it a regular habit and being focused will become second nature to you. You can also find ways to reduce distractions, which are the enemy to your focus. Activities (such as creating a product or doing a marketing campaign) that will make your business profitable take focus.

Unfortunately, your focus is put to the test when you're working from home. All sorts of things dilute or harm your focus. Everything from children and pets, neighbors and family, television and the Internet can put demands on your time and attention and distract you. Therefore, cultivate the discipline of having focus because doing so can put more money in your pocket in due course.

Striving for excellence

Being the best at what you do sounds may seem like I picked up that phrase from the positive thinking seminar I just took. Well, it does matter to your business success. When you get the reputation of being *really* good at your product or service, no matter what it is, you can attain success and bigger profits much easier.

Therefore, don't produce a weak product or service. Believe me, I know on a personal level. I have been self-employed for many years. I have lost clients because I made mistakes and I have gained clients when I did my best. Every entrepreneur experiences it, and you must learn from the lesson. Don't try to be a jack-of-all-trades. Stick to what you do well and what you know inside and out. Doing so can make being more successful in your business so much easier for you.

Being persistent

People give up too easily, especially when they're in business. For every businessperson who succeeds, dozens (and maybe hundreds) gave up. Some gave up because they didn't realize that being in business can be hard work. Some gave up too soon because they expected success to come easy — or fast — or both. What they lacked was *persistence* — the important trait of not giving up easily, which is important in being a successful micro-entrepreneur.

It's amazing how all roads lead to your passion. For more than 25 years, I have told my students (in my home-business seminars) to choose a business topic or niche that you passionately enjoy . . . that makes being focused and persistent in building and pursuing your goals and dreams easier. In that spirit, persistence isn't a driving force — it's a symptom of you choosing to do your passion.

Getting discouraged is easy, especially when you work so many hours in your spare time and late hours on the weekend, and no sales or money to show for it. I know, I have been there (more times than I can admit). This is a big reason I tell beginning home-base entrepreneurs to choose something they love to do because it helps you get through the tough times when you're not making money. Being persistent isn't easy, but doing so is easier when you choose your business activity wisely and stay focused, which will ultimately make money.

Showing creativity

When you're doing what is necessary in your enterprise, problems, glitches, and challenges will always pop up. Maybe the most frequent ones involve making money when you don't have a lot of capital to deploy. Being creative helps to overcome other shortcomings, particularly when you don't have money or resources.

For example, what do you do when you want to get customers for your service, but you have little or no money in your marketing and advertising budget? Well, here is where being creative comes in handy.

Being efficient in your environment can help you excel. These resources can help you spur on your creativity:

- ✔ **Read *Creative Thinkering: Putting Your Inspiration to Work.*** This book by Michael Michalko (New World Library) is praised for its ability to get the reader's creative juices flowing to help them handle personal and professional challenges.

- ✔ **Play around on Lumosity.** This website (www.lumosity.com) can help you increase your activity through a variety of mental exercises.

- ✔ **Experiment and use your creativity and imagination.** I can't tell you everything. Brainstorm, search the Internet, and see what you can find.

Beginning Your Business Life

As I write this book, I assume that you'll be home-based. When you're a micro-entrepreneur, starting at home is both logical and recommended. In these sections, I explain why starting at home is a wise choice and the logistical steps you can take to get up and running.

Recognizing why starting at home makes sense

Choosing to operate your business in your home has a number of advantages, including the following:

- ✔ **Cost:** The most obvious reason the micro-entrepreneur starts at home is the cost. Being home-based easily saves you thousands of dollars — money better spent elsewhere. You don't have to spend money on rent for an office, and you also can save money on gas, driving back and forth to work every day.

- ✔ **Convenience:** Working from home is convenient. Your home office is just a few feet away, so you can tackle issues or handle work almost whenever you need to do so.

- ✔ **Time:** Going back and forth to an office can take a lot of time, even if it's walking distance. A 10-minute commute translates to 20 minutes a day, an hour and 40 minutes per 5-day workweek, and hundreds of hours each year. In that time, you could write a book or serve clients, which can make you more money.

- ✔ **Tax advantages:** When you have a home-based business, you have great tax benefits. You have the ability to write off a home office, which includes a portion of upkeep, utilities, and so on. You can read more details about the tax benefits of a home business in Chapter 21.

- ✔ **Personal benefits:** If you're a single parent and have kids or pets, being able to work from home and keep an eye on those you care about is a great benefit. (I personally enjoy this benefit as a home-based entrepreneur.) The side benefit is that you don't have to pay babysitters or hassle your relatives about helping out. If course, you'll need to figure out how to work and keep your business focus, given the distractions that come with kids and pets.

The moment you run your business outside of home, you automatically have to think of rent, utilities, and so on. These costs start ticking immediately, and you haven't even earned your first dollar yet. Don't forget: You also have to furnish the place and consider the cost of commuting, auto expenses, and so on.

As I write this chapter, I am in my own home office. I first started my business as a part-time venture in March 1981 (probably before some of my readers were even born!). I owned a rental apartment in Hoboken, New Jersey, and although I have long since moved, I am still home-based and now full-time. The great thing about being home-based is that when I get out of bed, I am at work! Of course, the downside is that when I get out of bed, I am at work (no one said being a home-based business was perfect!).

Setting up your environment

If you go to a hundred different home businesses and see their set-up, you would likely see a hundred different set-ups. Some are very efficient, and some aren't, but home office arrangements are as varied and different as diet plans or financial planning needs.

In order for you to set up your business environment to maximize your business success and performance, ask yourself these eight questions and consider what works best for you:

- ✔ **Is your home area used regularly and exclusively for your business activity?** This question has two sides to it.

  - Consider the area you use, so you're efficient and also able to minimize distraction.

  - Focus on the involved tax issues (the potential tax benefits are fantastic), so discuss it with your tax professional (see Chapter 21 for more details on taxes and what you can possibly deduct).

- ✔ **Will clients be visiting you?** If clients are visiting, your set-up needs to be professional and appropriate for your type of potential clientele. Ask yourself if your business set-up enhances the image you want to convey. Of course, if your cousin is an interior decorator, get a second opinion. Finally, if you do have business visitors coming to your home office, talk to your insurance person about the potential liability.

- ✔ **What will be the location of your home office?** Determine whether it will be in the basement, a room at the side of the house with its own doorway, or a spare bedroom. Also look to see whether your home office is next to a noisy kids' playroom or in a room where loud traffic can bother you. Of course, if you're working alone, the possible distractions may not be an issue. But if customers come and go, the distractions may become an issue.

- ✔ **Is some type of permit or license needed?** Sometimes a municipality has a zoning ordinance that limits or prevents some types of commercial activity. See whether you need any special license as well (say if you're selling food items, and you need clearance from the local board of health). Flip to Chapter 21 for more advice about permits and licenses.

✔ **Will you be creating physical products on your site?** If what you're doing is noisy or smelly, find out what is suitable, appropriate, and allowable in your neighborhood. Check with local covenants or with your city's zoning department.

✔ **What type of equipment will you need?** Besides the typical computer set-up, sometimes you need more, such as scanners, digital cameras, DVD burners, and so on, to do your work. Just make sure that there is a significant business purpose before you acquire any equipment.

✔ **What safety factors should you consider?** This question is especially true if you have pets and/or children in the home.

✔ **Have you made provisions for business continuity?** Disruptions are a part of life, and that includes with your business. Are you ready for disruptions? For example, do you have a service or procedure for data back-up if a problem outage happens or a computer's hard drive crashes?

Chapter 4

Setting Up Your Internet Presence

In This Chapter

▶ Creating a website

▶ Starting a blog

▶ Looking at other ways to have an Internet presence

*L*ess than ten years ago, getting a website was a daunting task, right up there with doing your taxes blindfolded or landing on the sun (at night, of course). Thankfully, that's no longer the case. Now getting a website (or a blog) is as easy as ordering pizza or putting on loafers.

A website is almost a mandatory pursuit for a micro-entrepreneur, but fortunately, getting one up and running is relatively easy. In fact, you can actually do it initially for less than ten bucks — for an entire year! Interesting that setting up a website is officially cheaper than ordering pizza (or doing a load of laundry).

In this chapter, I explain the importance of having a web presence and how you can start to make your presence known with a website and/or blog. I also explain a few other ways you can do business without a website or blog if you choose. Just make sure you have some type of presence.

Having a Web Presence: Something You Need as a Micro-Entrepreneur

If you had all the customers you could possibly need or you're looking to stop your business in the coming weeks (retiring or getting a new job), then you probably don't need a website. But for just about every other micro-entrepreneurial reason, you'd be well served with a website. Here are a few reasons why:

- ✓ **Your website is a 24-hour-a-day, 7-day-a-week salesperson.** Both your existing customers and anyone considering doing business with you (prospects, partners, vendors, and so on) will need to know who you are, what you offer, and why they should do business with you. A well-designed website communicates provides all these reasons.

- ✓ **Your website is an inexpensive customer service and support arm of your business.** If people need answers about the technical features of your product, directions to your office, or details about your money-back guarantee, your website can save you time and effort. Furthermore, websites offer many other vital services that cost you next to nothing.

- ✓ **Your website can save you money.** Before the Internet, prospects called you for more information. Now they can be directed to the website for full information, saving you printing, mailing, and other related costs.

- ✓ **Your website allows you to compete with your competitors.** When your customers look for you, your website lets them know that you're here to stay and that you're serious about your business.

In your particular business, you may be able to do business without a website. If so, make sure you still have a web presence, such as with a blog or Facebook presence. If you want to grow your enterprise, however, I suggest you have a website because it offers much potential to help you grow.

Creating Your Website

If you decide to have a website for your business, you're ready to tackle the nitty gritty. You can't just jump in without having a crystal clear idea how you want your website to present yourself and what to include in it. That's where the following sections come into play.

Doing some pre-planning

One of the first steps in setting up your website is in the idea and planning stage. Take the time to figure out before you do anything in terms of actual set-up and ask yourself the following questions:

- ✓ What are my goals?
- ✓ What do I plan to offer?
- ✓ What will be my target market?
- ✓ What products and services will I offer or be an affiliate for?

The answers to these questions can tell you a lot about what type of website (and related services) you may need. If your goal is to simply communicate who you are, you can have simple site with just detailed information about you, what you offer, and your contact information. If you offer a catalog of products, then you can add a shopping cart. You'll need shopping cart software so that people can order what you have, choose options (such as how and where to ship), and be able to make a payment. The versatility and complexity of your website can mirror your business.

In addition, ask yourself the kind of set-up you're considering. For example, if your website is about vitamins, consider whether the site gives information about vitamins and tries to resell vitamin products or whether the site simply provides news and trends about vitamins and simply has affiliate links and/or Google AdSense.

In other words, you can have the same category or niche, but have a variety of ways that you could set up both the actual website and the actual ways to make money. Give this some thought so you have a clear purpose and a clear approach to making money (of course, if that is your ultimate goal).

Recognizing the four basic elements

Today, creating your own website is easier and cheaper (even free) than ever. Making sure you include the basic elements of a website is essential so that your web presence gives customers an accurate and complete picture of your business.

Look at other websites that cover your category to ensure you're in line with them. (For instance, if you sell gardening products, what do the leading gardening-related websites do to make it easy for visitors to learn about gardening and to easily buy gardening products?)

Here are the four basic elements of a functional business website to help you as you start to create your site.

Element one: Domain name

The most important part of a website is the *domain name,* which is the identity of not only your website but also (by extension) you, your company, and what you offer. A domain name is the specific URL that customers type into their web browser to pull up your page. The name should be an asset to you in the sense that it helps the public (actually your *target market* — the customers you want to attract) know the essential reason to visit you.

Some experts actually think that your domain name choice is more important than other generally prominent elements in the world of *search engine optimization* (SEO). SEO is the practice of utilizing the best methods and strategies for getting search engines to direct visitors to your site, such as meta tags and keywords. I discuss SEO and related topics in Chapter 15.

For instance, if you love gardening, then do your best to get a domain name that clearly projects the idea that you're into gardening and that your site is a great place for gardeners (people who buy gardening stuff) to visit.

To select a domain name, follow these steps:

1. **Determine what your domain name will be.**

   You need to figure out whether you want one that refers to your name, identity, or topic, although choosing a domain name that identifies your topic is a better choice. This decision is especially true if you're just beginning your company or Internet career because your target market isn't looking for you. They're looking for what interests them. In other words, they will seek out your topic versus who you specifically are.

   In addition, choosing your topic makes it easier for search engines to help your target market find you. So, for example, if your name is Irv Kowalski and you have a company named Kowalski Associates and you sell financial advisory services, the best website domain name for you would be `www.financialadvisory.com` (or something very similar) rather than `www.irvkowalski.com` or `www.kowalskiassociates.com`.

2. **Select an alternative domain name.**

   You want an alternative in case your first choice has already been taken. The odds are good that someone else also thought of it and probably registered it before you. Be ready to have alternative domain names because many of the good ones (especially with extensions such as .com, .net, and .org) are already used. Fortunately, more domain extensions have come on the scene in recent years, such as .cc, .biz, .info, .me, and so on.

   The .com domain names are the most popular (and likely the most expensive), so see if you can get that extension because it's still the most prized digital realty, although getting a .net or .org name isn't bad. When people hear the .com name and then find it online, the odds are good that they'll automatically type ".com" if they didn't hear (or remember) the extension.

3. **Register your domain name with a domain name registrar online.**

   The Internet Corporation for Assigning Names and Numbers (ICANN) licenses these places to be able to register domain names. You can find a complete listing of domain name registrars at sites such as the following:

- **About.com** (www.webdesign.about.com)
- **Go Daddy** (www.godaddy.com)
- **ICANN** (www.icann.org)
- **Internic** (www.internic.net)
- **Verisign** (www.verisigninc.com)

Try your first preference for a domain name. If someone has already taken it, try your alternate and keep looking until you find a suitable one.

The cost of getting a domain varies from registrar to registrar, so shop around. You'll probably be able to find something for less than $10 because the competition in domain name registering is fierce. I have seen many domain names available for even under $5.

Element two: Web pages

If folks type your domain name into their web browser, they expect to see something. You should have web pages there for them that give interesting and compelling messages about what you offer, who your company is, and so on. The good news: Creating the web pages isn't difficult.

In the Internet's early days, you needed a programmer to create web pages for your website. I chuckle when I write that because the "early days" sounds like history and that the Internet was invented right after fire was discovered and just before the iPhone came along. Actually the "early days" of the Internet are circa 1998 (give or take a few years).

Today, you can easily create decent-looking web pages in plenty of ways and without the need for figuring out HTML code or paying for expensive programming. You can even do it at no cost at all.

Here are some free or inexpensive ways (and resources) to easily create web pages:

- ✔ **Cnet's Download.com:** This great site (www.download.com) offers thousands of software packages that you can review and use as soon as possible.
- ✔ **File Hippo:** File Hippo (www.filehippo.com) is a great site with thousands of download software programs.
- ✔ **Hosting firms:** Most hosting firms (even the ones that offer free hosting) provide free software to create your web pages. Refer to the next section for a list of URLs.
- ✔ **HTML Goodies:** This site (www.htmlgoodies.com) has lots of resources and information that are useful for novices as well as the experienced web page designers.

✔ **Tucows:** This site (www.tucows.com) may be the most comprehensive site on the Internet for Internet-related software that is either free or inexpensive. You can find plenty of freeware, adware, free web page creation software, and free-trial software that you can try, at usually no cost. You can also probably find dozens that you can try out for free.

✔ **Web Hosting Free Reviews:** Many websites provide free or low-cost web page creation software. You can find them at www.webhostingfree reviews.com.

✔ **Web page templates:** They're available either free or low-cost. Do a search with your favorite search engine for "web page templates". They're also available on eBay as well as on Tucows and at Cnet's download.com page.

✔ **Word processing packages:** Many give you the ability to save a word processing document as a web page. They include Microsoft Word (www.microsoft.com) and Open Office (a free suite of software programs available at www.openoffice.org).

If you're proficient (or you're planning to be), these preceding resources can help you do web pages on your own at minimal cost. However, for most folks starting out, I recommend you get technical assistance. Outsourcing can prove to be very useful. For more on outsourcing, see Chapter 19.

Element three: Hosting

When people type in your domain name in their browser window, they expect to see you and what you offer (through your web pages) in their browser. But the only way that can happen is if your domain name and the accompanying pages are hosted. Being *hosted* means that a firm gives you space on its *servers* (computers that are connected continuously to the Internet) so that visitors do find and see your website.

A web-hosting firm generally hosts many web sites (maybe hundreds or thousands), and as such it requires a very fast connection to the Internet. The hosting firms typically charge *rent* (monthly, quarterly or annual fees) for anyone using their web hosting services.

You may find that you're dealing with a firm that directly owns that main server, or you may find you're renting your space from a company that, in turn, is renting its space from a larger web hosting company. In this case, the server of the smaller company is linked to the server of the larger company, so the larger company is actually enabling your website to be viewed online. This level of detail is really inconsequential to the website owner, whether he is directly dealing with the main company or a smaller subsidiary because the end result is the same.

To help you find a host for your website, check out these sources:

- ✔ **Free Web Hosting** (www.free-webhosts.com)
- ✔ **Free Web Space** (www.freewebspace.net)
- ✔ **Host Index** (www.hostindex.com)
- ✔ **Host Search** (www.hostsearch.com)
- ✔ **Web Host Directory** (www.webhostdir.com)

The preceding list includes sites that track and review those firms that provide free hosting, too (the clue is the word "free"). Although I include sources that track free hosting, they aren't necessarily the best for you. I include free hosting so that beginners don't face any entry barrier. I want to see you get started whether you're getting free hosting or paying a few bucks a month.

Free hosting is free for a reason. Remember that you get what you pay (or don't pay) for. Ask yourself whether that trade-off is worth any potential issues you may have. By not paying, you often allow the host to do advertising on the site, and you may also get limited services. You need to decide what services you need the most and carefully investigate and review several hosts and their various plans.

Element four: Accepting payment

This last element of your website is only necessary when you're trying to make money directly from your site. If you're directly selling something, such as products or services, to your visitors, you need to ensure the site has this capability. If you're not, I sell my audio seminars as downloadable programs at sites, such as www.ravingcapitalist.com, and I use PayPal (www.paypal.com) so that folks can use either PayPal or their credit card (PayPal can process payment either way.)

Paypal is an electronic intermediary payment service that gives merchants and buyers the ability to pay. Buyers can go to PayPal to set up an account so that they can pay for products and services. Merchants use the site to receive funds. PayPal has complete tutorials for how a business can add electronic payment services at a website or blog.

Accepting payment at your site is important, especially if you're selling products right there (versus soliciting that prospects contact you at your office, for instance, for services). PayPal is the leading source for making and receiving payments for Internet businesses, although plenty of alternatives available, such as:

- ✔ **Amazon Payments** (https://payments.amazon.com)
- ✔ **Google Checkout** (https://checkout.google.com)
- ✔ **Money Bookers** (www.moneybookers.com)
- ✔ **Pay Simple** (www.paysimple.com)
- ✔ **Payza** (www.payza.org)
- ✔ **Shopify** (www.shopify.com)

For resources to help you compare and shop for ecommerce payment services for your website or blog, use these resources:

- ✔ **Card Payment Options** (www.cardpaymentoptions.com)
- ✔ **Ecommerce Guide** (www.ecommerceguide.com)
- ✔ **Ecommerce News** (www.ecommercejunkie.com)
- ✔ **Payments Views** (www.paymentsviews.com)

These resources provide lots of news and guidance on the latest technology and services for businesses facilitate payment and do financial transactions online.

Tackling marketing considerations after your website is up

After your website is running, your work isn't done. In fact, your job has just begun. Now you're ready to market your site. People need to see your site and then make a decision about buying what you're offering. Or if you're presenting an affiliate link or offer from a direct party (and you make some type of commission from their sale of a good or service), you want them to proceed to the sales page of the merchant's offer, so you need traffic.

Getting visitors and building this audience is important if your website is to turn into a profitable pursuit. I discuss marketing in greater depth in Part III, but here is a brief list of some ways to get folks to your site (both free methods and methods you pay for):

- ✔ **Advertising in ezines:** *Ezines* are online newsletters that cover a particular topic and can reach a large audience. Most of them allow you to do paid advertising (refer to Chapter 16).
- ✔ **Article marketing:** You can write articles on your specialty and have links back to your site (check out Chapter 18).

- **Directories:** Submit your business for listing in directories such as Manta (`www.manta.com`). More about directories in Chapter 15.

- **Guest blogging:** Many active blogs allow you to post an article as a guest writer or guest blogger. You can then add links for readers to be able to visit your site (go to Chapter 16.)

- **Link exchanges:** Exchanging links with other sites can help increase traffic to your site (check out Chapter 14).

- **Search engines:** You can list your website with search engines such as Google and Yahoo (among others). Refer to Chapter 15.

- **Social media:** You can use Facebook, Twitter, and other social media venues to reach prospects and garner interest in your site (look in Chapter 17).

- **YouTube:** Video marketing through venues such as YouTube can help generate traffic to your site (refer to Chapter 17).

Marketing your website gets easier as you find out what methods work best for you. Internet or not, you must constantly test all the possible ways available for you and your potential customers.

Setting up Your Blog

Creating a blog is easier than you think. The word "blog" may even be a mystery to you, but fortunately, the resources are available to help understand you so you can quickly set up one.

A *blog* is much like a journal you write online, and the blog is hosted by a third party. Consider a blog much like a website, only easier and with less cost involved. With a blog, you don't need to figure out how to create a web page or set up and design an entire website. Running a blog can be as easy as doing word processing.

These sections give you the lowdown on blogs, including everything from knowing what to write about, figuring out how to set up a blog, deciding what to include in your blog, and marketing your blog.

Deciding on your blog's purpose

Before you do your blog, spend some time figuring out what you will do in your blog. Ask yourself these questions to give you a clearer idea:

✔ What am I interested in?

✔ What am I an expert in?

✔ Would my occupation be an interesting subject?

✔ What is currently missing online?

✔ Do I have a goal that I'm trying to achieve that I can document online?

✔ Will I be able to blog about the subject matter consistently over a long period of time?

✔ How many other blogs exist on the subject matter I'm interested in? Do I have a fresh take to stand out from the rest?

Do some research on how others are doing a successful blog. Check out the "Popular Blogs" page at Technorati (www.technorati.com). Also check the Webby Awards' list of blogging nominees (www.webby.com).

If you're a part-time blogger and work at a regular full-time job, be careful about doing a blog (or anything for that matter) that is about your job, workplace, or employer. Unless you're safe-guarding your blog (password-protected, for example), a blog is viewable in the public domain (which is the point of a blog to begin with) so it's easy for any employer to see if its employees are doing or communicating anything improper or illegal. Think twice (three times!) before mentioning anything about your employer, other employees, customers, vendors, and so on because whatever you write can haunt (and hurt) you.

Figuring out the blog's set-up in advance

Because a blog is basically an online journal wherein you can digitally write your thoughts, ideas, opinions, and practically anything that you want people to read, you may want to decide what form your thoughts will take.

Your blog can be any of the following (with the following equipment needed):

✔ **A written blog:** Folks read your *posts* (the updates and articles you write). This is the most common form (but audio and video blogging are catching up).All you need is your computer to start immediately writing and posting.

✔ **An audio blog:** You hope to get listeners to listen to what you post (often referred to as *podcasting* or *audio blogging*).

✔ You need a good quality digital audio recorder (most digital recorders are adequate for audio blogging). You also need a venue to upload your audio files. Many audio bloggers use iTunes (www.itunes.com). You can refer to Podbean (www.podbean.com) for advice on how to create an audio blog.

> ✔ **A video blog:** You hope to have viewers to watch what you posted (you guessed it, *video blogging*). For video, all you need minimally to get started is a good video recorder and a venue such as YouTube (www. youtube.com).

> ✔ **A mix:** Some bloggers write articles and also do some audios or videos. (I like to do both written and video commentaries.)

Some of my favorite blogs regularly feature both articles and videos. too. A mix is a good idea because many people who visit your blog can enjoy the mix and may be more receptive to your offerings.

To help you figure out which type is right for you, figure out what the easiest way for you to communicate is. If writing isn't your strength, don't fret because plenty of bloggers prefer the audio and/or video routes. Find the bloggers in your niche or topic and see how they do their blogging. What's more important is that you offer consistent content rather than the style of the content.

So blogging has a lot of power for you and gives you a great way to have a presence, communicate to the world and find ways to make money, too. After you decide what type of blog you want, you can check out these top places to go to get your blog started:

> ✔ **Blog.com** (www.blog.com)

> ✔ **Blogger** (www.blogger.com)

> ✔ **Posterous** (www.posterous.com)

> ✔ **Tumblr** (www.tumblr.com)

> ✔ **Type Pad** (www.typepad.com)

> ✔ **Wordpress** (www.wordpress.org)

I have a blog with www.blogger.com (a Google service), and I usually write, but I also post videos to YouTube and place the link on my blog so viewers can get a chance to view them and hear what I have to say. In the video, I usually take a moment at the end of my commentary (I talk about financial, business, and economic issues) to encourage the viewer to see something I am offering for sale and provide a link right below the video.

Understanding a blog's features

Besides being able to do a journal with regular posts is the main activity, a blog has other important features. Within your blogging, you have the ability to place links (read that as "affiliate links" so that you can make money). (*Affiliate links* are links that go to an affiliate offer that you make money from. See Chapter 11 for more information.)

In other words, having affiliate links to gardening products when you're writing posts on the topic of gardening in your gardening blog is smart.

Your blog can also give you the ability to

- **Do advertising:** You'll have the ability to add advertising to your blog and gain revenue from it. Chapter 12 contains more information about earning money from advertising.
- **Add Amazon:** You can gain revenue by adding Amazon products to your blog and gain revenue when visitors click and buy from Amazon.
- **Make permanent links:** Every article you post can have a permanent link that you can share with others.
- **Allow comments:** You can create interest in your posts when readers are able to add their comments.
- **Create a mailing list:** Your blog can help you create an email list or distribution list so that you can send reach many customers with an email that announces something or promotes a product or service you're offering or an affiliate link.

Tapping into blogging resources

If you're serious about blogging (and making money with it, too), then head to these sources for some great guidance to do some really neat blogging:

- **Blogging Bits** (www.bloggingbits.com)
- **Blogging Tips** (www.bloggingtips.com)
- **Daily Blog Tips** (www.dailyblogtips.com)
- **Pro Blogger** (www.problogger.com)
- **Successful Blog** (www.successful-blog.com)

You can also check out *Professional Blogging For Dummies* by Susan J. Getgood (John Wiley & Sons, Inc.) for a much more in-depth discussion in the friendly *For Dummies* format.

Take care and make sure that you don't run afoul of the law (especially when you blog about sensitive or controversial topics). Legal issues can arise, so make sure you're aware of them before you get in trouble. Many of these blogging resources touch on these matters, but make sure you check other sources, such as the Electronic Frontier Foundation (www.eff.org).

In addition, understand your rights and responsibilities with issues tied to copyright laws. Find out more at places such as the Copyright Office (`www.copyright.gov`) and Creative Commons (`www.creativecommons.org`).

Marketing your blog

After you launch your blog, you need to build awareness and readership (or listenership or viewership or some kind of ship). That means one word — marketing! (Chapter 16 provides more specific information about marketing your blog.) Here is a brief list of marketing approaches for your blog:

✔ **Check out blog directories.** You can post your blog to blog directories. People go to them to seek out blogs on a given subject matter. A top blog directory is Technorati (`www.technorati.com`).

✔ **Ping.** *Pinging* is just the process of blasting your blog's identity into the blogosphere to inform folks that you are there. You may say that pinging is to blogs what search engines are to websites.

✔ **Google.** Add your blog to the Google (`www.google.com`) search world. You can find more about search engines in Chapter 15.

✔ **Remind your readers that if they like a recent post or your blog in general, they can share it.** Check out these sites:

- **Delicious** (`www.delicio.us`)
- **Digg** (`www.digg.com`)
- **Reddit** (`www.reddit.com`)
- **Stumbleupon** (`www.stumbleupon.com`)

These sites are excellent venues for folks to share content and links with their contacts.

✔ **Comment.** Be a regular commenter on other active blogs and make sure you have a signature when you comment so that you can link back to your blog. A *signature* is when you end your comment with your name and a reference to your site (or a specific page at your site such as a landing page).

✔ **Spread the word.** Tell your family and friends about your blog. Use the social media world with tools like Twitter (`www.twitter.com`).

Considering Other Alternatives to Give You a Web Presence

Having a presence on the Internet doesn't necessarily mean that you need a website or blog. You can be on the Internet in other ways that are free and provide you with an easy platform to tell the world about what you do. The following are two alternatives:

Facebook

Facebook (www.facebook.com) is more than just about posting snarky comments and witty updates. You can do many of the things that you can do with websites and blogs (writing articles, sharing links, and so on) on Facebook at no cost.

To do so, keep in mind that Facebook is its own great tutorial for how to use it. With Facebook, stay focused; remember that you're a micro-entrepreneur, so use your online time wisely and stay focused on the greater financial good. Chapter 17 covers more about how you can use Facebook to market your business.

LinkedIn

LinkedIn (www.linkedin.com) is essentially like Facebook for professionals. You can find contacts, companies, and groups that cover most professional interests. In addition, LinkedIn provides a place for your profile and gives you the opportunity to connect with potentially millions of like-minded folks based on your interests and professional pursuits.

LinkedIn has plenty of information about itself with an entire site on how to use LinkedIn at http://learn.linkedin.com/. Chapter 17 has more discussion on LinkedIn.

Chapter 5

Honing In on Opportunities

This chapter is your treasure-hunting chapter. When you're a nimble micro-entrepreneur, the opportunities are endless. If you have the ability to serve others in some way, either with a product or service, then finding the people who have wants and needs can help you make a profit. (The most basic requirement of free market capitalism is serving others, whereas locating those people to sell it to them is the other basic requirement.)

As you go through this chapter, keep in mind that you can make money in any area or niche that I cover (and for you imaginative folks, even more). You can make money directly or indirectly with the areas and niches covered.

> ✔ *Directly* means that you're personally involved in that type of business, offering products and services in that category or niche. In addition, it may be an area or niche where you can create products such as ebooks and other information products to sell (refer to Chapter 10 for more information on self-publishing).

> ✔ *Indirectly* means that you make money through referrals or as an affiliate (refer to Chapter 11 for more about becoming an affiliate).

Profit is there to be made if you recognize it and seize the opportunity. This chapter explores some basics, including identifying people who need your service or product, knowing how to make money after you identify them, figuring out what to offer them, identifying and steering clear of bad opportunities, and knowing how to handle possible legal issues.

Identifying Customers; Differentiating between Their Wants and Needs

In order to earn people's money, you need to satisfy their wants or needs to the point where they say, "Thank you, here is your money." As a micro-entrepreneur, in order to make profit, you need to help the reader solve the problem of which needs or wants to fulfill. Keep this in mind about the two:

✔ *Needs* are simply those things that a person can't live without; they're necessities, such as food, water, shelter, and so on. Think of what people will keep buying no matter how good or bad economic times are.

✔ *Wants* are those things that people desire to have but aren't necessities, such as more vacation time, the latest electronic entertainment technology, or a bigger home. Wants are most likely fulfilled when economic times are good.

Knowing the difference can pay off. Understanding the general economy can also figure out how you can profit by serving others. Keep reading for more information.

Knowing the lifetime value of a customer

Being able to know the lifetime value of a customer is important. (The *lifetime value* of a customer means how much money that customer will potentially spend during the extended time that he or she may be buying your product or service.) If a product is typically bought once (such as a big-screen TV) and that purchase amount is $600 (and it's the only product you sell), then the lifetime value is $600. If a customer buys a $10 cream from you and he or she typically buy three jars of it per year, and the customer, on average, sticks with the cream for five years, then the lifetime value of this customer is $150. (Five years times three purchases of $10 each.) With that data, you can estimate how much of a profit each customer is potentially worth, and you can budget the marketing cost. For example, if you sold those $10 creams, you can afford to give free samples (that are relatively inexpensive to you) because the upside potential is five years of sales.

You want to find out (if possible) the buying power of a particular niche to see which niche gives you the bigger bang for your marketing buck (you can find more specific information about "Searching for Success: Finding the Information You Need" in this chapter).

Say you can choose between niche A where consumers buy $25 worth of products or niche B where consumers only buy $10 of products but typically buy $10 worth every year for five years. Which would you prefer?

In niche A, the lifetime value (in terms of total product purchased) is only $25. However, the niche B buyer has a lifetime value of $50 (5 times $10). All things being equal, I suggest you'd do business in niche B because it provides the opportunity to make more money.

Recognizing the type of market: Horizontal or vertical

Opportunities come in different shapes and sizes. Markets are the same. You need to know the type of market your niche falls into and whether that market has more opportunities. There are essentially two types of markets:

- ✔ **Horizontal market:** A *horizontal market* means you have a specific product or service that can apply to many types of buyers across many different categories of industry. An example of a horizontal market is a business that sells computers or office supplies. These types of products can easily apply to most businesses (as well as consumers and government agencies).

   Just because a product or service is applicable across a large swath of the marketplace doesn't necessarily mean that it will be a profitable choice. A good example is if you were selling the service of house key duplication. More than 60 million homeowners live in the United States, but ask yourself how many will buy more than one set of keys.

- ✔ **Vertical market:** A *vertical market* means you offer products and/or services that are targeted to a single industry. An example of a vertical market is a business that sells golf equipment; your business targets its products to the golf industry. All the products created, from golf clubs to shirts to ebooks are targeted at the golf industry. Vertical markets will always be more niche-focused than horizontal markets.

Eyeing the Basic Categories of Successful Home Businesses

The most common type of micro-entrepreneurs is that of the home business, although this section certainly applies to any type of small business. In order for you to succeed in your enterprise, you need to understand which following category of success you fall into.

When people decide to buy from you, they're deciding whether to buy from you or your competitor — either you or another business. Make sure you know why people would buy from you versus your competitor.

Category one: The problem solver

Think of when you last paid someone money and what you did. You wanted a problem solved, so you turned to someone who you viewed as an expert to help you solve the problem.

When you solve problems, you make money. When people have a problem, they pay to have that problem solved. Micro-entrepreneurs excel at finding profitable ways to solve problems. Think about what problems exist in society. The public reads today's headlines and it sees problems; micro-entrepreneurs see those same headlines and see opportunities. Look in the mirror and examine what you see.

For instance, I remember seeing the headline "13 million adults in America are illiterate" (and the ironic thing is that they couldn't read that). The public read that headline and saw a problem. Entrepreneurs saw that same headline and saw opportunities.

When the world perceives you as an expert at solving a particular problem, marketing is much easier and getting clients is much easier. (Refer to Part III for specific ways you can do so.)

Category two: Anticipating a megatrend

This category anticipates and gets to a big trend before the crowd, not at the same time as the crowd. In other words, if a large, definable trend is in its early stages now, a nimble micro-entrepreneur can start setting up (by finding products and services to offer, by doing a marketing plan, and so on) to take advantage of opportunities before others do and thus profit as the trend becomes larger and more obvious.

You may think that you can't readily forecast or see a megatrend coming, but you don't really need to do anything that requires a crystal ball or a session with a stargazer. All you need to do is see what megatrends are unfolding right now before your eyes and do some common-sense analysis of wants and needs that would logically arise in due course.

A *megatrend* is a very development typically involving or impacting millions of people (or entire countries) involving social, economic, technological, or political change. This change is deep-seated and usually lasts for years and possibly decades. Those with foresight and planning can make a fortune by anticipating the wants and needs of people as megatrends unfold. Determine which megatrends are unfolding today.

Imagine for a moment that you're looking at the cover of *Time* magazine's "Man of the Year" issue from 1982. That year, *Time* couldn't think of any man or woman, so it named a "thing of the year" — the computer. The magazine recognized that several million computers were showing up in homes, although in today's numbers, it probably was low. Now most households have multiple computers, such as desktops, laptops, tablets, and smart phones.

Several hopeful entrepreneurs saw that cover and rushed out to open — you guessed it — computer stores. But many of those computer stores went out of business because there were too many computer stores. Who made money from this megatrend? The nimble micro-entrepreneur would have looked at that cover and said, "If millions of people are buying computers today, what will those same people need tomorrow?"

I actually used that example as a creative-thinking exercise in one of my home business seminars. Imagine that you're one of my students and consider these ideas and the potential:

- If millions of people own computers, that means that millions of people will ultimately need training and education.

- If there are millions of computers, it means there will be demand for computer repair, computer accessories, computer cleaning, and so.

- If there are millions of computers, there will be need for software for a variety of functions, such as word processing, spreadsheets, and so on.

Eyeing former or ongoing megatrends

While other businesses are competing in markets in the here and now, forward-thinking micro-entrepreneurs can prepare for opportunities that come tomorrow. Some examples of past (and/or still ongoing) megatrends include the following:

- **Baby Boomers:** This group of folks was born during the post–World War II era (1946 to 1964). As of today, they number more than 85 million. Now they're an aging group that will need retirement planning, healthcare services, and so on. Micro-entrepreneurs also found opportunities in re-training middle-aged folks to re-enter the workforce, start businesses, teach and train on Internet technologies, and so on.

- **The Internet:** Generally starting in the late 1990s, this far-reaching technology has impacted every corner of society (and the world) and has ignited an explosion of change touching on information, technology, business services, customer service, and much more. Many micro-entrepreneurs made some macro-money!

- **Debt and more debt:** In recent years, millions have become over-indebted, which has had an impact in slowing economic growth in recent years. As of 2012, college debt hit $1 trillion. States and municipalities racked up billions in debt and ended up laying off many workers. Some cities even closed down their police departments. All of these events contributed to some of the worst economic times in history, which meant that micro-entrepreneurs had opportunities in helping folks find ways to save money, find jobs, and lower debt.

Category three: A combination

You can combine the previous two sections and launch a business that solves a problem and also anticipate megatrends. You then have two powerful factors helping you make money.

Years ago I had a student that did this very thing. It was 1997 when he took my class on Zero-Cost Marketing (www.zerocostmarketing.net). He was an affiliate to a program that helped bankrupt consumers gain credit cards. At the time, 1997 was the first year the United States had total bankruptcies of one million or more. He marketed a program that both solved a problem (gaining credit) and was a megatrend (for years since 1997 we have had one million plus people going bankrupt and needing credit). That business generated seven figures in revenues, and it was only a website! I doubt he had credit trouble.

Getting the Lowdown on Niches: What to Focus Your Business On

A *niche* is nothing more than a definable slice of the general market place, and a niche that you have chosen to make money in is your target market (also referred to as your *target niche*).

Whether it's rock music fans, insurance agents, or consumers dealing with hair loss, a niche is specific and small enough for the micro-entrepreneur to sell to. You want to know what your niche is for one simple reason. The general principle is simple: Don't spend your time targeting (marketing) 100 percent of the world. Instead, spend 100 percent of your time and effort targeting 1 percent. It is a more focused approach and it will make for an easier path to sales and profits.

The following sections give you an overview of the major niches that continue to have profitable opportunities for the micro-entrepreneur. Review them and use the resources later in the chapter to help you focus in on a niche that you can concentrate on for your marketing success.

Choosing the right niche for you

Selecting a niche isn't difficult. Just ask yourself the following questions to help you choose:

✔ **Do I enjoy the niche or have experience in it?** The more knowledgeable and passionate you are about a niche, the greater chances of success as that niche becomes your target market.

✔ **Is the niche big enough and popular enough to give me adequate income?** If you want a large income, the niche you choose to become your target market should be big enough to accommodate you.

There is no problem with trying to make money in a small market, but the question is how small it is. Is it still big enough to make money? If you're full-time or part-time in your business, it does matter.

Say that you're a real *Star Wars* fan (or *Twilight,* take your pick). Examine to see if it has potential for a business and whether it may be too micro, even for a micro-business. The size of the market matters, especially if your goal to make enough money to turn the activity into a full-time income.

Finding out if a niche is big enough or popular enough isn't difficult. Do a search with your favorite search engine for a quick test. If a search for niche A has 5,000 hits and niche B has only 200 hits, those search results tell you a lot. In this case, if all things are equal, then choose niche A. If you go to Technorati (www.technorati.com) and you find that niche X has 500 blogs discussing/covering that niche and niche Z has only 23, then in that case go for niche X.

Use the resources later in this chapter to do more research for a niche that you like, and that can be very fruitful.

Recognizing recession-proof niches

In good times and bad, as a micro-entrepreneur, you can find ways to make money by giving people what they want when they want it. Choosing the right niche becomes even more important during recessions. People will keep buying, but to a lesser extent, so here are some recession-proof niches (which are needs, and not wants).

Business opportunities

When people are hurting for cash, they seek alternatives — things to do in addition to their jobs (or their unemployment). For consumers, this business opportunities market is schizophrenic. They need to worry about scams that are competing for their attention along with legitimate providers of information and programs to make money. If your business helps folks make money, then you can double-up on marketing what you offer in bad times.

Helping make money can come in many forms, ranging from coaching and consulting to seminars, ebooks, and so on. You can also consider affiliate programs — not only for moneymaking programs but also for business services. (Check out Chapter 11 for how to find affiliate programs.) There are incorporation services, for example, that do offer commissions to those micro-businesses that help them market.

Job search

When unemployment is high, people need assistance finding and getting jobs. Offering services, such as interviewing, skills training, and resume preparation will do well. In addition, many job hunting websites have affiliate programs.

Examples of sites that offer affiliate programs in this niche are Monster.com (www.monster.com) and Employment 911 (www.employment911.com).

Health and wellness

Whether it be health insurance, vitamins, or medical information (such as to find out what ails you), people are concerned about their health in good times and bad. Lots of companies in this niche have affiliate opportunities for you. Hopefully, you can also enjoy some healthy profits (would hate to see your P&L be DOA).

A good example is eHealth Insurance (www.ehealthinsurance.com). It pays affiliate commissions when your prospects submit applications for health insurance (it has a network of more than 150 insurers). Another example is Market Health (www.markethealth.com), which tracks affiliate programs in the health and wellness niche.

Preparedness and self-sufficiency

When times are tough, the issues of preparedness and self-sufficiency become popular. Should the economy get deeper into difficulty, this topic will only get easier to market. If you went to places like Clickbank (www.clickbank.com), you can find lots of programs on this topic with good affiliate commissions (50 percent or better).

Escapism (entertainment)

In tough times, diversion is an important pursuit. The movie industry, for example, did very well during the Great Depression. Today's entertainment industry is larger, and the Internet makes it easy to find entertainment and for entrepreneurs to profit by it.

Some micro-entrepreneurs, for example, would go to a site like Internet Movie Database (www.imdb.com) and look up what movies are coming up to anticipate popularity and hopefully profit from it. Say that you sell toys and you know that a big Disney animated feature is coming out in six months. You can focus your marketing to profit from it. (Refer to the chapters in Part III for some strategies.)

And don't forget, companies like Netflix (www.netflix.com) and many other entertainment-related companies also have affiliate programs.

Financial concerns

Helping people with financial concerns is always an issue, but it's even more so in slow economic times. People need help with lowering their debt, lowering their taxes, saving money, and with budgeting.

A good example is Lower My Bills.com (www.lowermybills.com). This site specializes in lower costs in areas, such as mortgages and credit cards; it also has an affiliate program.

Education

When people can't find a job, many of them figure that they need to upgrade their skills and knowledge to make themselves more employable. Many education-related companies do well in both good times and bad, and many of them do have an affiliate program. A good example of a top educational site that pays affiliate commissions is Ed2Go (www.ed2go.com).

Seasonal niches

There seems to always be a reason for buying something for someone, all year round. Here are some great seasonal opportunities:

- ✔ **Holiday buying:** The most obvious is the Christmas and Hanukkah holiday season. Identify which gifts are popular. Shrewd affiliate marketers research places like Amazon (www.amazon.com) and eBay (www.ebay.com) to figure out the consumer buying trends and habits. Focus your strategy on this: If customers are going to buy something anyway, they may as well buy it through you or an affiliate link.

- ✔ **Winter and summer:** In the wintertime, people buy coats, boots, snow blowers, and road salt. Many retailers that sell these items are a good choice to make some cold cash (pardon the pun). In the summer, people are buying swimsuits, sunblock, and lawn-and-garden items. Whether they're buying from Amazon or other venues, find out.

- ✔ **New Year's resolution:** In January, people vow to make the new year better. Translation: They decide to improve their health (losing weight is the most common health-related resolution) or their wealth (increasing their income).

While you're at it, see how you can make money tied to Valentine's Day because it comes so soon after New Year's Day. (Who says that love and money don't go together?) Many sites that offer flowers, candy, and gifts have affiliate programs. In fact, the major affiliate directory sites highlight Valentine's Day affiliate opportunities in January. A good example of a merchant that uses affiliates for Valentine's promotions is Emitations (www.emitations.com).

✔ **Life milestones:** Weddings and graduations are generally big events in people's lives. Identify the products, such as photography, gifts, event planning, and catering, that people are most likely to buy during these times. Examples of niche businesses that do well at this are at The Knot (www.theknot.com) and Graduation Place (www.graduationplace.com).

✔ **Demographic niches:** Look to see how the demographics are changing in the United States and capitalize on them. For instance, the Latino market is growing in as well as the Asian market. Baby Boomers are also a huge market. You'll find plenty of opportunities if you're targeting large, definable sectors of society's large and diverse population. If they're buying, you should be selling!

Do your research on these niches. A good place to start is www.census.gov. You can then find out what products and services these demographic groups tend to buy. See if you can provide these products/services or if any affiliate programs are available that you can market.

Good times niches

When times are good, people are spending differently than when the economy is sluggish. Either way, the alert micro-entrepreneur keeps a watchful one for buying trends when the economy is thriving. Here are some areas to keep in mind:

✔ **Big-ticket items:** When times are good, both consumers and businesses tend to have greater confidence in acquiring big-ticket items. A consumer is more apt to make that big purchase like a new car or a new washing machine. Businesses are more apt to expand their operations and do things, such as upgrading their computers or other technology, or hiring more workers.

✔ **Vacation and travel:** When people are doing better, they have more discretionary income and can spend on things that seem like out-of-reach luxuries. In good times, vacations are more prevalent as more people either visit places or go on more cruises. Think of those places, products, and services that can excel as a result.

Hotel chains, airlines, travel agencies, and other companies do have affiliate programs to take advantage of at this time. Bon voyage!

✔ **Home improvement:** When people feel good about their personal economic conditions, they tend to improve or upgrade their property. Home improvement is more apt to happen when times are good and the real estate market is on an upswing.

Special interest niches

No matter what your interests (or whatever interests your target market has), you can also profit from some special-interest niches, such as the following:

- ✓ **Politics:** The blue-state, red-state debate has been raging for quite some time. You can take off your political lenses for a moment and view this environment as an opportunity. Look to see what progressives and liberals buy and identify what conservatives will buy. You can also identify what libertarians and centrists buy. Each group has measurable buying habits that you can identify from and profit from.

  By the way, the same dynamic occurs when you apply this thinking to other demographics, such as religion, teenagers, senior citizens, Millenials, and so on.

- ✓ **Embarrassing problems:** People who have embarrassing problems are actually a profitable niche. People who have issues that bother them will also seek relief. They frequent the Internet for confidential and low-key ways to address these issues. You can certainly imagine what some of those issues are (you may even be suffering from them right now).

As a micro-entrepreneur, your main goal is to help the customer. You solve their issue and make a profit doing it — a win-win situation. For more on doing market research to find potential customers, see Chapter 13.

Searching for Success: Finding the Information You Need

The Internet's greatest strength is the ease in finding stuff. Use the following sections to find what you need, depending on, of course, what you're looking for.

Researching niches

No matter what niche you're targeting (or researching), have a handy batch of resources to help you zero in on your best profitable opportunities. Consider some of these search engines, directories, and sites to help you:

- ✓ Alexa Top 500 Movers and Shakers (`http://alexa.com/topsites`)
- ✓ Amazon Bestsellers (`http://amazon.com/gp/bestsellers/books`)

✔ Barnes & Noble Bestsellers (www.barnesandnoble.com/bestsellers)

✔ Blog catalog (www.blogcatalog.com)

✔ Business.com (www.business.com)

✔ Google Alerts (www.google.com/alerts)

✔ Google Trends (www.google.com/trends)

✔ Search Engine Guide (www.searchengineguide.com)

✔ Search Engine Land (www.searchenginelanc.com)

✔ Search Engine Watch (www.searchenginewatch.com)

✔ Search Engine Colossus (www.searchenginecolossus.com)

✔ Squidoo's Top 100 Lenses (www.squidoo.com/browse/top)

✔ Super Pages (www.superpages.com). This is one of my favorite directories. It's similar to a national Yellow Pages online. If you need to find companies, vendors, and suppliers, this site is good.

✔ Trend Watching (www.trendwatching.com)

✔ What Sells Best (www.whatsellsbest.com) looks at best-selling products on eBay

✔ Yahoo! Directory (http://dir.yahoo.com)

For a more extensive look to help you with all things business (and especially marketing), check out Chapter 15.

Viewing educational tutorials

Educational tutorial sites provide you not only great info on various how-to topics but they're also good for research on what the public likes and what they want to discover more about.

Here are some great tutorial sites:

✔ About.com (www.about.com)

✔ Answer Bag (www.answerbag.com)

✔ eHow (www.ehow.com)

✔ Eli the Computer Guy (www.elithecomputerguy.com)

✔ How Stuff Works (www.howstuffworks.com)

✔ So You Wanna (www.soyouwanna.com)

✔ Video Jug (www.videojug.com)

✔ Wiki How (www.wikihow.com)

Searching news sites for information

Keeping an eye on unfolding trends for opportunities means that you spend some time watching what is going on in the world at-large. Here are some varied sites covering news and views:

- ✔ CNN (www.cnn.com)
- ✔ Drudge Report (www.drudgereport.com)
- ✔ Huffington Post (www.huffingtonpost.com)
- ✔ Market Watch (www.marketwatch.com)
- ✔ Mediaite (www.mediaite.com)
- ✔ NBC News (www.nbcnews.com)
- ✔ News Media Directory (www.newsmediadirectory.com)
- ✔ Yahoo! News (www.yahoo.com)

Perusing article directories

Article directories are a great source for information and ideas, as well as for generating traffic to your website, blog, or affiliate link. Extensive databases of articles that are written by thousands of writers on a variety of topics are available. In addition to being great content that you can learn from, they give you great insights on popular niches. If you simply do a keyword search for "whatever niche you want," you should have no problem seeing many great articles, especially if it's a popular (meaning profitable) niche:

- ✔ Article Base (www.articlebase.com)
- ✔ Article City (www.articlecity.com)
- ✔ Article Dashboard (www.articledashboard.com)
- ✔ Article Depot (www.articledepot.com)
- ✔ Ezine Articles (www.ezonearticles.com
- ✔ Go Articles (www.goarticles.com)
- ✔ I Snare (www.isnare.com)
- ✔ Search Warp (www.searchwarp.com)

Refer to Chapter 18 for more information on other ways to use article databases.

Testing opportunities

Sometimes you don't have to do guesswork about what opportunities are profitable or not. Consider doing some testing on what you offer.

Say that you found a good niche (digital cameras) that you want to offer. Find the top three hottest selling digital cameras at Amazon or other major venue. Then consider doing either a review or consumer report on your blog, website, or maybe an article that runs at an appropriate consumer blog. Make sure you incorporate affiliate links to all three cameras. This way, you can make money when consumers choose and buy the one they like.

Some enterprising micro-entrepreneurs will do the same technique using Clickbank or other affiliate offer. Refer to Chapter 11 for more information.

Relying on Your Background for Opportunities

Your background, education, experience, and expertise can instantly give you a business on a silver platter! Everyone has knowledge that others would pay good money for. Whatever you have learned or experienced, even the bad moments in your life, offer micro-entrepreneurial opportunities. You have the ability to teach others what you already know and make some good money, right from the comfort of home!

For years I did a seminar entitled "The $1,000 a Day Seminar Leader." In the early years (the 1990s, the clunky years before the Internet), the most common technology available to do seminars was in a live classroom setting. In fact, for smaller organizations, live events at hotels and other public meeting places were essentially all that were available.

Today you can now make money doing an educational program from the comfort of home (or your office). Here are some true-story examples:

- ✔ A retired person sold his window cleaning business. He then did an educational program on "how to launch a successful cleaning business." The program was in book and audio format, and it sold very well.

- ✔ An associate of mine years ago got a speeding ticket. He was so annoyed by it, he self-published a booklet on how to beat a speeding ticket. The topic was so interesting that he was constantly called to do a radio program. He did thousands of radio and TV programs. He sold thousands of books. The interviews were free advertising. His next project was another educational program — on how to get radio and TV interviews! He literally made millions with both of these educational programs.

✔ A client of mine was a tutor. To leverage his knowledge and experience as a tutor, he decided to do an educational program on how to have a successful tutor business.

✔ A business associate of mine self-published books on self-improvement and packaged the information as a Kindle book. He sells hundreds of them! He did so well that he wrote an ebook — on how to self-publish your own Kindle books!

Find out more about what's in your background, abilities, and interests. Assess yourself using Chapter 3.

Avoiding Fraud

Catching good opportunities is nice, but you want to avoid catching bad opportunities. Here, when I discuss _bad opportunities,_ I mean fraud. Today's economy (at press time) isn't the greatest. A lot of folks are unemployed, and many people are struggling. What does that have to do with fraud?

In bad times, fraud tied to "money-making opportunities" is more prevalent. People are more desperate, which means that they're more susceptible to fraud. No matter what the moneymaking program is, double-check any opportunities that find you.

I am of the school that you should find opportunities; they shouldn't find you. If you're presented with magical ways to make money, check and double-check.

Here are some additional ways for you to review opportunities before you pay your hard-earned money:

✔ Better Business Bureau (www.bbb-online.org)

✔ Consumer Reports Webwatch (www.consumerwebwatch.com)

✔ Federal Trade Commission (www.ftc.gov)

✔ Fraud.org (www.fraud.org)

✔ Scambook (www.scambook.com)

The world is filled with opportunities, so if you have any doubt about a program or opportunity, move on. Getting involved with something that could potentially cause harm to you or to your customers or others isn't worth the risk.

Tracking the get-rich real estate gurus

Remember those infomercials on late-night TV where the guy in the Hawaiian shirt tells you how easy it is to make fantastic money in real estate? Those glossy sales pitches become ubiquitous when the real estate market is doing well. Some of those guys actually made money in real estate, although most of them made more money selling get-rich-quick-in-real-estate kits through slick marketing.

One fellow that tracked most of them (the good, the bad, and especially the ugly!) was

John T. Reed. He rated them and gave you the gory details (such as which ones went to jail or got slapped with heavy fines by the law). You can see his exposes at his site `http://johntreed.com/Reedgururating.html`. You can pick up several lessons here. Don't fall for the hype. Secondly, don't adopt these types of overblown approaches as a marketer. Do honest marketing and provide real value for your customers, and you'll garner a good long-term reputation (and stay out of jail, too — what a bonus)!

Steering Clear of Liability Problems and Other Legal Issues

No matter how well you have tried to do business and how diligent you are as a businessperson, having potential legal problems is a reality you have to guard against in today's world. You can certainly try to produce a good product or provide a good service, but you also need to take preventative measures to avoid pitfalls with liability. How you take necessary precautions can prevent a potential problem from a disgruntled client.

Here are some points to keep in mind to minimize or avoid any legal issues that may come your way:

- ✔ **Get advice now (before you need to).** Have a consultation with an attorney familiar with business issues if you're concerned about your business. If you can't get referred to one, you can find an attorney at sites such as Find Law (`www.findlaw.com`) and Attorney Find (`www.attorneyfind.com`).

- ✔ **Check with your association.** If you're a member with a professional or trade association, check with the people familiar with legal issues facing your particular industry or niche. Some associations even provide guidance and/or a legal hotline for its members. You can find associations either with your favorite search engine or you can consult the "Encyclopedia of Associations" (published by Gale Research, `www.gale.cengage.com`) in the reference section of a well-stocked library.

✔ **Have your documents and agreements reviewed.** Whatever agreements you use in your business, having an attorney review and critique them is a smart decision. Your attorney can tell you if you have any vulnerability in your terms of agreement.

✔ **Review your marketing.** Honest and realistic marketing communication will keep you out of trouble (or at the very least keep legal hassles to a minimum). Take the time to ensure that your marketing isn't communicating anything inappropriate or that you're making promises that your products or services can't keep. Carefully peruse your materials to verify that nothing in your ads, sales letters, or other forms of communication could be misleading, either purposely or accidentally.

✔ **If you're short on cash, consider signing up for a prepaid legal plan.** For a relatively small monthly fee, you can sign up and have access to lawyers that you can speak with and also have other services, such as document review or legal writing on your behalf. Many prepaid legal plans are available, and you can find many of the more prominent ones through resources such as the American Prepaid Legal Services Institute (www.aplsi.com).

✔ **Check rules with third-party sources.** If you're working with third-party sources to meet clients, sell products, and so on, find out what their rules are and check out their recommendations for best practices. No matter whether the third-party sources you use are about products (such as eBay or Etsy) or about services (such as Elance or Odesk), they have plenty of experience and information about what are good practices (and what are not).

✔ **Use your common sense.** Don't forget your common sense. If you act with integrity and regularly communicate with customers, vendors, prospects, and others with honesty about your products and services, you should be able to keep legal risks to a minimum.

Part II
Finding Great Micro-Entrepreneurship Ideas

Five Things That Every Successful Affiliate Marketer Should Do

- **Understand your target market.** The more you understand your customers, the better chances you have of matching them to a product or service that can help them. When you fill the want or need of your customers with a product or service that you refer them to, you can more easily profit as an affiliate.

- **Offer more than one product to the same niche.** Not everyone will buy the same product, so why not profit by offering another product in the same category or niche? If you find three great products that are perfect for a particular niche, then you'll have more sales.

- **Know who reaches your target market.** Successful affiliates find out who has access to the target market. Spend time at the websites, forums, and blogs where your target market is likely to be so you can discover more about your target market. Find the ezines and other media that reach your target market, read the information and advice they suggest, and incorporate that advice into your marketing plan.

- **Make sure the product has popularity and quality.** If you see a good product that you want to market as an affiliate, find out what others think about it. Check to see whether the product fills a want or need for your prospective customers. If people generally like the product, you'll have an easier time generating affiliate sales.

- **Team up with supportive merchants.** Make sure that the merchant you choose has plenty of guidance on marketing strategies and supports affiliates with tools for success, such as sample sales copy and banners.

Visit www.dummies.com/extras/microentrepreneurship to find out the different options you have for making money as a micro-entrepreneur.

In this part . . .

- ✔ Find the right business opportunity that taps into your skills or interests so you can increase your income in even a struggling economy.

- ✔ Whether hand-knit sweaters, refinished furniture, or salvage that becomes one-of-a-kind art, take advantage of your creative spirit by making and selling products that people want.

- ✔ Sell stuff that you already own, using online auctions and other venues, and make money connecting desired goods with the people who are seeking them.

- ✔ Figure out how you can make some dinero with your own writing, no matter whether it's online articles, ebooks, or something else.

- ✔ See how you can self-publish on your own.

- ✔ Promote other companies' products on your website or blog and have your customers link to those companies' websites.

- ✔ Know how to incorporate advertising on your website or blog to generate income.

Chapter 6

Creating Your Arts and Crafts Micro-Business from Scratch

* *

In This Chapter

▶ Using your creativity for profit

▶ Buying low and selling for high arts and crafts profits

▶ Making money from renewing, repurposing, and recycling

* *

aking something from virtually nothing and creating a beautiful product that you can resell for a profit and provide someone with something that is unique and uplifting is a true joy. It's the essence of creativity. Many micro-entrepreneurs have started their own home-based businesses by making something beautiful or unique and selling it to others who appreciate the handiwork.

If you're interested in starting your own arts and crafts micro-business, you've come to the right chapter. Here I discuss how it all starts with an idea and your time, effort, care, and maybe a few bucks. You can then take your hobby and turn it into a satisfying business. This chapter also looks at the different types of arts and crafts you may want to sell and examines Etsy (www.etsy.com), the most popular website, and many other sites for selling arts and crafts.

From Nothing to Something Good: Entering the World of Arts and Crafts

Doing an arts and crafts business is a perfectly good way to make money because many folks are really good with their hands and most people have some spare time. Creating a physical product takes some handiwork. For me, my handiwork is creating something from nothing — in other words, writing and publishing. (Check out Chapters 9 and 10 for more on writing and self-publishing.)

If you're a whiz with your hands and can make interesting, useful, and/or unique items, you may as well as make your goods and make money, too. Fun and profit sounds like a good combo, and your options are almost endless. In fact, I know one guy who could turn a trashcan into a condo in two weeks (give me a hammer and in 30 minutes I could turn it into a doctor's visit). Okay, perhaps a bit extreme, but no matter what you can make, whether it be a unique handbag, an attractive piece of pottery, or a modern painting, you can turn your arts and crafts hobby into a business. These sections cover what you should consider before you officially start this type of business.

Making your art and craft and a profit at the same time

Creating a physical product is only half the battle — the greater half of the battle is to sell it. Therefore, you should only create a product that other people will actually pay for. Don't get me wrong; creating something that will beautify your home or make a nice gift is nice. However, that personal approach won't make you money. For the scope of this chapter, you want to make something that people will buy (and I don't mean your aunt!).

Therefore, before you do anything, do some market research. Market research basically is figuring out who your customers are and what they'll buy. Chapter 13 provides more in-depth discussion about researching your market. Here are some questions to keep you focused:

What do you want to do?

This question is simple, yet profound. Arts and crafts encompass literally thousands of different things that can spring from imagination and become objects of physical beauty (and may be useful, too). A simple list of all the ways your creativity can take shape could easily be hundreds of pages long. So you need to decide what you want to make and then sell. Ask yourself what types of arts and crafts excite you and what you really enjoy.

Choosing something you enjoy is the first (and probably most important) criterion. In fact, like I discuss in Chapter 3, following your passion is the primary way to succeed and having staying power. Big bucks don't come easily or quickly in this type of business; enjoyment will carry you through to where this hobby can be a viable for-profit activity.

For example, my wife loves to make decorative wreaths and silk floral arrangements to decorate our home and as gifts for housewarmings, events, and holidays. She can sell these to party planners as centerpieces. Because she enjoys teaching, she offers classes in adult education venues and has had a profitable business teaching others while having fun making crafts.

If you need some help to figure out what arts and craft idea to pursue (perhaps you're a crafty person, but you aren't sure exactly what options might work), don't worry. Great craft ideas are everywhere. Here are some places to do your research for craft ideas:

- Directory of Arts and Crafts Online Marketplaces (`http://artsand crafts.about.com/od/sellingonline/tp/Selling-Arts-And-Crafts-Online-Marketplaces.htm`)
- Homemade Money Guide (`www.homemade-money-guide.com/best-selling-crafts.html`)
- The Arts & Crafts Society (`www.arts-crafts.com`)

What is your experience?

Any experience you have in terms of constructing or creating something can be a big plus, particularly if you plan to offer a variety of items. You obviously want to stick to something you enjoy, but you also want to select something for your business that you have hands-on experience doing in order to achieve greater success.

If you have enjoyment in some area of art and crafts but you don't have experience, then take the time to read and master the skill. The good news is that a wealth of education is available to help you excel in any craft niche, right at your fingertips.

Here are some great resources you can tap into to help you become more familiar and master a certain area of arts and crafts:

- **Michael's and other arts and craft stores:** Places like Michael's (`www.michaels.com`) regularly offer arts and crafts workshops. These works are usually free or low-cost.
- **Local adult education programs:** Thousands of arts and crafts courses are offered inexpensively through adult education programs sponsored by local boards of education across the country and through local community colleges, adult education companies, and so on.
- **Your local library:** You can find a plethora of resources, all for free, at your local library. If your library doesn't carry a specific book, you can often ask for an exchange with another library that does carry it.
- ***For Dummies* books:** This helpful series of books has a wide range of books on arts and crafts. You can find books on nearly any topic you can imagine, from knitting and crocheting to watercolors and acrylics to jewelry making and stained glass windows. Check out `www.dummies.com` to search.

- ✔ **Spotted Canary:** This website (www.spottedcanary.com) offers craft projects to make yourself. This offers you the opportunity to get a head start on a project and add your own personal touch and uniqueness for sale. You can also search for online craft classes.

- ✔ **eHow:** This great site (www.ehow.com) is a resource to find out more just about every craft. It also includes great information on ways to sell crafts online and at fairs.

- ✔ **Arts and crafts at About.com:** You'll be surprised at all the great hands-on articles and helpful pieces of information you can find at this site (www.artsandcrafts.about.com).

Even if you're well versed in a niche, you can keep on learning. The more you know about your craft, the better your products will be and the more you can create. The more you can create, the more you can sell.

Who is your customer?

You also need to find out who will buy what you have to offer. To do so, you need to research your target market. To find out who your target market is, study your customers to determine their buying habits, what they like, and where they buy this type of product. You can read more about researching your target market in Chapter 13.

You don't want to try to sell all sorts of crafts to all sorts of people. You need to study local trends and styles. For example, a silk floral arrangement of high-quality wildflowers will sell to customers with country decorating themes in their homes.

If you do stretch yourself too thin, you'll end up providing lots of average stuff rather than offering your specialty — the item that you can provide better (and more unique) than anyone else. Stick to your specialty so you can build your reputation and your *brand identity*, which is the name, term, design, symbol, or any other feature that identifies your goods or service as distinct from everyone else. Focus on knowing who your customers are and providing them the best maker of whatever product you're selling in a specific niche.

How do customers buy your product?

You want to know where customers can buy your product so you can better market and sell it to them there. Etsy (www.etsy.com) is a great online way to sell your arts and crafts. Etsy specializes in handmade items, so buyers coming to the site are specifically looking for unique finds. I discuss Etsy in greater depth in the "Selling your Creations: Focus on Etsy" section.

For other places where you may be able to sell your arts and craft creations, check out the later section, "Identifying Other Online Selling Venues for Your Crafts" in this chapter.

Who is your competition?

You not only want to reference the people who are your competitors but also the organizations and websites. Buyers will buy whatever product you're selling from you or your competitors. Understanding how you stack up against your competitors (including strengths, weaknesses, price differences, and so on) is important because this information allows you to price effectively (so your products sell quicker than your competitors') and also gives you a better sense for the latest trends in color, style, and so on.

If your prospects are buying from others, find out why. Study your competitors' marketing strategies and tactics to see how your product stacks up against the competing product. For example, if wreaths sell well in flea markets, find out how best to position yourself so customers see your products first or ensure you prominently showcase your products' difference.

Finding the raw materials

If you're making anything, you'll need to obtain the raw materials and know where to find them. Where you get them all depends on what you're making. If your creation is made using paper, for example, you may be able to set up an account at a local office supply store like Staples (www.staples.com) or Office Depot (www.officedepot.com) as you start out.

Ultimately, you'll need a wholesale account from a paper vendor like Paper Papers (www.paper-papers.com). For specialty paper needs (like card stock, invitations, vellum, and so forth), you can use vendors such as

- **LCI Paper** (www.lcipaper.com)
- **Paper and More** (www.paperandmore.com)

For more craft-oriented supplies, you can check out these places:

- **Create for Less** (www.createforless.com)
- **DCC Crafts** (www.dcccrafts.com)
- **Michael's** (www.michaels.com)
- **Fire Mountain Gems** (www.firemountaingems.com)
- **Wholesale Supplies Plus** (www.wholesalesuppliesplus.com)

Buying wholesale

Buying wholesale allows you to buy in bulk and create an inventory for your arts and crafts business. If you're able to purchase your supplies at low wholesale prices, your business will be more profitable.

To buy wholesale, research online for companies that manufacture the product you require. After you locate some companies, directly contact them and ask for bulk discounts if you order a certain amount. Many manufacturers have a wholesale price list for the available items and what constitutes wholesale for them. You may need to partner with other crafters to get bulk pricing.

Some manufacturers will be willing to give you a bulk discount on a limited quantity if they see a potential for future orders. You may not have the bulk order yet, but if you can convince the manufacturer that you'll be promoting its product and project many sales in the future, the manufacturer may give you bulk prices from the first call.

Touring the World of Crafts

The types of possibilities for what you can create are endless. Here I break them down into six basic categories. When starting a home-based arts and crafts business, your best bet is to choose a single category and master it so that you can become a dominant seller.

- **Wearable crafts:** Some call this category *textile crafts* because it's about taking materials like cotton and wool and turning them into sweaters, hats, or whatever you can wear. You can create something beautiful and something useful, too.

  Doing crafts in this category definitely needs to be a labor of love because creating a sweater or a scarf can take a relatively long time, easily days and sometimes longer. Knitting, macramé, quilting, and similar skills/activities apply here.

- **Paper crafts:** Think of what you can do with paper. Origami, decorative paper works, and even greeting cards fall into this category. Supplies can be inexpensive and easily available. However, unless you've made an amazing piece of handiwork, don't count on getting big bucks for your individual pieces. On the other hand, if you crank out lots of items, you can make it up on volume.

✔ **Usable crafts:** This category includes everything from making pottery and utensils to crafting soap to making a unique stool and chair. In other words, making a unique craft that people will buy for their daily use is usually a hit. For example, purses and wallets can be knitted from supermarket plastic bags. The idea of re-purposing an item makes it unique, fun, and usable. Soaps and homemade hand or skin lotions are other useable craft items that sell well because the ingredients are typically organic and natural. You don't have to be the town blacksmith and need to fashion horseshoes from molten metal, but you can still command some good money in this category.

✔ **Fashion crafts:** Unique handmade jewelry, including earrings, bracelets, necklaces, and so on, are the types of crafts that make great gifts and offer a good market for either birthdays or holidays like Christmas.

✔ **Edible crafts:** They look good and taste good. too. Edible crafts are a niche that you may not think of. I saw a local franchise that creates what looks like a flower bouquet but was actually made of berries and melons. Use your creativity here and conjure up some delicious profits.

✔ **Holiday crafts:** Holiday crafts are always a strong market, so see if this category suits you. Can you make some unique Halloween items? How about for Valentine's Day? You know, making some unique decorations for the Christmas tree may be right up your alley.

This list includes general categories. You may be able to think of something else. Crafts are suitable for many markets, demographics, cultures, ethnicities, age groups, and so on. Keep researching to find a suitable niche for you.

Adding Beauty and Profit

Perhaps you have an eye for beauty and you have a real flair for creating something visual. Maybe you are a painter or you can draw with the best of them. If so, you may want to take your passion for artwork, start your own business, and sell your artwork. Doing so is easier than ever.

Here are some websites that can help you sell your art:

✔ **The Abundant Artist** (www.theabundantartist.com)

✔ **Empty Easel** (www.emptyeasel.com)

✔ **Imagekind** (www.imagekind.com/sell/art-photography.aspx)

✔ **Proud Artists** (www.proudartists.com)

✔ **Yessy** (www.yessy.com)

✔ **Zazzle** (www.zazzle.com/art)

Keep in mind that some of these sites also provide a selling platform for crafts. Sometimes one person's craft is another person's artwork. Visit some of the sites in the previous section on crafts because some of them offer sales opportunities for artists too.

Selling Your Creations: Focus on Etsy

If you want to sell your arts and crafts, you have many options. The big kahuna for doing so is Etsy (www.etsy.com). You may already know that Etsy is an online marketplace, but I suggest you take a closer look at what it all has to offer. It prides itself on being a robust marketplace for handmade goods while being the crafter's best path to global buyers (more than 15 million members worldwide). The recent stats show that Etsy has monthly traffic of 8 to 9 million visits, and that number pops up to 11 million during the gift-buying season of October through December.

If you have handmade goods, then Etsy is worth checking out to find your buyers. The following sections take a closer look at how you can use Etsy. You can also check out *Starting an Etsy Business For Dummies* by Allison Strine and Kate Shoup (John Wiley & Sons, Inc.).

Setting up on Etsy

Whether you are buying or selling (or both), you need to register (the account is free). When you put in your location, the site figures out what currency you'll be using (Etsy is truly international). You also need to enter information, such as arts and crafts shops that you like, find people that you may deal with or are seeking (perhaps people well known for their handiwork).

Take some time and research the types of crafts being sold on Etsy. Pay special attention to the types of crafts that are in your niche or area of expertise to see how other crafters list them, how much they charge, and other appropriate information.

When you create your listing on Etsy, make sure you post great pictures of your crafts. To do so, here are some great sites that offer guidance on how to take photos of crafts for Etsy (as well as eBay and other selling venues):

✔ About.com's photography site (www.photography.about.com)

✔ Crafts Report (www.craftsreport.com)

✔ Your Craft Business (www.yourcraftbusiness.com)

Selling on Etsy

When you choose to sell on Etsy, you have three basic categories that your selling falls into:

- ✔ **Handmade goods:** These are the main category and consist of quality handmade crafts.

- ✔ **Vintage goods:** They don't have to be handmade, but they should be at least 20 years old.

- ✔ **Craft supplies:** They're supplies that go into creating quality handmade crafts.

You don't have to pay any membership or maintenance fee on Etsy, but you do have to pay listing fees (similar to eBay). To list an item (which can last up to four months), you pay 20 cents. When it sells, you pay 3.5 percent of the sale price. If your item doesn't sell after four months, there is an option for auto-renewal.

When you're setting up shop on Etsy, you're literally creating an online shop, so you want it to be attractive where you can showcase your wares (upload sharp digital photos) and provide full details to your visitors regarding product details, your policies, and so forth. (Etsy has templates for much of this.)

Don't think you'll get rich by offering a few items; remember that your site on Etsy will be similar to a crafts boutique, so have a nice array of offerings to entice buyers.

Identifying Other Online Selling Venues

Arts and crafts have lots of opportunities for you to have a rewarding business. You want to sell your handiwork and want an online outlet to do so. In addition to Etsy, which I discuss in the previous section, you have many other options. Feast your eyes on a list worthy of any arts and crafts marketer:

- ✔ **Art Fire** (www.artfire.com)
- ✔ **Artful Home** (www.artfulhome.com)
- ✔ **Bonanzle** (www.bonanza.com)
- ✔ **Cargoh** (www.cargoh.com)
- ✔ **Chictopia** (www.chictopia.com)
- ✔ **Coriandr** (www.coriandr.com)
- ✔ **Da Wanda** (www.dawanda.com)
- ✔ **Ecrater** (www.ecrater.com)

✔ **Folksy** (www.folksy.com)

✔ **Handmade Artists** (www.handmadeartists.com)

✔ **I Craft** (www.icraft.ca)

✔ **Made it Myself** (www.madeitmyself.com)

✔ **Not on the High Street** (www.notonthehighstreet.com)

✔ **Novica** (www.novica.com)

✔ **Poppy Talk Handmade** (www.poppytalkhandmade.com)

✔ **Ruby Lane** (www.rubylane.com)

✔ **Silk Fair** (www.silkfair.com)

✔ **Storenvy** (www.storenvy.com)

✔ **Supermarket** (www.supermarkethq.com)

✔ **Tophatter** (www.tophatter.com)

✔ **Uncommon Goods** (www.uncommongoods.com)

✔ **Yokaboo** (www.yokaboo.com)

✔ **Zibbet** (www.zibbet.com)

Tons of arts and crafts items are sold regularly through eBay and other auction sites. You can find out more about selling on auction sites in Chapter 7. In addition, many people sell their wares through their own sites and blogs. Many places on the Internet can help you set up a relatively inexpensive store site. A good example is Webstore (www.webstore.com).

If you want to boost your product sales, don't just list them and wait for results. Do some active marketing, too. Here are some strategies to consider:

✔ Search for art categories in the free classified ad sites, such as craigslist (www.craigslist.com) and Backpage (www.backpage.com).

✔ Set up a Google alert (www.google.com/alert) with keywords like "craft" or a brief description of your item. When new pages with your keywords are set up on the Internet, you can go there and check for any new marketing opportunities for you.

✔ Find blogs and forums on arts and crafts and participate. You can create opportunities to link back to your craft page where you sell your item.

Keep in mind that the sales of products may be subject to sales tax. Although you, the business owner, don't pay the sales tax, you may be obligated to collect it from the customer and subsequently submit it to the appropriate sales tax authority. The sales tax is considered a state and local tax issue. Check with your tax professional for specifics, depending on where you live.

Eyeing Offline Selling Opportunities

Don't think that the only selling opportunities are just online. The offline world also has plenty of opportunities for you. Here are some venues and ideas too:

✔ **Events and shows:** Craft fairs and shows are everywhere, and they aren't difficult to find. Do your searches with your favorite search engines. Also check with sites such as the Trade Show News Network (TSNN) (www.tsnn.com) to find local trade shows and related events. Every event is run differently, but you can get contact information for the event organizer at the TSNN site. If an event is running in your area, go first as a visitor. Doing so can give you a chance to see how the event is operated and if many people attend. Then you can meet the organizer to determine when he will be back in your area and other details (costs, benefits, and so) so you can decide if you want to participate the next time the event is in town.

✔ **Consignment shops:** Just as there are consignment shops for clothing, there are also similar shops for items such as arts and crafts. You place your item at the shop, and if it sells, you split the profits with the shop. To find them in your area, use Super Pages (www.superpages.com) or you can get referred to local shops through their trade group, the National Association of Resale Professionals (www.narts.org).

✔ **Fund-raising vehicles:** I was at a craft fair recently for my church. It was successful for both the crafters and the church. You can find and create plenty of opportunities in this venue. Approach your favorite charity and discuss the possibilities! You'll probably split the profit with the organization — a win-win.

✔ **Branding considerations:** Remember that arts and crafts can pave the way to bigger and better things. When you have a reputation and a brand that you have created, you can forge a very successful business. Some good examples of arts and crafts leading to big things are Thomas Kinkade (I love those paintings!) and iconic craft items such as Precious Moments.

Focusing on the Four Rs

I'm a real stickler about not wasting. In fact, many times I have even reused aluminum foil or a paper plate. The fact that this practice is good for the environment is a plus. It can also be a bonanza for crafters! Lots of items could have ended up in the garbage bin and clogged up some landfill, but that actually has utility and sales value.

Imagine making a nice profit by selling something that effectively cost you nothing — even common items that you find in your kitchen or garage or in a junkyard. Try out a website like Earth 911 (www.earth911.com) to find lots of great ideas about turning items that would have been discarded to reuse or repurpose them. You'll never look at garbage the same way again! You can find materials that are cheap and readily available and convert them into a profitable item — and reduce waste that would otherwise pollute the environment — all in one fell swoop. Cool!

I refer to this practice as the four Rs:

- ✔ **Reuse:** Is there anything that you can reuse? In your house and your neighborhood, many things can easily head into the trash bin and clog up some junkyard or landfill. Use your creativity (and a chance to profit) and reuse items.

- ✔ **Recycle:** If you find raw materials, consider foregoing on the creative stuff and make a buck by recycling. Think of the materials that are valuable and that you can get paid for just because it is what it is. Aluminum, plastic, and so on all have value because society can use it again in another form.

- ✔ **Renew:** Look to see if you can refurbish something, renew it, and then resell it. For example, I saw one example where a creative person took aluminum cans and remade them into decorative pencil holders.

- ✔ **Repurpose:** It's amazing how you can take things that seemingly lost their usefulness and have a creative person turn it into a great new item. Check out Ehow (www.ehow.com). I went here and did a simple search using the word "repurpose" and found some great examples.

As you scour the world of arts, crafts, and all things creative, keep in mind an aspect of your business that can reap some good bucks without being creative or decorative at all — finding raw materials and waste items for profit and benefiting the environment.

Chapter 7

Selling Other Stuff: The Golden Rules of Success

. . . .

In This Chapter

▶ Seeing what you can sell

▶ Implementing strategies to buy low and sell high

▶ Using eBay to the max

▶ Identifying other venues for selling

. . . .

*W*ith the Internet, you get a real chance to earn some money by selling your own stuff and other people's stuff. In fact, doing so has never been easier.

Auction sites are a great way for buyers to find sellers and vice-versa. For you to make money, sites like eBay help you find potentially millions of buyers for what you offer. On these action sites, people place bids on items the want. The more desirable or popular an item, the better chance you have to turn your auction into a viable and profitable business.

I recall when I used to sell products during the 1980s and 1990s and if it wasn't in person; it was through mail order. Remember mail order? I'm dating myself, right? Actually, mail order is alive and well, and plenty of "high-tech" companies are involved (like Amazon and eBay) are doing it day in and day out, today!

Auction sites are still the cat's meow when selling stuff on the Internet, with eBay being the biggest lion. You also have other online options for selling stuff. This chapter focuses on the fundamentals of selling stuff on auction sites (and also addresses your other options). Here I help you figure out what you can sell and offer you some strategies for acquiring products to buy low and then strategies on how to sell high. This chapter also explores how you can maximize your potential on eBay (and other auction online sites) to sell your stuff to make money.

Identifying Your Selling Options

As a micro-entrepreneur, you have several choices for how you can sell merchandise and make some extra money. Here are your options. You may choose to go a couple of routes to maximize your profit:

- **Online auction sites:** For many people, online auction sites are the best way to begin selling products. There are two types of online auction sites:

  - **Horizontal:** A *horizontal* auction site is a site that basically sells all sorts of offerings in many categories with a wide variety of both buyers and sellers. The most popular is eBay. I focus on more on how you can use eBay in the later section in this chapter, "Listing on eBay."

  - **Vertical:** A *vertical* site is an auction site that specializes in a specific category. Say that you're selling a rare collector's item that is in baseball. Maybe the best way to find a buyer is to try to sell this item at a vertical site that specializes in baseball or sports collectibles. This type of site won't have the same traffic of buyers and sellers like eBay because it's smaller, and the buyers and sellers are all interested in only that particular category.

  Here are other auction sites that compare with eBay:

  - **Online Auctions** (www.onlineauctions.com)

  - **Overstock** (www.overstock.com)

  - **Quibids** (www.quidbids.com)

  - **Ubid** (www.ubid.com)

  - **Upillar** (www.upillar.com)

  If you're looking for an auction, horizontal or vertical, offline or online, go to Internet Auction List (www.internetauctionlist.com), which is one of the most comprehensive sites on the Internet for auctions.

- **Online garage sales:** Buyers and sellers can conduct a garage sale online. Sellers can set up a virtual garage sale. Good examples of online garage sale sites are Garage Sale Home Page (www.garagesalehome page.com) and Online Garage Sales (www.online-garage-sales.com).

  You can also sell stuff at an offline garage sale. Organize a twice-yearly garage sale in your neighborhood to sell some odds and ends.

✔ **Online classified ads:** You can list your items for free and reach a wide audience of classified ad shoppers. Craigslist (www.craigslist.com) and Backpage (www.backpage.com) are perfect examples.

✔ **Other online spots:** You can list your stuff without the auction process. You can sell it by simply setting the price and seeing who would buy it. That way, you can keep it simple! Here are some sites to explore including the following:

  • **Amazon:** You knew that . . . right? This site (www.amazon.com) is the most active retailer online; you can register and become a reseller.

  • **Deep Discount.com:** This site (www.deepdiscount.com) doesn't sell everything, but buyers and sellers can get into CDs, DVDs, books, and similar products.

  • **Half.com:** This is Ebay's fixed price site (www.half.com) (with no bidding); it's similar to Amazon.

✔ **Mail order:** You can always sell products online and ship out goods the way mail order was done for decades. Find out more with sources such as the National Mail Order Association (www.nmoa.org).

✔ **Consignment shops, thrift shops, and resale options:** You can sell items offline in retail venues such as consignment and thrift shops. You can search for ones in your area through sites such as Super Pages (www.superpages.com). Another good place to start is with the consignment industry's trade group, the Association of Resale Professionals (www.narts.org).

✔ **Booth space:** If you're selling collectibles and antiques and you have a large enough inventory, you may consider renting a small booth in a local antiques store. You have to ensure you keep the booth stocked (see the later section, "Finding merchandise for resale"). Having a booth along with listing stuff on eBay, for example, can give you two platforms for selling your merchandise. Just make sure you don't have the same item in your booth that you list. If it sells in your booth, you may not be able to honor the sale on eBay if it sells.

✔ **Auctions:** Many cities have auction houses will sell your items to the highest bidder, usually in person, but some also are going online. You can also search for auctions at private homes where you can often purchase items for resale. Be warned that if you want to sell your goods in person at an auction, that many auctioneer companies have added extra fees that make this option one of your last resorts for selling stuff. In addition, the National Auctioneers Association has a great site (www.auctioneers.org) that can help you locate auctions.

Understanding What You'll Sell: Specialize and Understand Value

When you're first starting to sell, it makes sense to sell whatever you have on hand. Everyone has stuff in the attic, basement, garage, or junk room that they want to get rid of. This stuff is good practice for selling on eBay or in an online garage sale, until you get to what will be your business activity.

But you can't sustain a business just selling your own stuff. You have to figure out what you're going to sell and then locate those items to ensure you have an inventory.

When figuring out what to sell, the No. 1 rule is to specialize and sell in a category that you really enjoy. The most successful entrepreneurs on eBay and other auction sites stick to a specialty and get to know that niche inside and out (you can find out more about niches in Chapter 5).

When I say specialize, don't overdo it. For example, selling just elephant-foot umbrella stands will greatly limit your profit potential. Make your offering specialized enough that you can project competence and dominance in your chosen area but large enough to give you growth potential. Selling toys would be a good example of a specialty; it's large enough to generate a good income but small or specialized enough for you to build a reputation and gain prominence.

Your options are endless. Here are the major categories at eBay to give you an idea what you can specialize in:

- ✔ Collectibles and art
- ✔ Deals and gifts
- ✔ Electronics
- ✔ Fashion
- ✔ Health and beauty
- ✔ Home, outdoors, and decor
- ✔ Jewelry and watches
- ✔ Motors
- ✔ Sporting goods
- ✔ Toys and hobbies

Any of these consumer categories is a multibillion-dollar area with plenty of room for you to do business. Each category has subcategories. Take the collectibles and art category, for example. Popular subcategories include coin and paper money collecting, sports memorabilia, antiques, art, stamp collecting, and entertainment memorabilia. You can probably get even more specialized (each subcategory has its own subcategories), but don't get too specialized to avoid shrinking the size of your potential market (and potential profits).

After you do decide what to sell, proceed with selling items that you already have that are applicable and also find sources for new items to sell.

When you start selling merchandise on an online auction site (or even on an online garage sale site), the No. 2 rule is understanding value to be profitable. When you understand value, you know when you're getting (or giving) a good deal. After all, when you buy stuff, you want to know you're getting a good value. On the flipside, if you sell stuff, you want to know that get the top dollar.

Finding Items to Sell: Buy Low

When you're building your inventory of items, you want to focus on paying the smallest amount. You can buy low and then sell high, especially if you're intent on turning it into an ongoing business. Before you buy anything, you want to find out if the product is in a desirable niche. It's not that difficult to see if it is selling well. These sections help you buy products so you can then sell them. The earlier section, "Identifying Your Selling Options," spells out places where you call sell.

Buying from individuals

Lots of people on any given day are trying to get rid of stuff and get some cash for it. They may not be worried about getting top price; they just want to get money and move on. In other words, you can find lots of motivated sellers in today's economy, which translates into buying opportunities for you. The shrewdest sellers understand that making a good profit starts with paying the lowest possible price first.

The individual selling the item just wants to get rid of it and get cash; he doesn't want to wait and spend time looking for a better price. For you, you can use this opportunity to get something at a greatly reduced price and then turn it around and offer it through your venues (online auctions and so on) at a higher price.

Selling mass items: Drop-shipping

Who in their right mind would try to sell thousands of products from home? Well, how about you? People think that to sell thousands of different products that you must store, finance, and ship out those same thousands of products. They think that to compete with the likes of Amazon and Wal-Mart that you need a home the size of an aircraft carrier, but you don't have to. Just remember this important word is drop-shipping. *Drop-shipping* gives you the ability to sell goods that you don't need to store, finance, or ship out. All you need to do is sell goods (through your website, blog, or eBay, and so on) that are drop-shipped.

Drop-shipping means that the source of the product (the manufacturer, for example) is able to ship as little as one of the product to any shipping address. It's very simple. You sell the product (at $10, for example) at retail, and the product is available wholesale (at $5, for example, from a manufacturer). When someone sends you an order for the product, you keep $5 of the retail price and send the remaining $5 (along with the shipping address) to the source. After the source of the product gets the $5, it ships the product with your label (your return address and the customer's address). You make a profit, the manufacturer makes money, and the customer gets his order. Drop-shipping is big business and it's done every day (even Amazon does it).

To find motivated individuals who want to sell their stuff, you can check out the options in the earlier section, "Identifying Your Selling Options," because they also apply for ways you can buy stuff.

Another great way to find real value is go treasure hunting at places such as Goodwill (www.goodwill.org) and the Salvation Army (www.salvation armyusa.org). Both organizations have many locations across the country where you can visit and find some amazing bargains. You can get everything from gently used clothing, toys, sporting goods, and collectibles. People have donated these items because they just want to get rid of them. I bought a really nice, dark-blue, name-brand sports jacket (that retails for $75 to $100) for only $5. I bought it for personal use, but if I decided to sell it at an auction site or other venue, I could probably sell it for $50. My buyer would get a good deal, and I would have a good profit.

Buying from businesses

Lots of businesses have unsold inventory (especially true in a slow economy) that you can buy for a great discount. If these discounted products are in your category or niche, then consider buying them for resale. No matter how you sell products, you want to find products that you can buy low and have the potential to sell high. Check out these places:

✔ **Alibaba:** Thousands of buyers and sellers converge here (`www.alibaba.com`) to buy and sell all sorts of products both in the United States and internationally.

✔ **National Mail Order Association:** This organization (`www.nmoa.org`) maintains a database of manufacturers that cumulatively offer more than a million products available for resale, and done via drop-shipping (see the nearby sidebar for what drop-shipping means).

✔ **Public storage companies:** Public storage companies regularly have auctions over storage units that are considered abandoned and the contents are available in a public auction. In fact, you may have even seen some reality TV shows that highlight these auctions and some buyers. To find out more, go to the Self Storage Association (`www.selfstorage.org`) for more details.

✔ **Liquidation.com:** At this site (`www.liquidation.com`), you can find many businesses and individuals buying and selling surplus inventory at great prices.

✔ **Trade Show News Network (TSNN):** Many products get their start at trade shows. Hundreds of vendors showcase thousands of products at trade shows. TSNN (`www.tsnn.com`) has a searchable database of hundreds of trade shows that you can attend and find new and exciting products available for resale.

✔ **Wholesale products:** Places such as Wholesale Central (`www.wholesalecentral.com`) offer sources that give you the ability to resell thousands of products through drop-shipping.

✔ **Worldwide Brands:** This site (`www.worldwidebrands.com`) is a directory of verified drop-shipping sources that offer thousands of products available for resale through drop-shipping (see the sidebar, "Selling mass items: Drop-shipping").

Buying from the government

Government, alas, is probably the worst entity on the planet when it comes to understanding value. Government constantly overpays for virtually everything and it regularly sells property for less than market value. However, if you're a seller, you should be encouraged. Many products (both used and new) are available from the government and (ironically) much of it is sold via government auctions.

Government agencies at all levels have products that you can buy at a fraction of the actual value. Here is a sample of what you can find:

✔ **US Post Office:** The Post Office (`www.usps.com`) frequently has unsent and unclaimed stuff that it periodically sells through auctions. Contact the main post office in your area or visit the site.

  ✔ **Government Services Administration (GSA):** The GSA (www.gsa.gov) conducts most of the federal government's auctions. It actually has a website to help you find government property (www.govsales.gov).

  ✔ **Usa.gov:** Check out this site (www.usa.gov) that offers property and surplus items for sale from the government.

  ✔ **State governments:** Most state governments have property (confiscated or otherwise) that is made available to the public. You can find the state government websites listed at www.usa.gov/Agencies/State-and-Territories.shtml.

  ✔ **Municipal auctions:** Many local agencies have property available at deep discounts to the public typically at public auctions. Many police departments, for example, sell seized property through police auctions. You can find them by using your favorite search engines (you can also start searching at the usa.gov site previously referenced).

While you're at it, you may as well use some of the proceeds from what you've already sold to pay for your taxes. Refer to Chapter 21 for important tax considerations for micro-entrepreneurs.

Making a Profit: Sell Higher

Your success is a combination between buying as low as you can and selling as high as you can (and then, of course, repeating as often as you can). In today's economy, you shouldn't have difficulty finding merchandise that others are selling at bargain prices and then proceed to resell at a profit. Before you list your products and sell them, keep these pointers in mind to help you list at the highest amount possible for your product:

  ✔ **Search for you own stuff as a make-believe buyer.** Doing so is probably the most important rule of selling, no matter where you're selling. When you come across a batch of listings (selling similar items to what you're selling), make sure you thoroughly analyze them. When you see how others are selling and take note of what the successful sellers are doing, you can discover valuable tips to improve your selling approach. In addition, you can find out from those that aren't selling well (and then avoid any obvious mistakes).

  For example, if you were selling discount shoes on eBay, then first do a search for "discount shoes" as if you were an interested buyer. When the search pulls up a batch of listings, analyze the first 25 or 50 listings, and ask yourself how successful (or unsuccessful) each listing is and why. This approach can help you know what to do and what not to do. The education you will get will be very valuable.

Resources for eBay and other auction websites

Online auctions are a wonderful place for the micro-entrepreneur, and a plethora of information is available for you to become familiar with online auctions. Here are some great resources to help you become more successful in your auction business:

✔ **Auction Bytes:** This site (www.auction bytes.com), run by Ecommerce Bytes, offers lots of news and information on the auction business.

✔ **Ebay's education center for novice (and experienced) sellers:** Go to http://pages.ebay.com/education/index.html to get a great education on buying and selling on eBay (straight from eBay!).

✔ **LinkedIn:** This site (www.linkedin.com) has several large and active auction sellers' groups. Some of the more prominent are "eBay sellers," which is an official eBay group, the "eBay Powersellers" group, and the "Professional Ebay Sellers Alliance" (PESA).

✔ **Skip McGrath:** This site (www.skipmcgrath.com) has some excellent resources for both beginners and experienced auction sellers.

✔ **Make sure that your item isn't prohibited.** These days, people will sell almost anything because times are difficult and people's imagination about what they can sell can sometimes go beyond the bounds of good taste — or the approval of legal limits. If you're thinking about selling your deceased uncle's spleen, you may want to rethink that. If you're selling on eBay, check (www.ebay.com) to find out what is prohibited. In the meanwhile, help your uncle's widow sell some more appropriate items, such as his collection of Buster Keaton memorabilia.

All the major sites have information on what is prohibited in their venues. Use your common sense about what you're selling. If you're not sure, find out if there is an association for your particular product or category and inquire with it. Lastly, you may be selling something appropriate, but it may be difficult to ship or be possibly prohibited by shippers, such as the Postal Service (www.usps.com), so inquire before you attempt to sell and ship something.

Going the eBay Route

The first time I taught a class about eBay, I loved it (it was 2001 and eBay was hitting its groove as "the" hot Internet trend) and yet it's just as good now as it was back then. Yes, it has matured and it isn't the exciting site it was some time ago, but it is a huge billion-dollar market and it's a still a great way to make money. These sections walk you through the listing process on eBay, what to do during the auction, and what to do after the auction.

Listing on eBay

When you're ready to sell what you're offering and you want to sell on eBay, you need to create an auction listing. The listing form at eBay (and many other auction sites) has the following elements:

- ✔ **Category:** The *category* signifies a group of products that have obvious commonality such as toys or personal electronics, so carefully choose the category you're offering. Many people at eBay and other auction sites are *browsers*, and they like to look through a category. For example, I like to look for advertising deals on eBay (you never know when you can find advertising at a bargain price for your marketing needs). In that case, I browse the "Business and Industrial" category. I plug in "advertising" in that category and see what comes up.

- ✔ **Second category:** Some sites allow you to choose a *second category* (some second categories are free, whereas some charge a small fee). If, for example, you're selling an item that can easily be in two categories, consider listing it in two categories. That way it will be easier for buyers to find your listing. For example, I was selling a James Bond collectible comic book. To improve my chances of selling it, I listed it in two categories: "James Bond" and "comic books."

- ✔ **Title of the listing:** The *title* of your listing serves as a headline or an attention grabber. When folks look through the auction site, they do a keyword search. If they find your listing, the title will either entice them to look at your full listing or not. Make sure that you analyze the titles of other, similar listings so that you have the ability to have more people visit and view your listing.

- ✔ **Description:** The *description* is the body of your listing. It's supposed to provide full details so that the buyers can make that buying decision (preferably in your favor!). Remember that when you write the description, provide benefits of what you offer besides just merely describing what you have. People buy benefits, so be honest about your product because honesty pays dividends on eBay! They should know why what you offer is good for them.

- ✔ **Pictures:** Provide a picture of what you're offering. If it's a common product, you may be able to find a photo that is appropriate. Pictures are very important, especially if the item is unique, expensive, or decorative. Check out the nearby sidebar about what to remember when taking pictures. Typically, it doesn't cost anything for up to 12 photos, but find out more at eBay because its pricing policy changes regularly.

Including pictures in your listing: What's important?

Pictures in your eBay listing can help you increase sales by giving the bidders a better idea of what you're offering. Good pictures can also set your listing apart from others. You can have up to 12 pictures for each listing (with some types of listings, there may be a fee, such as with eBay motors). When uploading pictures to your listings, keep the following in mind:

✔ Each picture should be no more than 7 MB in size and preferably in .jpg format (but eBay does accept other picture formats).

✔ The first picture is referred to as the *gallery picture,* and it appears next to your listing's title in the search results.

✔ Use a high-quality digital camera and find a well-lit area to take your pictures. Take the same picture several times in several ways (with the lights on, with the lights off and shades open for full sunlight, and so on).

✔ Make sure that you also take photos from different angles. Be sure to include close-up photos of important areas or aspects of your product. If it has an imperfection, take a picture of it. Give your bidders full pictorial details so no issue pops up about what you're selling.

Ebay's customer support pages offer great assistance and guidance for sellers on all issues (go to `http://pages.ebay.com/ help/sell/selling-basics.html`).

As technology advances, selling your stuff online becomes easier. eBay has mobile apps that allow you to sell products from your smartphone. Simply take pictures of the product with your phone, set your price, and list your product. The application can be used on almost all smartphones and tablets. In addition, eBay's website keeps getting streamlined to make your selling process quicker and easier.

✔ **Location:** Find out if the location is a relevant matter for what you're trying to sell. The listing will have a field for the location of the item. Location is important because the product may be better off being picked up versus shipped to save on the costs and the hassles. For instance, if you're selling a large entertainment unit sitting in your living room, the location indeed matters. Shipping it would cost a small fortune. If the buyer can pick it up, everyone wins.

✔ **Quantity:** Are you selling one item or more? If you're selling more than one unit of an item, consider doing a *multiple-item auction,* which is also referred to as a *Dutch auction.* (I guess the Swedes got there too late.)

✔ **Minimum bid:** Figure out what the absolute minimum bid is you're willing to accept. Doing so is both a selling strategy and a legal one. It's a selling strategy because a low price encourages bidding. It's a legal transaction, too, because if the only bid comes in at your minimum bid, you're required to sell it at this price even if it isn't as desirable a price as you like. Be careful setting your minimum bid. Make sure you do a lot of research and see what others are doing in setting their minimum.

✔ **Auction duration:** Determine how long you want your auction to last — you can select a listing duration of 1, 3, 5, 7, or 10 days. A longer duration may be better, but it may also cost you more to do. Look to see what your competitors are doing and see what is typical for your category. eBay tweaks the duration at times, depending on the type of listing, so check eBay's guidelines (`http://pages.ebay.com/help/sell/selling-basics.html`).

✔ **Auction timing:** Many auctions are timed to expire when they get the greatest exposure. For example, eBay's hottest night of activity has usually been on a Sunday night. Many successful sellers time their auctions to end by late Sunday night or very early Monday morning so that they can take advantage of the traffic. Still others time their auction based on the unique buying habits of that category. Find out this timing aspect to maximize your auction's exposure to your target market.

✔ **Reserve price:** Sometimes you want to sell an item at a much better price than at the minimum bid, but you don't want to be stuck selling below your desired price. You can use the *reserve price,* which is a way to protect the seller from selling an item for too little. Say you really want to sell a product at $50, but you want to start the bid much lower to generate excitement for what you're offering. In that case, you can set a minimum bid at $20, but you won't be obligated to actually sell the item until your reserve price is met, which is really at $50. The reserve price helps you get the price you want.

The reserve price isn't revealed to the bidders until a bid actually hits that amount or higher. In this example where the minimum bid is $20 and the reserve price is $50, the listing will be labeled "reserve price auction" while bidding is still below $50. At this point, the bidders are aware that the seller isn't obligated to sell the item until the reserve price is hit or surpassed.

✔ **Private auction:** Maybe you're selling something that is too sensitive for a public auction. If so, you can consider a private auction. In a private auction, the buyers are anonymous.

✔ **"Buy it now" feature:** Some auction sellers use this feature to get their desired price immediately and avoid the back-and-forth of auction action. It alerts the buyers that with the specific price you set, they can get the item without fear of being outbid. This feature is particularly popular if you're selling several versions of the same item. For example, if you have 1,000 iPads, you can offer a buy-it-now price for the people who don't want to bid.

✔ **Best offer:** This designation gives your buyers a chance to offer you a price that they're comfortable paying but you aren't obligated to accept.

✔ **Shipping details:** In this part of your listing, you offer the specifics of shipping, such as cost and carrier (post office, UPS, and so on). eBay now automatically determines and calculates the shipping costs, based on the shipping information provided in the listing (shipping address, shipper, and so on).

✔ **Exposure upgrade fees:** Maybe you want greater exposure of your offer. Many auction sites give you the ability to pay a little more for greater exposure, such as a more prominent position. You can pay for greater prominence either in those particular listings or for greater exposure at the main website.

✔ **Escrow feature:** If you're selling an expensive item or dealing with overseas buyers, *escrow* is a way to protect and guarantee payment if you're worried that the buyer may not pay.

✔ **Payment methods:** In this segment you indicate what payment methods you accept, such as PayPal, credit card, checks, and so on. (Refer to Chapter 4 about setting up a PayPal account.)

✔ **Shipping terms:** Here you indicate how you'll handle shipping. The buyer may pay based on which carrier you use. You may waive shipping chargers if the buyer purchases a second item.

Managing ongoing auctions

While your listing is active, watch it carefully and see if any actions are necessary during the process. If it's going well (good bidding activity and price is rising), you don't have to do anything unless a bidder has a question. If so, respond promptly.

When a bidder sends you a question, it may be a clue that the listing is missing some information (other bidders that didn't inquire may have the same issue). Revising the listing to add more information or to clarify something is easy to do. You can't do some changes during a live auction (such as raising the minimum bid, especially if someone has already bid).

If an auction isn't going well, you may be able to end the auction early. Because guidelines can change for revising a listing or ending it early, check with eBay at `http://pages.ebay.com/help/sell/selling-basics.html` before you do so. If you're at a different auction site, check its guidelines.

Keep in mind that if you change or end a listing, you may have to pay a fee, so find out before you even do a listing.

When your auction expires

If your auction was successful, make sure you send off your item as soon as possible. When both the buyer and the seller are satisfied, make sure you put in a positive review (feedback) about the buyer and request positive feedback from the buyer. *Feedback* on eBay is its way of giving buyers and sellers the ability to provide a rating and some short comments about their experience with the buyer or seller. Buyers can leave a positive, negative, or neutral rating and a comment for sellers. Sellers can leave a positive rating and a comment.

Feedback is important because by maintaining a positive feedback as a seller, you'll have an easier time selling to buyers because you become a trusted person to buy from. Keep in mind that after you provide feedback, changing it is very difficult, so think carefully before you submit your feedback, especially if it's negative. Negative ratings can have an adverse impact on someone's ability to do business on eBay. Try what you can to resolve the matter (whether you're a buyer or a seller) before submitting feedback and use negative feedback as a last resort if the matter still isn't resolved. In addition, submit a query to eBay about the matter to get it resolved.

If you're a seller and you have consistently had trouble with a particular buyer, eBay can allow you to bar that buyer from your listings. Check their selling guidelines for details.

If your item didn't sell or didn't meet your reserve price, then consider relisting the item. If it still doesn't sell, check out other auction sites. Just because eBay is the most popular auction site doesn't mean it's always the best site. To find other auction sites, go to a directory such as Internet Auction List (www. internetauctionlist.com).

Flipping for more information on eBay

This chapter only covers the basics to selling on eBay. If you want to read more about the topic of selling items through auctions and other venues, I suggest you check out the latest edition of the following books (all published by John Wiley & Sons, Inc.):

✔ *eBay For Dummies* by Marsha Collier

✔ *eBay for Seniors For Dummies* by Marsha Collier

✔ *Starting an eBay Business For Dummies* by Marsha Collier

✔ *eBay Business All-in-One For Dummies* by Marsha Collier

A big reason I focus on *For Dummies* books is that I know that John Wiley & Sons, Inc. produces quality products, and the authors do make sure to address the readers' questions. (I have done several *For Dummies* titles, so I know the drill!). You can also find plenty of free resources for readers at www.dummies.com. The books I mention here actually have some great free resources at the dummies.com site, so take a peek.

Chapter 8

Selling Your Services

In This Chapter

▶ Offering your services online

▶ Deciding what services to offer

▶ Knowing how to find prospective clients

▶ Becoming a virtual assistant

▶ Looking at micro-task opportunities

Doing some time and effort and providing value to others for money is the essence of being a micro-entrepreneur. Not so long ago, the intrepid entrepreneur who offered services to others spent time knocking on doors and making calls, soliciting their business.

Fortunately, in today's Digital Age, making connections between people and organizations that need services and those individuals who offer services is easier than ever. In this chapter, I highlight how you, the micro-entrepreneur (also known as a freelancer), can find the best places and how to proceed with them.

Ironically, a bad economy can actually help you get assignments (believe it or not). Companies and organizations that need services, but can't afford to hire permanent employees, turn to small businesses and freelancers to help them finish necessary work. Even struggling government agencies are getting the same type of help. This is where you (and this chapter) come in.

Read Chapter 3 for help with assessing your strengths and weaknesses so you can sell corresponding services. That way you not only get hired for your services but you also can get rehired.

 This chapter looks at you, Mr. or Ms. Micro-Entrepreneur, as a freelancer, also known as an *independent contractor* — someone who owns his or her own business and who is offers a service. I refer to you as a freelancer in this chapter.

When you're providing services as the nimble micro-entrepreneur that you are, keep in mind that your efforts are paid as an independent contractor — not as a W-2 employee.

As a freelancer, you're responsible for your own taxes and reporting. The person or firm that paid you simply paid your fee and nothing else. The taxes you may be responsible for include federal income taxes, Social Security taxes (also referred to as *self-employment* taxes), state taxes, and local taxes. Consult with your tax person. For more information on taxes, refer to Chapter 21.

Knowing Who Your Prospective Clients Are

Before you can offer any service (or sell any product), having a firm grasp of your customers is important. I go into greater detail about your clients (*your target market*) in Chapter 13, but for now, I simply show you the two types of customers you'll have so you can understand how to focus your services toward them.

The two types of customers are consumers and businesses — okay, three if you add government entities. All three have different motivations for rendering a buying decision.

Focusing on consumers

As a freelancer, consumers are the first group to consider when figuring out who your clients are. Look to see what services consumers want. If you have products and services geared toward consumers, then you need to discover as much as possible about what motivates them to buy and what information and services they want and are willing to pay for.

Here is what happens when consumers need assistance. Familiarize yourself so you can hone your approach in selling services to consumers:

- Consumers recognize that they need help. You won't catch this moment yet; it's too early for you to recognize it.

- Consumers search for information, more than likely on the Internet. They do some simple researching to find potential solutions. Here you have your first chance to gain their attention. An easy way to do so is with article marketing. You can write a free article that links the consumer to what you offer to help meet her need. Refer to Chapter 18 for more on article marketing.

- ✔ Consumers then evaluate the options. They'll ask themselves whether they can solve it alone or whether they need help. Many micro-entrepreneurs create DIY articles, audios, and/or videos to help the consumer. They also make themselves available for services. Many consumers will opt to get help (and contact an expert — ideally you).

- ✔ Consumers make the decision to buy. I hope they made it with you.

- ✔ The post-buying period begins. Consumers may have either a buyer's remorse or a desire to purchase more. If you provided a service, follow up with some communication, thanking them for the service and reminding them about the benefits of what you provided. Doing so also gives you an opportunity to invite them to consider other things you're doing (such as subscribing to your blog or inviting them to an event where you'll be, either online or offline).

Defining this group of consumers may be easier if you can build a picture of them with specifics. For instance, say that the ideal person you want to approach for your services is a webmaster. This category is clear, and finding webmasters isn't that difficult. After you know your ideal customer, you can then focus on ways to find webmasters, such as with a professional organization or an affinity group of some kind.

Whether you're looking for webmasters or any other definable group, here are some places to help you start your look:

- ✔ **LinkedIn** (www.linkedin.com)
- ✔ **Meetup** (www.meetup.com)
- ✔ **Yahoo! Groups** (www.groups.yahoo.com)

After you identify the group, in this case webmasters, you can then target your skills to individual webmasters, probably by sending individual emails.

Capitalizing on companies

If you're offering services to companies, you can probably find them easier than finding consumers. Because they know the cost of a permanent part-time or full-time W-2 employee, companies may be more receptive to using freelancers for services. Pitching them your idea may not be that difficult because you can point out the cost savings to them.

Business buyers are sophisticated and need to see the value of what you offer from a cost-benefit analysis (whether the value of the benefits exceeds the cost of paying for them). Businesses buy services that keep them profitable, competitive, and successful. If you can show how your services can help them increase sales or lower costs (or maybe do both), you chances of success increase.

To find individual companies, do a search in venues such as these:

- ✔ **Business.com** (www.business.com)
- ✔ **LinkedIn** (www.linkedin.com)
- ✔ **Manta** (www.manta.com)
- ✔ **Super Pages** (www.superpages.com)

Say that you received an assignment to work for a florist. The florist was happy with your services. Perhaps your services are appropriate and very helpful to other florists, too. In that case, you can use the previous resources to find other florists. If the service you provided was bookkeeping, for example, and you know the ins and outs of bookkeeping for florists, it can be an advantage for getting more business with other florists.

Selling to government agencies

A third potential source of business for your services is the government. In the grand scheme of things, the government (federal, state, and local agencies) spends trillions. No matter how you slice it, several types of opportunities are available for you to provide valuable and reasonable services for the benefit of government (and taxpayers, too).

What this means for you (and other micro-entrepreneurs) is that government agencies will buy your services if what you offer makes sense to them. Government regularly buys all manners of services, ranging from technology to written communications. Even better: The government is transparent about what it wants and what it will pay for. The federal government, for example, has the General Services Administration (GSA) (www.gsa.gov), which provides guidelines on how you can sell products and services to the federal government.

The GSA even set up an agency solely to help small businesses in their pursuits to sell more goods and services to the federal government; the Office of Small Business Utilization (OSBU). For more information on the OSBU, go to www.gsa.gov/aboutosbu. If that link doesn't work, go to the federal government's official search engine at www.search.usa.gov and look up either GSA or OSBU.

Meeting and Finding Prospective Clients

The great thing about looking for potential clients for your services is that they're usually also looking for you. Of course, for every paying client that is looking for help, dozens or hundreds of folks are looking for the assignment.

Finding out where these clients hang out will pay off for you. You can look in three places that are generally considered work-for-hire venues.

Horizontal venues

A *horizontal site* has all sorts of clients with all sorts of assignments, and the competition is among all sorts of service providers (freelancers). In other words, a horizontal site crosses all specialty services and needs. A good example of s horizontal site is Elance (www.elance.com), which is really like eBay (and also owned by eBay), but it's primarily for services. Other horizontal venues include the following:

- ✔ **Odesk** (www.odesk.com)
- ✔ **Freelancer** (www.freelancer.com)
- ✔ **Get a Coder** (www.getacoder.com)
- ✔ **Guru.com** (www.guru.com)
- ✔ **Ifreelance** (www.ifreelance.com)
- ✔ **Project 4 Hire** (www.project4hire.com)

Refer to the later section, "Hooking Up with Elance and Other Horizontal Sites" in this chapter for a more complete discussion on how these types of sites work.

Vertical venues

A *vertical* site is a site where the services provided are very specialized; they concentrate on a particular type of service or maybe a particular industry or sector.

The best way to find a site that specializes in a particular service is to do a search with your favorite search engine with phrases such as "work for hire in [type of service]" or a similar phrase. Here are other examples of vertical sites:

- ✔ **Agents of Change:** If I were part of a company seeking a pre-screened webmaster, this site (www.agentsofvalue.com) is a great consideration. If I were a webmaster seeking to provide service, this site would also be a good marketing venue.
- ✔ **All Graphic Design:** This site (www.allgraphicdesign.com) showcases a community of graphic designers.
- ✔ **1-800 Contractor:** If you're handy with tools and enjoy home improvement projects, check out this site (www.1800contractor.com).

✔ **House Keeping Wanted:** If you do house cleaning or housekeeping, make sure you review this specialty site (www.housekeepingwanted.com).

Directly via search engines and directories

Maybe you already figured out what type of client is right for you. Perhaps you already landed your first assignment and you now have a good idea of the ideal client to approach. In any case, you may be able to find new customers directly through search engines and directories that would cut out the middleman fees that most freelance sites charge. (A *directory* is a website that has its own searchable database and can help you find businesses based on your category or geographical area. A good example is www.superpages.com, which is a searchable database similar to the Yellow Pages.)

Other useful directories to find businesses are as follows:

✔ **Any Who** (www.anywho.com)

✔ **Switchboard** (www.switchboard.com)

✔ **Yellow Pages** (www.yellowpages.com)

For example, say that you found a paying client who was a florist. You figure that other florists would make good clients too. To find more of this type of client, you can search for "florist" (and similar phrases, such as "flower," "florist business," and so on). At that point, proceed to contact the search results, either via email or telephone (For more details on communicating with your clients, refer to Chapter 14.)

Hooking Up with Elance and Other Horizontal Sites

No matter what type of services you offer, a website is probably available to be helpful in getting connections with prospective customers that need your services. The leading horizontal site is Elance. These sections take a closer look at how Elance works if you're ready to list your services. Keep in mind that the other horizontal sites operate similarly to Elance.

One of the benefits of using Elance is that payment is assured. This way, if your client is on the other side of the country or in a remote town in Uzbekistan, getting paid for your services will be covered.

Identifying the client

So you have a clear idea what prospective clients who are looking to hire you, you need a basic grasp of the other side of the transaction. Those individuals, organizations, or companies that hire freelancers can register on Elance for free with no cost to post a job or assignment.

Elance makes it as easy as possible for the clients to hire freelancers. The site even provides job post templates and other guidance to avoid any problem or confusion in posting an assignment.

When the assignment is posted, freelancers like you that see it and then put in proposals (these act as *bids*) to gain that assignment. The prospective client views all the proposals and narrows his choice. He gets a chance to see each freelancer's profile along with important information such as

- ✔ Work history
- ✔ Tests passed
- ✔ Portfolio of your work (with images or screenshots)
- ✔ Feedback and rating from prior assignments

The client can then make a decision and hire the freelancer (hopefully you!). After the assignment is started, both the client and the freelancer manage and collaborate on a page referred to as a *workroom*. Both can view the progress of the work and can set milestones toward completion of the work. Video conferencing can also be part of the process.

When the freelancer completes the assignment, the client makes the payment after approving the work.

- ✔ For short assignments, a simple fee is part of the assignment (referred to as a *fixed price job*), and the payer puts the amount of the fee in a licensed escrow account; the freelancer receives payment after satisfactorily completing the assignment.
- ✔ For long-term assignments, the client pays the freelancer when whatever portion of the fee is agreed upon and when the freelancer successfully meets each milestone.

The process must be working. As of November 2012, more than 175,000 companies have hired freelancers on Elance.

Signing up and understanding the set-up process

As a freelancer (also referred to as the *service provider* or just *provider* on Elance), you sign up and registration is free. You fill out a profile detailing your skills, experience, work history, and so.

To sign up, follow these steps:

1. **Complete your profile.**

   Pay special attention because your profile acts like an advertisement for you. Of course, you want an honest and accurate showing of your skills and experience, but make sure you highlight the benefits of hiring you. Cover anything that a prospective client would want to know about your skill set.

   I can't emphasize enough that everything everyone sees of you and what you offer (your great service) is marketing. Companies won't hire you just because you're a nice person (okay, most of the time); they'll hire you because you offer a service they need and hopefully at a price they're willing to pay (and be happy with it, too). Refer to the chapters in Part III for general marketing advice.

   In your profile, include work samples (if available and suitable for that type of work). Your potential clients will be easier to win over if they're convinced of your competence and see the quality of your work. Some types of work can lend themselves well as samples such as graphic design, writing (articles or blog posts), or a video production.

   Some types of work aren't as easy to offer as a sample, such as data entry. In those instances, get good reviews from clients who were happy with your service. Of course, you should solicit good reviews from any former client.

2. **Designate the categories in which you're seeking work.**

   Some categories may require the freelancer to be tested regarding her skills in order to be qualified to submit proposals (keep reading for more information about skills testing).

3. **Choose whether your account will be a basic level or a premium level.**

   A basic level lets you make up to job 40 proposals per month (submitting a job proposal is referred to as a *connect*, and 40 is the monthly quota). A basic membership is free (you just are charged the 8.75 percent fee per assignment). The premium plan has three levels: individual, small business, and large business. Each has a monthly membership with added benefits, such as increased proposals (up to 60 per month for individuals) and other services (such as hosting for your portfolio work). By the way, at any time you can have more than your allotment of proposals per month with a small fee per proposal.

No matter which level you choose, Elance makes its money as a percentage of your fee. As of 2013, that fee is 8.75 percent, which is deducted from your payment. Say that you win and complete a job where the client pays $200. You would net $182.50 ($200 less a deduction of 8.75, which in this case is $17.50).

4. **If you know anyone who runs a company, invite her to register at Elance so she can peruse the site from a prospective client's point of view.**

   She may be able to view what freelancers have presented in their profiles and get back to you with some pointers about what was good (and not so good) to include. I always think it's helpful to view things from the perspective of the client because it will be helpful in your marketing.

As you get familiar with Elance, take the time to go to its Elance University. It's loaded with tutorials for both clients and freelancers to maximize your success and effectiveness on Elance. For more details, go to www.elance.com/q/elanceuniversity/index.html.

Grasping how the bidding process works

Because hundreds of jobs are available at any given moment to bid on (send your proposal), take your time and scrutinize what work is listed. Don't bid just because the work sounds easy, you're eager to get an assignment, or you need money. Bid only on work that you'll be happy to do. Be just as selective finding clients and assignments as your clients are in seeking freelancers.

When you're bidding for work, keep in mind what you'll minimally accept. Don't put in such a low bid that you're working too hard relative to the money you're receiving. Don't be reluctant to walk away from bidding for an assignment. Other assignments will come along.

Don't automatically assume that a client will accept only the lowest bid. If the project is a complicated one, clients know that work quality is more important than the cost. Don't be shy about what you charge because quality work is worth it. Keep in mind that the clients already know (or assume) that hiring a freelancer will save them money because it's less costly than hiring and retaining a standard W-2 employee.

For example, put yourself in an employer's shoes: What is less costly, hiring an employee to do a short-term project for gross pay of $10,000 or paying a freelancer that same $10,000? When you add in statutory costs that come with an employee (such as Social Security taxes, state taxes, unemployment taxes, worker's compensation, overhead, and so on), the cost of a W-2 employee in that scenario can easily rise by another 25 to 40 percent (depending on the state, industry, and so forth). In other words, hiring that W-2 employee can easily increase the cost to $12,500 or as high as $14,000 when all costs are factored in.

Gaining the assignment: Now what?

When you get the job, you'll work and communicate directly with your client (whether it's via telephone, email, and/or Skype). Elance provides the facility for tracking and reporting work and processing payment for both parties.

Do your best with the assignment. After all, the assignment is itself a form of marketing when you really think about it. In other words, you want your work to speak for itself because it reflects the type of work you do. You want the client delighted. If the client knows that he can expect a great job from you, then you have a better chance gaining a second assignment when you have a reputation for great work (at a fair price).

Always finish your work on time and be responsive to the client's questions and concerns. As you gain a good reputation and build your client base, you'll eventually be able to increase your fee.

Maximizing your Elance success

After you have nailed your first assignment, keep your success going. Here are some important points for your ongoing success:

- ✔ **Keep updating your profile.** This page communicates to the Elance world about how competent and adept you are, so you should continuously add to your profile when you increase (and improve) your skill set and as more and more folks are happy with your service. Make sure that your summary is updated and your keywords accurately reflect your skills and desired assignments. Don't forget that how you present your profile also tells clients how careful you are in your work, too. A sloppy or incomplete profile doesn't convey a positive message to potential clients.

✔ **Make yourself unique if possible.** Focus on presenting something that makes you and your skill set stand out among the fray. If a client said to you "You are one out of a thousand," ask the client what he means and then focus on that skill as something that makes you different (better) than your competitors.

✔ **Focus on improving your bidding (also known as *proposal writing*).** Writing a good proposal isn't a skill you pick up in the beginning and then no longer utilize. Each time you do an assignment — and even each time you don't get an assignment — you figure out more about what makes (or un-makes) a good proposal. Realize that this skill is like any other skill or service: It can keep improving.

✔ **Be responsive.** Act fast when you see desirable assignments posted. Be quick (within 24 hours or as soon as possible) when clients and others communicate with you or have questions or concerns. Doing so pays dividends in terms of total overall income. Being quick to call back can be the edge you have over your competitors. Many freelancers lose opportunities because they forget that a successful freelancer is also a salesperson who understands the value of customer service.

✔ **Do skill tests.** According to Elance, a majority of clients surveyed said that verified skill tests and credentials were very important considerations in their hiring decisions. Although Elance doesn't require skills testing, some employers may. Skills testing can be a good marketing tool for you because many employers can see how well you performed. Elance uses an outside firm (Expert Rating at www.expertrating.com) for skills testing. If, for example, you're looking for assignments in Joomla programming, you can take a skills test on Joomla. Your results are then displayed on your profile at Elance. If you scored in the top 10 percent, you'd be a more attractive candidate.

✔ **Upsell and cross-sell.** When you go to bagel shop and buy a coffee and the clerk asks if you want the large size, she is *up-selling*. If you get the coffee and you also said yes to getting the blueberry muffin, that is *cross-selling*. Most businesses do this to some extent, and freelancing is no different. Don't just thank your client when the assignment ends. If your client was happy, discuss other ways you can help him at that moment. If you wait for your client to just call you back, you may lose the opportunity to make more money with this satisfied client.

You can discover new opportunities, new pitfalls, and new ways of doing business and freelancing. Here are some more resources and freelance sites to help you make money providing service to others.

Perusing other freelance resources

Like any worthwhile business activity, you should stay informed. Freelancing and similar pursuits (like consulting, counseling, and tutoring) are active areas where many folks are making money either part-time or full-time. Here are places to turn to for more information and guidance:

✔ Freelance Folder (www.freelance folder.com)

✔ Freelance Switch (www.freelance switch.com)

✔ Freelancer Job (www.freelancer-job.com)

✔ Freelancer Life (www.freelancer-life.org)

✔ Job Stock Blog (www.jobstock.com/blog)

Before you think that freelancing is a must, keep in mind that micro-entrepreneur opportunities abound elsewhere, even if you don't have very technical skills.

Becoming a Virtual Assistant

A growing profession right online is that of the virtual assistant. A virtual assistant doesn't have to be an expert in anything like programming, writing, or graphic design (although the more you know, the more you earn). A *virtual assistant* is a freelance helper who has basic business and administrative skills. The virtual assistant is a perfect choice for those individuals who want to help an organization, without the cost and hassle of commuting downtown.

These sections explain what types of jobs you can do as a virtual assistant and how you can locate those jobs.

Recognizing what a virtual assistant does

Think of a virtual assistant as someone who does what administrative assistants and secretaries do in a general office environment but from the comfort of their home. They perform tasks such as the following:

✔ Basic bookkeeping

✔ Basic research

✔ Customer service

✔ Data entry and maintaining databases

✔ Office organizing

✔ Proofreading

✔ Secretarial work

✔ Transcription work

✔ Typing

✔ Word processing and spreadsheets

As you can see, a virtual assistant can do a wide range of activities. As a virtual assistant, you may not need to know all these tasks, but the more you know, the more employable you are.

Do a complete assessment and inventory of your skills. Don't just include those things that you learned in high school and college; think of what you already do currently that you may not have formal education in but that you do have a high degree of competence.

If you have some shortcomings, such as lacking knowledge or skill in a major function that virtual assistants carry out, consider getting some training.

Marketing yourself and finding work

If you want to be hired as a virtual assistant, you want to market yourself and showcase your skill set. The chapters in Part III provide some concrete and specific ways you can do so. In addition, to get clients, check out these resources:

✔ **Network online.** Find small businesses (any business in fact) using venues such as

- Super Pages (www.superpages.com)

- LinkedIn (www.linkedin.com)

- Business.com (www.business.com)

✔ **Network offline.** You can find businesses at places, such as your local Chamber of Commerce and local business associations.

✔ **Join online forums.** Plenty of online forums exist where small businesses and entrepreneurs meet and exchange ideas. Find out more about forums in Chapter 5.

✔ **Network at virtual assistant sites and organizations.** These sites can help you make contacts with firms and individuals that hire virtual assistants. Check out these suggestions:

- **Administrative Consultants Association** (www.administrative consultantsassoc.com)

- **Alliance for Virtual Business** (www.allianceforvirtualbiz.com)

- **Hire My Mom** (www.hiremymom.com)

- **International Virtual Assistants Association** (www.ivaa.org)

- **Real Estate Virtual Network** (www.revanetwork.com)

- **Virtual Assistant Forums** (www.virtualassistantforums.com)

- **Virtual Assistants Network and Forum** (www.vanetworking.com)

- **The Virtual Link** (www.thevirtuallink.com)

A virtual assistant has the potential to make a full-time income and can net as much money as an administrative assistant working in a standard job. Although the virtual assistant doesn't usually have the typical expenses of an employee (commuting time and expenses, for example), he does have the potential to work for more than one employer because he has the opportunity to work beyond a typical 40-hour weekly routine. In terms of an hourly rate, experienced virtual assistants have earned as much as $25 to $35 per hour.

Micro-Tasking for Small Bucks

You can make some good money, just a few bucks at a time. Plenty of folks are making some good spare time cash by doing *micro-tasks* — in other words, small jobs or assignments for a small amount of money. These sections focus on one of the most popular micro-tasking websites and provide more resources and other sites.

Using Fiverr

The pioneer for micro-tasking is Fiverr (www.fiver.com). This site is popular, and if you go to the site, you may be surprised to see what people will do just for five bucks.

These offerings are called *gigs*, and you'll see gigs that sound useful ("I will put up a blog for you for five dollars") to interesting ("I will sing 'Happy Birthday' in Swahili to anyone you like") to the off-beat ("I will do a video of myself with your name written on my forehead"). Ask yourself what you would do for five bucks.

Of course, you don't make a fortune on this site, but some folks do it in a way that helps them make sometimes hundreds of dollars with not as much effort as you think.

For example, one person's gig was "I will show you 101 ways to gain traffic to your site". It really was an ebook, and the gig did well. Another gig was "I will show you in detail how to use Twitter to make money," and the person did it with a YouTube video. In these two examples they did a task that they could easily duplicate, and all they had to do was keep selling and re-selling the gig.

Other ways that you can use Fiverr and other similar micro-tasking sites include these ways:

- **Arbitrage:** *Arbitrage* is essentially buying something at a low price and simultaneously selling it at a higher price and netting the difference. For example, one micro-entrepreneur I know freelanced graphic design work and sometimes used graphic design work he got on Fiverr gigs and simply sold it and charged a higher fee.

- **As a loss leader:** A *loss leader* is a product or a service that is initially sold at a deep discount or even below cost (at a loss) to stimulate the potential for future sales that can be profitable. I saw a financial adviser offer a half-hour financial session — for five dollars! Of course, he won't make money at that moment, but he figured that doing so was a great way to find prospects that he could then sell more of his regular fee-based services.

- **Marketing:** I have found many gigs that offered some marketing potential for micro-entrepreneurs. Gigs cover topics, such as Twitter marketing ("I will tweet your message or affiliate link to my 5,000 followers") and Facebook ("I will share your message with my 500 friends on Facebook").

Fiverr and other micro-tasking sites are great reminders that your creativity is an important business tool.

Investigating more about micro-tasking

If you're seriously interested in micro-tasking, plenty of places offer tips and information on Fiverr (and other sites) and the art of micro-tasking. Do a search for "micro-tasking" or specific sites by names at the following places:

- **ehow:** This site (www.ehow.com) contains lots of great articles on micro-tasking and other topics.

- **YouTube:** At this popular site (www.youtube.com), you can find lots of material and how-to videos on Fiverr (as well as other topics that I discuss in this chapter, including Elance and virtual assistants).

✔ **EzineArticles.com:** This site (www.ezinearticles.com) has more than 800 how-to articles about Fiverr (while you're at it, do a keyword search on the other topics in this chapter as well).

As Fiverr's popularity took off, similar sites soon popped up. Here are some more micro-tasking sites that offer you some micro-task opportunities:

✔ **Gigwalk** (www.gigwalk.com)

✔ **Gigzon** (www.gigzon.com)

✔ **Mechanical Turk** (www.mturk.com)

✔ **Micro Workers** (www.microworkers.com)

✔ **NetTradr** (www.nettradr.com)

✔ **Ten Bux** (www.tenbux.com)

Chapter 9

Writing for Money

In This Chapter

▶ Finding the writer who lives within you

▶ Knowing what to write about

▶ Locating the places that pay for writing

You're reading this book, which is proof that you can get paid for writing. Granted, getting a gig for writing a *For Dummies* book is nice but it's only an example of what you can do — getting paid to write. This chapter is about how you can tap into your inner writer and earn some cash for your written word.

Everyone has thoughts, feelings, ideas, and information that you can share with others through the printed (or digital) word. This chapter explains how you can make some bucks writing, including what you can write about and where you can submit your writing.

Discovering the Writer inside You

Writing from home and finding a way to make money at it is a pursuit that many people dream about. The good news: Plenty of work is available, and many different types of writing work are available for freelance writers. You just need to know a bit more about yourself and your skills before you can start writing. These sections point out some important writing and business skills you need, some basic equipment freelance writers you need, and some pitfalls to avoid as you begin writing.

Cultivating important writing skills

In order to be a good writer, you need to be a good reader. A good reader notices both the style and the content of the writer, which in turn helps you become a good writer. Read other people's work and as much as you can about the topic you want to write about and what sites and blogs they're at.

Being a good reader can help you develop a sense for writing because you read the other experts and ideally take note of what they write and how they write it. You can also get a better idea of your *market* (the people and organizations that will pay you for your writing).

With that, here is a list of writing skills you can cultivate:

- ✔ **Figure out the type of writing that interests you.** Selecting the type of writing you enjoy will be critical to your success. For example, do you enjoy humorous or serious writing? Do you enjoy short stories, fiction, professional, how-to, commercial (or business), or technical? Write what you are good at and what you enjoy and success will be easier.

- ✔ **Develop the ability to logically communicate your ideas and thoughts in your writing with clarity.** When you read other people's work, notice the structure and the style of writing. Look to see how your favorite writers craft their articles and essays. Model your style and pick up your own content. Write about the topics that you enjoy and have expertise with. When you go about your day, have a notepad (or maybe a digital recorder) and record ideas as they come to you.

- ✔ **You have to keep on improving your writing abilities.** To do so, regularly read the leading writers and bloggers in your specific writing specialty to see what they're doing and not doing. Even if you aren't in a writing-for-hire situation, you should have a blog and write weekly to maintain your writing edge and to remain visible. To me, a successful writer keeps producing, but does so in the entrepreneurial frame of mind.

- ✔ **Be a self-starter.** No one will be hovering over you to get you to do your assignment. Part of the character of a successful entrepreneur in the writing world is to have initiative, discipline, persistence and the ability to handle rejection with aplomb (I handle it with a plum).

  Being a self-starter means that you take the initiative; you get the work started because no one else will. Give yourself a self-imposed deadline and a list of specific steps to keep moving forward.

- ✔ **Develop researching skills both online and at the library.** The Writers Market (www.writersmarket.com) regularly does research and surveys into what are the various payment levels for various types of writing.

- ✔ **Pick up good habits.** Focus on having good time management and managing your workflow. Set up your office to minimize distractions. Procrastination is your enemy (and can zap your ability to make money). The bottom line: Analyze your situation and see what is reducing your effectiveness and productivity.

Grasping some important business skills

As a micro-entrepreneur, your business is the craft of writing. You can pick up the skills for writing in the preceding section, but you also need to couple them with the skills and responsibilities of a business person. Here are some important business-related skills that you need to master to be a successful freelance writer:

✔ **Understand the legal side of writing.** You need to understand the basics of copyrights. A *copyright* is the legal and exclusive ownership of intellectual property (such as a written work or audio or video work), which are produced by an author or publisher. Basically you need to know whether what you're writing is your property or someone else's (the website, blog, publisher, or someone else). For example, I am the author of this book, but it's not my intellectual property (it belongs to the book's publisher). I'm a writer for hire. (A *writer for hire* means that you're paid for your efforts to produce a work, but you have no ownership rights to the work.)

Make sure you bone up on your knowledge of copyright and related laws. These laws rule over what you produce; either in written, audio, or video means. This is important to know whether you're producing your own works (such as when you're publishing) or if you're a writer for hire

You also need to know what legal phrases, such as first rights and all rights reserved mean. (*First rights* means that the publication, website, or media outlet has the right to be the first to publish your original material; *all rights reserved* means that no one else has rights to the work except for the author/writer). *Writer's Digest* and *Writers Market* cover legal issues for writers regularly; check out these sources later in this chapter.

In addition, find out more about copyright laws at places, such as the Copyright office (www.copyright.gov) and the Copyright Clearance Center (www.copyright.com). I would also recommend checking out the Electronic Frontier Foundation (www.eff.org). When you're at these websites, get familiar with the Digital Millennium Copyright Act (DMCA), which was enacted in 1998 and intended to deal with copyright law with the new and growing electronic and digital environment.

✔ **Understand business agreements and protocol when dealing with publishers and other entities involved in your work.** When you work for someone in terms of writing and editing, you need a clear understanding of what you're expected to do and what you'll be paid. If you write and the client isn't pleased, it may be just cause to not pay you. Whatever work you produce, you want to do it right according to the agreement so that your client is happy and you get paid (and ideally be invited back for more writing work).

✔ **Know how to market and sell your services as a freelance writer.** You have to consider these important skills every day as a freelancer. You can do a lot with both your writing skills and your content in terms of marketing. Check out the Chapters in Part III for how to market your skills.

✔ **Build equity.** Consider creating content that you can copyright and own. You want to have your own intellectual property that you can sell in whatever way you see fit. Having intellectual property is an asset that can keep producing income. Refer to the later section, "Getting Paid Multiple Times" for more details.

✔ **Build your portfolio along the way.** The more work you have and the more clients you have worked for, the better your chances of getting more and better assignments.

Identifying your equipment needs

Fortunately, a writer's tools aren't difficult to come by. Here is the raw minimum you need:

✔ **A computer with Internet access:** If you want to write on a bare-bones budget, you can access the Internet at your public library.

✔ **An email account:** You need an email account. You can go with a free one, such as from Gmail or Yahoo, to keep in contact.

✔ **A blog or website:** A blog or website can publicly showcase your writing prowess and take advantage of more ways to make money with your writing (Writing good content means more visitors to your blog, and you can make money from advertising programs such as AdSense) or get into publishing (creating published product that you can sell at your site). You can find out more about marketing through blogs in Chapter 16 and more details about publishing in Chapter 10.

✔ **Word processing software:** Use the mainline software packages for word processing and related document types (depending on the type of work you do). If you don't have the money to get the higher-level software packages, you can consider the Open Office software suite that you can download free at `www.openoffice.org`.

Avoiding pitfalls in freelance writing

Being a freelance writer (or any type of business that you own) is that you have freedom to control your time as you see fit and to be your own boss and control your destiny. Being a freelancer means that no one is forcing you or cajoling you to work. This freedom can be a pitfall. Here are some other pitfalls you should watch out and avoid, especially when you're starting your freelance writing (or any other type of) business:

- ✔ **Getting distracted.** TVs, refrigerators, family, friends, neighbors, and members of the Water Buffalo Lodge can distract you. Don't let anything keep you away from writing.

- ✔ **Settling for lower pay for your work.** Research the market to see going rates for various types of writing work and make sure you aren't selling yourself short.

- ✔ **Failing to create your own content.** You don't want to just earn income; you want to create intellectual property that can build wealth. As a result, you want to create products (ebooks, ezines, audio programs, and so on) that can make money for you (check out Chapter 10).

- ✔ **Ignoring what successful writers are doing to convert their craft into greater income.** Many great writers took their content and parlayed it into much more income. Some writers have taken a single article and have sold it multiple times.

- ✔ **Failing to think outside the box.** Successful writers parlay their work into opportunities, such as consulting, seminars, and even product sales.

I personally love the freedom and that is definitely a nice perk of being self-employed. When your business is flourishing and money is more readily flowing in, then I encourage you to indulge yourself with some time for fun. However at the beginning when you're just starting as a freelance writer and trying to get established, you need as much time as possible to get things situated where cash flow isn't a problem. At that time, save the indulgence for after you reach some durable success in your endeavors.

Choose Your Writing Specialty

In order to be a successful writer, selecting what type of writing you will do is important. Writing is a very diverse activity, so you don't want to be a jack-of-all-trades writer. For instance, trying to write a mystery novel, a business how-to book, and a technical manual for manufacturers wouldn't be a smart decision.

To determine your writing specialty, do the following:

1. **Choose your content category.**

   Your initial decision is to write fiction or nonfiction.

2. **Determine the subcategories.**

   If you're writing fiction, you can go into mystery, romance, sci-fi, and so on. For nonfiction, your choices are endless, and they include everything from human interest to how-to.

3. **Choose the structure.**

   If you decide to write fiction, determine whether you want to write short stories, novels, and so on. If you decide to write nonfiction, figure out whether you want to write short articles, manuals, and so on.

4. **Select your style.**

   Figure out whether you want your style to be humorous, corporate, and so on.

The following sections discuss some fruitful areas that you may consider pursuing as a freelance writer.

Blogging in the blogosphere

Blogging is a very active area with plenty of room for new writers. Many blogs involve commentary on a variety of topics. In fact, blogs need a steady stream of new content to remain relevant and popular. Many blogs pay writers, although most may compensate you in nonfinancial ways, such as free advertising. (Chapter 18 discusses article marketing in greater depth.)

If you want to find actual paying assignments for blogging, here are active sites that post paying assignments and jobs in blogging:

- ✓ **Freelance Writing Gigs** (www.freelancewritinggigs.com)
- ✓ **Performancing** (www.performancing.com)
- ✓ **Writers Weekly** (www.writersweekly.com)

You can make money both by writing for other blogs and by writing for your own blog, which is your platform for your content and also a launch pad for sales of your products and services. To create your own blog, find out more in Chapter 4. Don't stop there. Refer to Chapter 16 for more about how to locate blogs and how you can use blog writing in your micro-entrepreneurship.

Providing website content

Lots of websites need content ranging from product descriptions and reviews to articles and information/instructions for site visitors, guests, and/or members. Some sites, for example, are *catalog sites,* which need content, such as sales copy for products that customers can order from the website or sales copy for an email blast for an upcoming sale. Other sites are *news sites* that need writing on current events (whether those events are national, local, or maybe industry news). The need for content is endless, which means that the nimble writer stays employed.

The following sections describe several of the types of text you can write for different websites. Use the resources in the "Locating Places That Pay for Your Writing" later in this chapter to find specific opportunities.

Creative writing

Creative writing is any writing where the purpose is to express thoughts, feelings, and emotions in an imaginative way rather than to simply express facts and figures. Creative writing can come in many different forms, from articles, short stories, or novels. If you have a great imagination and a flair for writing, creative writing may be the venue for you. Maybe you're the next J.K. Rowling. (If you are, please mention that my book helped you get your start.)

Humorous

If you have a funny bone, you may be laughing all the way to the bank by writing humorous material. The world loves a laugh (or at least a smile), and humorous writing is constantly in strong demand.

The opportunities for humorous writing range from jokes for humor websites and greeting card companies to longer articles and books. Probably one of the better known buyers of funny comments is *Readers Digest* (www.readers digest.com), but virtually any source where you can read some funny stuff is a potential market for you. You can start with the *Writers Market* (see the section later in this chapter).

Ghostwriting

A *ghost writer* is someone who can write articles, reports, books, and so on, but doesn't claim credit for the writing in the form of a byline. Typically the person paying for the ghostwriting takes the credit and gets the byline.

If you don't mind not getting credit, ghostwriting is an active area and worth considering. You can search online for "ghost writing opportunities" to get started. Many of the resources in the "Locating Places That Pay for Your Writing" section later in this chapter are also helpful.

Technical writing

You can find *technical,* also referred to as *professional,* writing in many corners of the writing world. Sources, such as corporations, government agencies, and educational institutions (like universities and technical schools) need your writing services.

Technical writers are a stout breed. Experienced technical writers don't have difficulty getting lucrative assignments. Qualities include an attention to detail and not falling asleep at your desk.

Business writing

Many businesses need help with everything from writing fliers to catalogs and news releases. Just think about what all that companies do to produce for the benefit of customers, employees, vendors, and so on. They may need a writer to help them with their next promotion.

Focus on a specific sector and ensure that you're extremely knowledgeable and proficient about it. Some successful writers specialize in technology or maybe the bed-and-breakfast industry. After you decide on the industry or sector, use the sources in this chapter and review the chapters in Part III for additional help.

Consumer markets

Consumers read everything they need to make an informed decision. Tons of publications and websites cover everything from how-to and product reviews to investigative writing and topics and so on. You can write for websites that cover consumer markets. Search online for different options. You can also find publications and websites in the "Writers Market" section later in this chapter.

Sales copy writing

Writing sales copy is a specialized skill set that every writer should get into, even if they don't plan on getting formal assignments on sales copy writing for businesses and other organizations that sell products and services.

Sales copy writing is about writing copy with the intent to persuade or motivate the reader to do something ("Supplies are limited . . . get your widget today!"). Being able to write sales copy is a valuable skill, and very experienced copy writers are among the biggest earners in the writing world. Their work ends up in direct marketing venues, such as mass marketing emails, direct mail pieces, and online and offline advertising.

If you're serious about building your writing business, you should look into sales copy writing because it's a valuable skill to have, even if it isn't your chosen writing specialty. Writing with the intent to persuade is certainly a valuable writing skill necessary in activities such as

✔ Getting clients to hire you.

✔ Inquiring with editors and content buyers

✔ Sending your emails to new prospects and potential publishers

Here are some of my favorite resources on the topic of sales copy writing (I personally know some of these individuals):

- **Bob Bly** (www.bly.com)
- **Jeff Dobkin** (www.dobkin.com)
- **Clayton Makepeace** (www.makepeacetotalpackage.com)
- **Ted Nicholas** (www.tednicholas.com)

You can read more about sales copy writing in Chapter 14.

Radio and TV

Thousands of opportunities exist as the explosion of entertainment venues spring on both TV and radio as well as their numerous (and growing) digital equivalents on the Internet. These opportunities range from program reviews and commercial advertising writing to infomercials and screenplays. For more information, check out sites such as the following:

- **Screenwriting Science** (www.screenwritingscience.com)
- **The Script Lab** (www.thescriptlab.com)
- **Watchers Watch** (www.watcherswatch.com)
- **Writer's Write** (www.writerswrite.com)

Locating Places That Pay for Writing

The bottom line: You're a freelance writer, and you want to be paid. These sections provide some helpful resources to help you locate the places that can pay you for your writing.

Finding websites for cold, hard cash

Many sites directly pay for articles that you write and that they post. They differ in method of payment and how much, so you want to do some investigative work and see which of the following sites offer you the best opportunities.

- **About.com** (www.about.com)
- **Associated Content** (www.associatedcontent.com)
- **Constant Content** (www.constantcontent.com)

> ✔ **Demand Studios** (www.demandstudios.com)
>
> ✔ **Ehow** (www.ehow.com)

These sites pay for your content. Just know that you won't make a fortune writing for them. You may get $10, $25, or $50 for a single article. Some pay based on how popular the article is and calculate your payment based on a percentage of ad revenue generated by the site with your article, whereas others have a different formulation. Many writers have had various experiences, both good and bad.

Look at these sites not as a writer, but as a micro-entrepreneur. A writer may view these sites and say, "Fifty dollars isn't much money. I will keep looking elsewhere." A micro-entrepreneur can look at the same sites and say, "I can write an article that potentially dozens or hundreds or possibly thousands of people could read and become my customers. Writing the article also can give me a solid credential, offer me traffic to my sites, and possibly boost my list of ezine subscribers, and they even pay me $50 to do that!" Some see a glass as half empty whereas others see it as half full.

Make sure to search online for these types of sites because new ones are always popping up. Search with phrases (include the quotes), such as "websites that pay for writing" and "blogs that pay for writing". Be creative. I also do phrases such as "top-paying sites for writers" and "list of writing websites that pay".

Perusing freelance writing resources

The following three are the best resources available for the freelance writer. You'll probably get excited by the possibilities when you explore these various sources.

Writer's Digest

Considering how varied and involved the topic of writing can be, the *Writer's Digest* (www.writersdigest.com) is the go-to source for the beginner. This hard copy monthly magazine is great, and its digital version is equally worthwhile. You can find lots of how-to articles from experienced writers and veteran editors on various topics, including working with editors, finding new markets, and becoming a better and more successful writer.

I recently signed up for its free ezine, and I was pleasantly surprised by the freebie for new ezine subscribers — a free report in PDF format entitled "101 Best Websites for Writers."

Writers Market

The *Writers Market* (www.writersmarket.com) is a must-have book for writers of all kinds. This thick book lists thousands of publications and media outlets that pay for written content. Each listing offers plenty of details on the paying source, including the source's writer's guidelines, which tell you exactly how to proceed. You can uncover what they want and what they don't want.

The main book is an annual compendium that you can buy from your local bookstore or online. However, you may want to consider signing into the website and paying a reasonable subscription fee to access the database.

Media Bistro

Media Bistro (www.mediabistro.com) is a great place for the truly serious freelancer. You can find plenty of information on industry news and trends in addition to job postings. This site provides in-depth reports on how to pitch a particular magazine or media outlet on what you want to write about.

Media Bistro also has other benefits as well, such as how-to information and group rates on health insurance. You can sign up for free, but then get the full benefits of the site; it costs $55 per year.

Accessing other freelance resources

Here are some additional options you can use to build your freelance writing business. Check out these sources:

- ✔ **Freelancer** (www.freelancer.com)
- ✔ **Places for Writers** (www.placesforwriters.com)
- ✔ **Writers Weekly** (www.writersweekly.com)
- ✔ **E Byline** (www.ebyline.com)
- ✔ **WritingHood** (www.writinghood.com)

You can also use your favorite search engine (along with Facebook and LinkedIn) to locate writers' associations and groups that offer you many benefits. Hundreds of writers' organizations and groups exist, and many are specialized (such as for travel writers or science fiction writers), so you should be able to find one that fits your needs.

Getting Paid Multiple Times

Writing becomes truly profitable when you can combine your content, some creative marketing, and a good structure or framework to implement your action plan. Here are some ideas for turning your writing into ways to continuously make money long after you finish your work. Here is a residual income plan that I think any competent writer can do (just remember that you're a micro-entrepreneur).

1. **Create your content.**

   Write an ebook or other type of digital content that that can be easily sold and downloaded over the Internet, such as a PDF or other common publishing format. (Chapter 10 goes into greater detail about creating self-published products.) Make sure that it includes good content and that it's *evergreen* (it's a topic of interest that will be good years from now).

2. **Set up the structure.**

   Put this content (along with the sales copy for the page) at a digital delivery service venue such as Payloadz (www.payloadz.com) or E-Junkie (www.e-junkie.com). Feel free to shop around for others.

   At a digital delivery service site, you can set up a page, upload your content, and add your PayPal information (www.paypal.com). You can usually find great tutorials on setting up at these sites. You'll then effectively have a page at this site that has both the sales copy and the ability to both buy the product and download it instantly.

3. **Set up the marketing.**

   The marketing will be from your writing. Write articles on the same topic as the content found in your ebook and place them on your website or blog. Create articles for sale (at paid sites) and create other articles than can be used for article marketing (Chapter 18 shows you how). All the articles and blog posts have the same link to your product. The more articles you have, the greater the funnel that guides all interested parties to your offering.

4. **Keep track and manage.**

   Make sure it's working and check your PayPal account. If you have done all the steps and made sure the articles were good content and the product you're offering is an excellent one on a topic that is in demand from your target market, then you should have success. If it worked well, go ahead and repeat it. The more articles your write, the more products you create for sale, the more marketing you do all mean the more sales and profits you generate.

Chapter 10

Getting Into Self-Publishing

*Y*ears ago, the power to create *intellectual property* (a legal term referring to works you produce that are creations of the mind), such as reports, books, and other information products that are the fruits of your labor was a relatively difficult pursuit. Fortunately, doing so today with self-publishing isn't the case anymore.

Self-publishing is when an author of a body of work (or the creator of an audio podcast or video) takes on the additional role of creator and distributor of that work. Traditionally, self-publishing meant that you created your own book (or report, newsletter, and such), but today self-publishing means your creative work can take the form of a website, blog, ezine, audio, video, or other work that can inform or entertain.

As this chapter explains, self-publishing isn't just about the written word in its various formats (article, report, book, and so on). It's also about taking that content and repurposing it in audio and/or video form for the intent of resale. You can build your wealth by putting together some valuable content (which everyone has in their lives) and creating a product that can be sold again and again in different formats — even in the modest corner of your spare time and effort.

Tapping into Written Self-Publishing

You have information and knowledge that someone will pay good money for, so you decide to self-publish the material. The following sections give you the lowdown on written self-publishing, including the basic how-to to help you start, the tools you need, the different avenues of written self-publishing you can pursue.

Getting started

Here are the basic steps you can take, no matter what type of written self-publishing you want to pursue (I refer to the different types in the "Identifying the different types of written self-publishing" later in this chapter).

1. Find out if a market for it exists.

What good is publishing a product that no one will buy? Of course, publishing something that no one will buy is okay; just don't call it a business — call it a hobby. A market is nothing more than a group of people who are willing and able to buy what you offer. Making sure a market exists first can help you make a better product and also ensure more sales for your business. Your written product isn't valuable if no one wants to read it. The same goes for your audio or video product. Refer to Chapter 13 for how to investigate your market.

2. Decide on your topic.

You should be proficient and enthusiastic with the topic and have some experience and/or expertise with it.

3. Create the product.

Determine your product's shape (physical book, ebook, audio podcast, or video). In the next section, I discuss the publishing tools, which you probably already have, to help you create your product.

4. Market it.

Marketing is the process where you find those that are willing and able to buy from you and communicate to them why and how your product should be bought. You can discover more about marketing in the chapters in Part III.

Naming your self-publishing tools

Here are the products you need to have or to acquire (you can either borrow or buy them) in order to self-publish.

Technology requirements

First and foremost, you need a computer. In recent years, desktops and laptops have become very affordable. In fact, I recently saw some desktops and laptops going for under $350 at a major electronics retailer chain (of course, you can do your shopping at sites like Amazon.com, Ebay.com, and Craigslist.com, among others. If you can't afford a computer, you may want to consider renting one until you have enough money or borrowing a used one from a friend or family member. You can also use the free computers at your local library or find an inexpensive one at a pawn shop.

In any case, the computer you use should be minimally loaded with the necessary software to do basic word processing and some ancillary tasks (see the next section).

In addition, you also may need a printer or scanner to print sales pages, which are typical peripheral pieces of equipment, unless you're self-publishing only on a digital platform.

Necessary software

On your computer, you need the following software to help facilitate your self-publishing endeavors:

- ✔ **Software that allows you to view and create PDFs:** A PDF, which stands for portable digital format, is widely used and makes for a good format for your report or ebook.

  Although Adobe pioneered this type of software, you don't need to purchase Adobe Acrobat or other expensive high-end software. In fact, most popular word processing programs give you the ability to save a word processing document as a PDF. If you computer doesn't have this capability, you can consider some lower-priced software packages you that give you the power to create documents as PDFs.

- ✔ **Software that helps you create information documents:** Whether you're using Microsoft Office or the free Open Office Productivity Suite (find it at www.openoffice.org), you may need some basic software to create reports, instructional pages, spreadsheets, presentations, or other documents that may be part of your product.

✔ **Software to help you be creative:** If you plan to do audios or videos, you may need software to help you edit these types of files. I personally use software such as Roxio's Creator suite (www.roxio.com), which helps you to create and edit audio and video files. I also like audio and video creation and editing software from Movavi (www.movavi.com).

✔ **Other software tools:** Make sure you have software to create zip files. Zip file software can help you take all the files needed for your product/ program and condense them into a single file for easy downloading and transfer.

For any other software needs, consider going online to find free trial software at the following places:

- **Tucows** (www.tucows.com): This site is one of the most comprehensive sites for free software downloads. Some of the software is totally free and fully functional (referred to as *freeware*). Most of the software is either a free trial version (which you can then pay for the full version if you like) or fully functioning software with limited features (which provides more features when you pay to upgrade).

- **Download.com** (www.download.com)

- **File Hippo** (www.filehippo.com)

- **Softpedia** (www.softpedia.com)

Considering your delivery option: Digital and physical together

You can easily create digital products and resell them. You may also want to consider the ability to create the same products in physical form, too. *Digital* form allows your buyers to be able to buy, download, and use your offerings at any computer connected to the Internet, at minimal cost and hassle to you. If your product is in physical form, then you have to physically create it, package it, and ship it with all the effort and associated costs. I suggest that you do your products in digital form, but that you also make them available (at a higher cost) in physical form for your customers who prefer a hard copy.

Creating physical products isn't difficult. You can make the following:

✔ **CDs:** Most computers have the ability to read and/or create CDs so you may only need software that helps you create and burn CDs in the CD drive.

✔ **Books:** For books you can hold in your hand (either hard or soft cover), you may consider a print on demand (POD) service. With this service, you can print a small quantity of hard-copy books for a modest cost. Some examples include

- **Book Masters** (www.bookmasters.com)

- **The Book Patch** (www.thebookpatch.com)

- **Blurb.com** (www.blurb.com)

- **CreateSpace** (www.createspace.com)

- **Lulu** (www.lulu.com)

To ensure you're ready to sell and market your digital products, check out the later section, "Setting up your ecommerce for digital content," for more information.

Identifying the different types of written self-publishing

If you decide to self-publish your written word, you have several choices. The following sections describe your main options and what you need to do for each type.

Making articles and reports

Creating your own articles and reports is the easiest and best way on the path to being a successful self-employed self-publisher. Furthermore, when you produce them, you can directly make money (you can get paid for your articles; check out Chapter 9 for more details) or you use articles for marketing purposes (refer to Chapter 18 for more discussion on article marketing, which I highly recommend as a powerful marketing technique for virtually any business).

Selling your articles and reports can become profitable. However, sometimes you can make money selling other people's content. If you want to profit from content you didn't create, consider the next two sections.

Master resale rights

With master resale rights (MRR), you can purchase a document, report, or ebook, and resell it and keep 100 percent of any sales generated. In addition, you can use those documents for ideas for content creation and marketing.

If you've written material, you may also want to contemplate selling your material through an MRR agreement. From a publisher's standpoint, MRR provides a way to generate sales through viral marketing. (*Viral marketing* is any marketing technique that encourages people to pass on a product that also has a marketing message to others, creating a potentially exponential growth in the message's visibility and effect, ideally for more sales or other business objectives.) You may want to sign an MRR agreement because if numerous copies of that ebook (or other information product) are sold, you indirectly benefit. The book (or product) may include numerous links that either go to your website or your affiliate links.

I have done the same. I created a PDF ebook with MRR, entitled *Job Hunter's Encyclopedia,* which was packed with hundreds of links to job-hunting resources. I tell buyers that they can freely pass along this publication to others. It has links back to my website and to some other offerings (including affiliate links; I cover affiliate programs in Chapter 11).

To find out more about MRR, you can do an online search or refer to the resources throughout this chapter.

Private label rights

You can buy information products that come with private label rights (PLR). PLR is a great way to get content that you use or change in any way and claim it as your own. In fact, PLR is a great way to get started with content. You can then change and edit it to suit your purposes.

Creating ebooks

One of the most obvious forms of written self-publishing is the ebook. Ebooks come in a variety of formats, including the following:

- ✔ **PDF:** This type, which stands for portable document format, is the most common. Files have the extension .pdf.

- ✔ **ePub:** Short for electronic publication, the type is also presented as ePUB, Epub, or epub. This is a free and open ebook standard. Files have the extension .epub.

- ✔ **Kindle:** Amazon (www.amazon.com) launched this format for its Kindle book reader. Creating a Kindle book is relatively easy and it has become a very popular ebook format.

   After you create it, you can upload your manuscript to the Amazon site and Amazon manages everything — including servicing, hosting, and delivering it when someone purchases a copy. Amazon also takes care of customer service. Amazon transfers your portion of the sale to the bank account of your choice. Buyers can get Kindle books either for their Kindle (or other electronic reading device) or for their computer (Kindle software is available for the PC).

I love Kindle. As a matter of fact, I initially did my ebook, *Job Hunter's Encyclopedia*, as a PDF, but I immediately did a second edition as a Kindle book. Find out more about Kindle publishing by heading to `www.kdp.amazon.com`.

The great thing about today's formats is that you can add features, such as making them password-protected or limit what people can do with them. Some advanced features allow you to limit how many copies can be made or how many you can physically print out. Review the features and decide what you would like to do.

Blogs and websites

Blogs and websites are certainly a popular form of self-publishing. Having one or both can definitely complement your publishing efforts and provide a platform for launching and marketing your published products. Go to Chapter 4 for details on how you can set up blogs and websites.

Electronic newsletters, also called ezines

If you're publishing information that is in a popular topic that is constantly changing, consider doing an electronic newsletter, also called an *ezine*.

Producing an ezine (either free or paid) can be a smart choice. You can take advantage of ezines in many ways to help you either sell your products directly or build your business. Refer to Chapter 16 for more about using ezines.

To find out more about ezines and the related opportunities, check out these resources: You can also check out Chapter 16 for more information and resources for creating your own ezine and for how to use ezines to market your business.

My own ezine adventure

I publish a free ezine that I call Prosperity Alert (`www.ravingcapitalist.com`), which I use to communicate with my clients and students. The world of finance, economics, and business has plenty to write about, and this ezine gives me the opportunity to tell my students about pending projects, new videos at my YouTube channel, and new seminars coming up at the adult schools where I teach. Also, once in a while if I see an affiliate product that I think is appropriate, I send an email to my ezine subscribers.

Using resources for written self-publishing

Here are some resources for your self-publishing pursuits that can get you on the right track:

- ✔ **Author Link** (www.authorlink.com)
- ✔ **Book Market** (www.bookmarket.com)
- ✔ **Independent Book Publishers Association** (www.pma-online.com)
- ✔ **Dan Poynter** (www.parapub.com)
- ✔ **Small Publishers Association of North America** (www.spannet.org)
- ✔ **Smash Words** (www.smashwords.com)
- ✔ **Writer's Guide to E- Publishing** (thewritersguidetoepublishing.com/)

Trying the Audio Publishing Route

The information you publish and sell to your clients doesn't have to be the written word. Armed with a digital recorder and your mellifluous tone, you can tap into audio publishing. Your digital audio files can in several formats, but the most common are MP3, WAV, and WMA. Your listeners can listen to your audio either from an online source (such as a website or blog) or they can downloaded the file to their computer, smartphone, or other device capable of accessing and playing digital audio.

In terms of what form your audio publishing can take, you can sell your offering in the following forms:

- ✔ **Downloadable digital product:** People can purchase your audio file the same way they would buy your ebook (they just use a PayPal account or some similar site).
- ✔ **Subscription-based venue:** They may pay a flat fee or other pricing method for a period of time for access to your audios.
- ✔ **CDs or flash drives:** Your digital audio may be digital and physically packaged on a CD (imprinted CD in a sleeve, jewel case, or other packaging). Some audio can be sold on a flash drive, but doing so isn't common.
- ✔ **Redbook CDs:** These are regular, standard CDs that your customers can play in a CD player at home or in their car. Places like music stores use this standard, which is different than digital audio. Most audio production software that burns (or creates) CDs can do your CD as a digital data CD (to house digital files) or as a redbook CD, which also means that you're

limited to approximately 70 minutes of standard audio time. (They're referred to as *redbook* because the technical guidebook for this industry standard really is red).

✔ **Other sale-able forms:** Other forms are available, but they're obscure right now. Just don't be surprised if new forms appear.

To understand the technical side of doing audio (from the latest technology to tips on how to create quality sound recordings and so on), visit sites, such as Digital Tips on audio (`www.digitaltips.com/audio/`), the audio section of Techspot (`www.techspot.com`), and other sites with audio information and technology (by doing a search at your favorite search engine).The following sections briefly explain audio publishing, including its formats and pros and cons, outline how you can use audio self-publishing as another way to make money. Here I explain how to create an audio product and include important tools you need to start.

Recognizing the formats you can use

Audio self-publishing includes these formats you can incorporate into your micro-business:

✔ **Audiobook:** The *audiobook* (actually a digital audio ebook) acts like a complete topic that the buyer can listen to versus reading. The same component breakdown of a book applies here (opening, body, and conclusion). I suggest you buy an audiobook or two (preferably of the topic you're planning to do) and discover from others. Most audiobooks run from 45 to 90 minutes, but there is no set length. Just make sure yours is long enough for the listener to get a complete treatment of a given topic. The audio file format may be MP3, WAV, or some other widely used format.

✔ **Podcast:** In the same way people listen to a regularly broadcast radio program, you can do the same with an audio podcast. In fact, a podcast is an ongoing series of regular recordings that have an identity and a structure. A podcast may be a 30- to 60-minute format done on a regular basis (like every week) and regularly uploaded to a site (like every Monday). Listeners can then listen to it at their computer while the audio is playing at the site; or they can download it and play it or transfer the file to listen on their MP3 player, smartphone, or other personal electronics device.

✔ **Other audio formats:** Your creativity matters here; as long as you have good content that can be heard and people are willing and able to pay for, you have a sale-able product. I have recorded entire seminars (typically about three hours' long) and sold them as audio seminars either online at my sites or as physical CDs either in person or via mail order.

Audio does have some downsides, too. Being profitable with audio may be challenging because of lots of competition in this medium. In addition, keeping the sound quality consistent in each podcast or broadcast can be difficult. If you aim to do audio podcasting, finding or creating content on a regular and constant basis can also be difficult.

These resources can help with going forward with audio publishing:

- ✔ **Audible** (www.audible.com)
- ✔ **The Audio Publishers Association** (www.audiopub.org)
- ✔ **Blog Talk Radio** (www.blogtalkradio.com)
- ✔ **iTunes** (www.apple.com/itunes/)
- ✔ **Listen and Live Radio** (www.listenandlive.radio)

Creating your audio product

If you decide you want to provide an audio product for your customers, you've made a smart choice. In fact, an audio product is one of the easiest information products you can make. To make a simple audio product, follow these steps:

1. **Research your market.**

   Before you create an audio, find out whether there is a market for it. Make sure your market has some type of demand or interest in your audio topic. If people are buying products and services in that market and you have good content that they can listen to related to that topic, you can proceed.

   The markets best suited for audio products include those related to education and where how-to information is helpful, as well as news and views and the entertainment market (ranging from music to fictional stories to other types of entertainment). The sites in the previous section can help you do your research (along with the information in Chapter 13.)

2. **Create a script.**

   You want to be specific and write down the points you want to cover, what you plan to explain, and so on. You don't want to just ramble. Make sure the opening minutes are a clear introduction with the title of your audiobook, a verbal table of contents (what you plan on covering), and your introduction.

If you are stumped about what to write in your script, take clues from other audiobook authors. Listen and take notes on how they say what they say and how they pace themselves with the structure and style. In my case, I'm more of an extemporaneous speaker. I don't use a full script. I just list some topic headings and important points I don't want to forget, but otherwise I speak off the cuff and in a conversational style.

3. **Practice your recorded session.**

Your first recording likely won't be your best. You'll be a little nervous, so practice it several times and record it each time. Listen to it and have others critique it as well. Remember to use a quality digital recorder that can easily connect to your computer (see the next section for what equipment you need).

4. **Record your audio product.**

You want to sound relaxed and confident in the final product; after all, you're talking about something that you're proficient in. You're talking about your specialty so you should sound confident with strong content.

5. **Prepare it with instructions.**

Include some written introductory instructions with the audio, including a table of contents or agenda of what you're going to cover. The intro can be a text or PDF file. (You can call it something like Read-Me-First. txt.) This file has written information about the program and the author, suggestions for a better listening experience, and any links to your website and other products or services that are related to this audio topic. You may also include your copyright notice and perhaps a disclaimer (see more on the disclaimer later in this chapter). The agenda can be a simple list so that the listener can follow along, or it can be a little more elaborate, such as a PowerPoint presentation. It just has to reinforce your audio content.

6. **Added profit centers.**

Your information is also an indirect form of marketing. You can briefly mention at the beginning and end of the audio content where listeners can get more information your website and blog.

7. **Upload the final product to a digital delivery service.**

When finished, take all the files and put them into a single zip file (a compressed single file that is created with file compression software). You can then upload it to your digital delivery service (such as pay loadz.com or shopify.com). At those sites you'll also need to write the ad copy for your item because they have a products section (much like Amazon) where visitors to the sites can see and ideally buy your stuff.

8. **Market it.**

   You can market to sell your audio program in many ways. Peruse the chapters in Part III on marketing strategies.

Seeing what equipment you need

To create your own audio self-publishing products, you need the following tools:

✔ **Quality digital recorder:** Being able to record your voice clearly and having the ability to readily connect to your computer are the two musts. Many quality brands are available from manufacturers, such as Olympus, Sony, and Phillips. For years I have used an Olympus digital voice recorder, and I'm satisfied with the voice quality. If you're doing a lecture-style program, then standard voice quality is acceptable. Many computers now have the ability to make a digital audio recording so see if your computer provides a suitable recording for your purposes. However, some audio experts say that you'll get better voice quality with other equipment, such as digital voice recorders.

✔ **Editing software:** Many free or low-cost audio editing software programs are available to help you edit the audio to make corrections and re-record material. I have used the Roxio Creator software program that edits audio and video.

Look online for Audacity Audio editing software (`www.audacity.sourceforge.net`). Movavi has an excellent suite of audio (and video) editing software programs that are affordable (`www.movavi.com`). Another great audio editing program is Sound Forge, which is in Sony Vegas Movie Studio HD Platinum 11 Productions Suite. This suite of software offers HD editing.

I recommend that you find free trial versions of some of these programs and others as well at active software sites, such as Tucows (`www.tucows.com`), Softpedia (`www.softpedia.com`), and SnapFiles (`www.snapfiles.com`).

Considering Video Publishing

Not long ago, a small businessperson faced a difficult challenge if she wanted to create and market a decent video. You needed expensive equipment, a decent-looking venue (such as a professional studio), and assistance from a videographer. Today's technology has made it very easy for you to create and market your own videos.

The following sections explain more about the advantages (and disadvantages) of using video, how you can create a video and use YouTube, and what equipment you may need.

These resources can help you with discovering more information and resources in helping you create and market your own videos (including how to create videos that are for sales and marketing purposes).

- ✔ **Reel SEO** (www.reelseo.com)
- ✔ **Tube Mogul** (www.tubemogul.com)
- ✔ **Video Maker** (www.videomaker.com)
- ✔ **Vimeo** (www.vimeo.com)
- ✔ **Web Video University** (www.webvideouniversity.com)

Spelling out the ins and outs to video

The Internet has created a platform that makes doing and marketing videos easier than ever. You can easily upload your first video to YouTube or other video platforms within hours of reading this chapter. You just need to have a plan and purpose.

A video has three main components that you need to figure out:

- ✔ **Content:** The content will be what your topic or specialty is. In addition to making sales videos and videos that you can sell, you also want to offer videos with free content.

    Free content isn't difficult or costly to do, and it can help you connect with your audience and build a relationship. People like to buy from people and businesses they like and have a relationship with, even if it's only through videos. The free content also acts like a nice sample of your knowledge and your insights. If people see that you're generous with your content through free videos (or free reports or other content), they're usually more conducive to buying from you. However, don't give away your bread-and-butter content that you make a living on; give away free content that helps you better sell the content you specialize in.

    For example, at my YouTube channel (www.youtube.com/paulmlad), I provide plenty of free content, such as my commentaries on economic, financial, and business issues. I even provide free lessons on economics and how they relate to today's political and economic issues. Because my paid-for content is meant to help people navigate the economy and financial markets, they work well together. I provide free content (about today's problems) and content that my customers can buy that provides solution (from my knowledge and experience).

✔ **Style or presentation:** This means both technical concerns (such as the video equipment) and cosmetic concerns (such as your video recording environment; and your clothes, lighting, and so on). Review the next couple of sections for more info.

✔ **Residence:** The site for the video(s) can be a simple and free venue, such as at YouTube (www.youtube.com). Refer to the later section, "Using YouTube" for more specifics on setting up a channel.

Creating your own video

Making your own videos (from a technical point of view) has never been simpler. To create your videos, stick to these steps:

1. **Research your market and competitors.**

   By now, you should have decided on your topic or specialty. You should have also analyzed and reviewed your competitors' videos, too.

2. **Decide on your video's content.**

   Figure out what you want your video to do, such as provide how-to information, news, or just entertainment. You can take any topic and have ten different spins on it — and ten different ways to make money. Just make sure you figure out before you start recording what you want your video to look like.

3. **Choose your video equipment.**

   Plenty of good video recording products are available. I have even used a Flip camera because I don't need sophisticated equipment. (I do commentary and don't need lots of special effects). Refer to the next section for specific help.

4. **Choose your studio where you'll record.**

   Decide whether you'll use a professional venue or some suitable place in your home. For my video commentaries, I actually use my basement. I set up a whiteboard to write some comments. I use a brick background with adequate lighting. It's simple, but it works for me. Your topic or approach may be totally different, but you need to choose what works for you. You can also hire a local videographer. A client of mine actually hired a college student that was a communications major who specialized in video. Some entrepreneurs also outsource some of the video production (see Chapter 19 for more on outsourcing).

5. **Create your script.**

You need a script that spells out what your video is about. Your script doesn't have to be a detailed Hollywood production, but you do need to jot down what you're going to say. When you write a script, you can stick to the plan, and viewers can tell whether you really know your stuff.

When I do my video commentaries, I do practice them a few times, but ultimately they're spontaneous because I'm talking about what I research and comment virtually everyday in my business. If you don't write a script, make sure you stay focused and talk only about what you know.

6. **Record your actual video.**

Make sure you dress comfortably and appropriately for the video you're recording. When all is ready, do your video and do it several times. Watch it and critique it. Ask others you trust to watch it and critique it. Rerecord until you produce something meets your satisfaction.

7. **Edit your video.**

From the video recorder you're using, transfer the video to your computer to edit. If you flubbed a word or didn't speak loudly enough on one take, edit parts of the many takes to create a final take. I use Roxio software to do things, such as add text to my videos. I also add my website where viewers can go to sign up for my ezine to increase my subscriber list.

8. **.Place your finished video online.**

The simplest and most versatile may be on YouTube. You can also email the video to your customers. You can also host it on your website.

Knowing what equipment you need

To produce your video, consider getting the following equipment and accessories:

✔ **Recording equipment:** You can use a camcorder, flip camera, or some other recording device; just shop around to check for the features and pricing. Start your research with the video sites I list earlier in this chapter in the "Considering Video Publishing" section. Websites such as Bizrate (www.bizrate.com), Pricegrabber (www.pricegrabber.com), and Shopzilla (www.shopzilla.com) offer product features, ratings, reviews, and price comparisons. As smartphones improve their technology, they may provide suitable recording capabilities, so use the same sites to shop for them, too.

✔ **Accessories:** You may need accessories, such as lighting, a tripod, or any props for your production, such as costumes. It depends on your production.

✔ **Video software:** To help edit and produce your video, consider the necessary software programs. I like programs like Roxio's Creator software (`www.roxio.com`) and Movavi's video editing software (`www.movavi.com`). Many computers with Windows 7 (or higher) come with video editing software. In this chapter I provide other sites to help you research video editing and production software.

✔ **Other software:** You may also consider screen capture software and presentation software for some types of videos (such as instructional videos where you need to guide viewers step-by-step through a process, such as filling out a form on your computer screen). You can find some great screen capture software at Camtasia (`www.camtasia.com`) and at Movavi.

The good news: You can quickly discover that indeed anyone can be a video producer.

Using YouTube

When talking video and the Internet, I must discuss YouTube (`www.youtube.com`). YouTube is the most heavily trafficked video website on the planet, and it's in the top three of all websites when it comes to total traffic.

You need to set up your own video channel to have your venue to present your videos to the world. Setting up your video channel is free and easy. Go to YouTube and click on "Sign In," to go to a Google page (Google owns YouTube). There you can click on "Create an Account" and fill in the basic information (name, email address, and so on). Keep in mind that you can have more than one YouTube channel. I prefer to have one for my business and one for personal use.

Having a YouTube channel means folks can subscribe to it. If you develop a following, every time you upload a video, your subscribers will automatically be alerted via email (think of the marketing possibilities). In addition, you can have your YouTube channel connected with your accounts at Facebook and Twitter, giving you even more marketing power.

When you make videos and post them to YouTube, you can designate them as public or private. A public video means that anyone searching for videos can find them (your videos can have keywords associated to them). You can also do private videos, which means that only people with the link can find it.

For your business YouTube channel, make your free content videos and your marketing videos public so that anyone can view them. However, you can use the private video feature for your products. For example, when I did my tax program, I created more than 35 videos for it, and I made them private videos. When people bought my program, they received all the videos through the private links that were provided with the purchase.

Handling Legal and Management Stuff

If you delve into the self-publishing world to make money, sell products, or market your business without first handling important legal and management issues, you may face some potential problems. The following sections cover some important points on legal and management matters.

Getting an ISBN

When you create a product, you have the ability to sell it where you see fit. In order for your ebook to appear on Amazon, in other large book buying networks and in major bookstores, or online in venues that sell similar products, you need to acquire an International Serial Book Number (ISBN). Not acquiring an ISBN won't stop you from self-publishing, but without one, you won't get the potential sales. For more information about getting an ISBN, go to www.isbn.org.

Respecting copyright

In the world of producing intellectual property, you must be familiar with the copyright laws. Copyright is legal protection for you — the publisher — in the event that someone takes verbatim (word-for-word from your work) what you have produced. Other people can write about the same topic, but they can't use it in the same manner that you did.

Make sure that you protect yourself and your copyrighted material. At the same time, respect other people's copyright.

Fortunately, you can get a great resource on not only copyright but also other forms of protection for your intellectual property (such as trademarks). Check out *Patents, Copyrights, & Trademarks For Dummies,* Second Edition, by Henri J. A. Charmasson and John Buchaca (John Wiley & Sons, Inc.).

Stating your disclaimer

Did you ever park your car at a parking garage and see the sign "This garage is not responsible for any damage to your car or for the theft or loss of anything in your car"? That is a disclaimer and whenever you write or produce a self-published product, find out (from your attorney) whether you need to include a disclaimer somewhere prominent in or on your product.

A *disclaimer* is a formal statement telling the reader what you can and can't guarantee and what you can't be held responsible for when the reader takes action with your content. The disclaimer is meant to hold you harmless and prevent any potential legal issue if the readers have a problem when they attempt to enact any strategies or actions described by your product. The disclaimer is also intended to protect the reader as well.

If your ebook, for example, is about how to save on taxes, then include a disclaimer in the book that states the book is only informational or educational and not meant to be formal advice. Then tell the reader to seek appropriate professional counsel.

 Make sure you put the disclaimer statement in a prominent spot within your program. The front page (or close enough) is best. Your readers or viewers should immediately see it. If the topic is serious or sensitive, it may be a good consideration to put the disclaimer statement in several places, such as at the front of the book (or in the beginning of the audio or video program) and a reminder at the end. Placing a disclaimer statement in the sales page or other point of purchase is a good idea so readers are aware of the risks even before they buy.

 Find out how other authors and established publishers handle the same situation in the same topic. Read their disclaimers, which are prominently displayed either in the front or back of their book (or both).

 In addition, make sure that whatever you write or produce has integrity. Don't, for example, give medical advice if you don't have a medical degree and license to practice. Don't lie about someone or say fraudulent stuff.

Setting up your ecommerce for digital content

When you finish creating your PDFs, audios, and so on, you want to make sure you're ready to sell and market them so your customers can easily purchase and download them. To ensure that your market can buy them, follow these three steps:

1. **Get PayPal or some other payment option.**

   You need a way for people to pay for it. PayPal (www.paypal.com) is one of the leading payment processors for Internet commerce. Find out more about PayPal and other payment alternatives in Chapter 4.

2. **Acquire a digital delivery service.**

   You still need a mechanism in place so that when your customers pay, they can download what they purchased to finalize the purchase. A digital delivery service integrates with your PayPal account to make a delivery of their purchase. Consider these places:

   - **E-Junkie** (www.e-junkie.com)
   - **Payloadz** (www.payload.com)
   - **Shopify** (www.shopify.com)
   - **Trade Bit** (www.tradebit.com)

   Some of these sites also feature a shopping mall area, which can work much like a mini-catalog site for your digital products. If you can't or choose not to do a website or a blog, this can serve as a site for one or more of your products.

   When you investigate these sites, find out how they charge. Some charge a monthly fee (such as E-Junkie), and others may charge a percentage of the sales (such as Payloadz). Some may have different rate structures based on your volume of sales, transactions, or activity. The pricing can impact when you start doing larger volume of sales.

   In the beginning when you don't have a lot of sales, use a digital delivery service that charges a percentage of the sale. That way, if you only sell $100 worth of product, your cost may only be, say, $5 if the site charges 5 percent. If you anticipate that your sales will substantially increase, price out a digital delivery service that charges a flat monthly fee. One service I work with charges a flat $15 per month for its basic plan. The price is the same whether you sell 1 unit of your product or 1,000 units of it.

3. **Market your product.**

   Refer to the chapters in Part III about how to market your products.

Chapter 11

Being a Successful Affiliate

In This Chapter

▶ Defining the term "affiliate"

▶ Finding success with affiliates

▶ Focusing on some popular affiliate opportunities for you

An enterprising person can find money in many different ways and make things happen. I've taught home business seminars for nearly a quarter century. I have had many students who told me why they couldn't succeed. "But Paul, I don't have a product, and I don't know what to sell!" This lament sounds familiar with today's economy.

However, finding a product to market is as easy as going to a website and deciding. If you don't have a product and you're clueless about creating a product (or service), then you may want to consider the world of affiliate marketing.

This chapter examines the world of affiliate marketing, including what it is, why you would want to be an affiliate, how you can be a successful affiliate, and several different real-life websites you may want to look at to see if affiliate marketing is right for you.

The Lowdown on Affiliate Programs

An *affiliate* is someone who gets paid a referral fee from organizations (typically online companies) when that referral results in a sale. The affiliate doesn't make the sale; the affiliate simply makes the referral by getting a prospective customer to click on a link. After the prospective customer clicks on the link, she is sent to the web page that does the actual sales pitch. The affiliate earns a commission when the merchant successfully makes the sale.

Differentiating between an affiliate and reseller

An affiliate gets paid for making the referral and isn't responsible for other aspects of the sale (such as customer service or product distribution). On the other hand, a *reseller* typically buys a product from a source (such as a manufacturer) at wholesale prices and hopes to resell them at higher prices. The reseller has a more involved role and does get involved in billing, shipping products, and answering inquiries from customers. I like the way one insider described the difference between an affiliate and a reseller: the affiliate pre-sells (makes that introduction between the customer and the vendor), whereas the reseller actually sells.

Keep in mind that although affiliate marketing is about getting paid on product sales, you can get paid as an affiliate in a variety of ways. Affiliates can also get paid per action or per lead. For the merchant, paying the affiliate on a *cost per action* (CPA) means that the affiliate gets paid when the potential customer does a particular action, such as filling out a form or providing an email address.

If the prospective customer does buy whatever is offered, the merchant then pays a referral fee to the affiliate. Variations of this type of transaction vary, depending on the merchant that an affiliate works with on the Internet. Being an affiliate marketer can be a great business for anyone, especially because it usually doesn't cost anything and because you can do it with little more than a computer and an email address.

These sections examine closer the advantages and disadvantages of being an affiliate and the different types of affiliate programs available.

Eyeing the pros and cons of being an affiliate

Becoming an affiliate is probably the single easiest home-based online business. Here are eight advantages of becoming an affiliate:

- ✔ **Affiliate marketing has been known to be a cost-efficient, assessable method of conveying long-term results.** In fact, you can start even with a shoestring budget.
- ✔ **You usually don't have to pay anything to become an affiliate.** Merchants want folks to sell their stuff.
- ✔ **You don't need special education.** Choosing an affiliate program and signing up for it is very easy.

✔ **You get the tools and guidance to make operating as an affiliate easy.** Most affiliate programs want to make sales, so they'll help you. They usually provide guidance and information along with sales tools, such as ad copy for sites and emails, banners, and other sales tools.

✔ **You can do it full- or part-time.** You get paid for the results you help to produce, not your time. There is no 9-to-5 routine or a clock to punch. Of course, the more time and effort you put in, the better results you will produce.

✔ **You don't have to drive anywhere or go to some meeting.** You can do it from the comfort of your home.

✔ **You can do it all at your desktop or laptop computer.** Even if you don't have a computer, you can do it from a public computer (such as at the library).

✔ **You just have to refer folks to the offer or product/service web page.** You don't have to worry about customer service or administrative support after you make the referral.

This list tempts me to do more affiliate marketing. As you can see, affiliate marketing can be an attractive business, especially when the economy is as tenuous and uncertain as it has been for quite some time.

However on the flip side, affiliate marketing does have a few downsides that you need to consider:

✔ You still have to sell. Sure, you're hoping that people will click the link and go to the sales page, but it still takes some convincing to do so.

✔ You need to build a list or find a way to reach an audience of prospects. The most successful affiliates spend a lot of time and effort building their list or garnering targeted traffic. It's nonstop marketing.

✔ Not all merchants have integrity. No matter where you go, online or offline, you have to watch out for unscrupulous merchants. Other times the product may have flaws.

Knowing the types of affiliate programs

To better understand how affiliates work and pay you, I need to explain the several types of affiliate payment methods:

✔ **Single tier:** This means that you get paid a percentage of the sale. Commissions typically range up to 50 percent and can sometimes be much more. I know of some programs where the payout is 100 percent because the merchant is more concerned about profiting from sales after the initial sale.

✔ **Two tier:** This type means you get paid at two levels:

- The first level comes from sales that are directly connected to your efforts.

- The second comes from commissions you get paid on the efforts your *subaffiliates,* those individuals who have signed up through you as affiliates.

If you're better at recruiting than direct selling, then a two-tier program may be better for you. Another version of the two-tier program is the multi-tier programs (referred to as *multi-level marketing* or MLM). MLM (also called *network marketing*) is a marketing system that has multiple levels of commissions, and you could have many subaffiliates. In MLM, you can make commissions from direct sales you generate and you can paid (an *override*) on the efforts of others that join due to your efforts as a recruiter. Because MLM is based on many levels of affiliates, you can potentially get override commissions from the efforts of many that are under you (the string of sellers or affiliates under you are referred to as your *downline*).

✔ **Residual:** This type means that you get an ongoing or recurring commission because the purchased product (or service) is charged on an ongoing basis, such as membership programs that may charge monthly or quarterly fees.

When you choose an affiliate program, select one based on both style and content. *Content* means you choose based on what is being offered (products and/or services in a niche or topic you're interested in) and a compensation plan that you like. All things being equal, as a beginner, choose a product/ service you really like and the compensation plan has two levels (or tiers) or more. If the plan has two or more tiers to it, it means that others in the compensation plan have an interest in helping you succeed. It becomes a team effort, which means that an inexperienced person can get the benefit of working with someone more experienced.

Viewing additional resources for more info

Here are some websites you can peruse to get additional information on affiliate marketing:

✔ **About.com:** At this site (www.about.com), you can read lots of great information and how-to articles by simply doing a search for "affiliate marketing."

✔ **Affiliate 1 on 1:** You can find lots of information and how-to for beginners and experienced affiliate marketers at www.affiliate1on1.com.

✔ **Affiliate Tip:** This site (www.blog.affiliatetip.com) includes affiliate marketing news and a tips blog by marketer Shawn Collins.

✔ **Affilorama:** This site (www.affilorama.com) is a leading site on affiliate education.

✔ **Associate Programs:** This site (www.associateprograms.com) has lots of great tips and tutorials for beginners; it also has a comprehensive directory of affiliate programs.

✔ **Ecommerce Guide:** At this site (www.ecommerce-guide.com), you can find plenty of news and information on affiliate marketing and related Internet marketing and commerce topics.

✔ **eHow:** Go here (www.ehow.com) and search with phrases such as "affiliate" and "affiliate marketing" and find some great how-to articles.

Starting As a Beginning Affiliate

Having the Internet is truly a blessing, no matter whether the economy is chugging or sputtering along. With just a few clicks, you get access to thousands and even millions of pieces of information and data on virtually any field of interest. The Internet's fast-growing popularity provides entrepreneurs — both micro and otherwise — a ready-made venue, especially for earning money in affiliate opportunities.

The affiliate marketing world has matured into being an established venue with established practices for both merchants and affiliates. Even a beginning affiliate like yourself can get started much easier now than even five or ten years ago.

The diversity of products and services that you can market as an affiliate is the greatest ever. You have thousands and thousands of products and services to choose from and thousands of merchants and affiliate programs to sift through. Don't forget that in affiliate marketing, everything won't take place overnight. And it won't happen without a strong commitment of time and effort by you.

To help you get started, these sections break down the simple steps that you, a beginning affiliate, can follow. They can get you moving on the right track.

Step 1: Discover your interest

First, ask yourself what topic interests you. Maybe you like fashion, education, electronic gadgets, gardening, automobiles, or furniture. Your options are endless, and the odds are good that your interested area has affiliate programs.

For example, any product sold on Amazon can earn you an affiliate commission. Whether it is a book, a lawnmower, or an elephant foot umbrella stand, you earn a commission.

Step 2: Identify your competence

You next want to identify your competence. Go with your strengths. If you have years of experience in a topic, get involved with affiliate programs related in that field. For instance, if you're an automotive mechanic, then consider affiliate programs tied to the automotive field. Affiliating yourself with affiliates that you're competent in is important for several reasons:

- **You'll have an easier time seeing the value if the product or service is good.** You can also determine whether it's good before marketing it to your contact list.

- **People will respect your opinion more.** When you send the link to people (especially people you know), they can respond more positively because they trust you and know you're credible about this offering.

- **You can offer regular, informed opinions on a blog, website, or on your Facebook page.** Doing so can result in more sales for you. Refer to Chapter 16 (marketing with ezines and blogs) and Chapter 17 (social media) for more information about this approach.

Step 3: Investigate before deciding

You can select from thousands of merchants, so you need to do your homework before making the final choice. You want to choose a program with the following features:

- A reputable company
- A quality product or service
- An in-demand product or service
- Acceptable compensation
- Ample tools offered to help you succeed

Various affiliate networks and affiliate tutorials can give you info on the most profitable products and best paying merchants. Make sure you take the time before you choose the right one for you.

Some people who tried affiliate marketing failed, perhaps because they lacked the knowledge or tactics. If you're a website owner and you want to join in an affiliate marketing business, you should know where to get good affiliate programs. Just keep in mind that you don't need a website to be involved in affiliate marketing. You can just as easily do affiliate marketing through a blog, a Facebook presence, or even through email marketing.

To help you start your search for suitable affiliate programs, here are some popular and active sites that have comprehensive listings and descriptions of affiliate programs:

- **Affiliate Directory** (www.affiliatedirectory.com)
- **Affiliate Programs** (www.affiliateprograms.com)
- **Affiliate Ranker** (www.affiliateranker.com)
- **Affiliate Seeking** (www.affiliateseeking.com)
- **Affiliate Tips** (www.affiliatetips.com)
- **Associate Programs** (www.associateprograms.com)
- **Lifetime Commissions** (www.lifetimecommissions.com)

Keep in mind that you should spend time reading and discovering the trends and changes in the affiliate marketing business. By doing so, you can remain on top of what is happening. If you're knowledgeable about online marketing, you can understand how important it is to stay up-to-date. In this kind of business, what worked last year may not work this year. Consumer tastes and behavior changes regularly.

You can promote multiple affiliate programs on your website or blog but don't promote everything you see. Just choose the affiliate programs that are appropriate for your site and are a good match for your target market.

Step 4: Select your marketing approach

After you choose what to market, your next step is selecting your approach to marketing. The chapters in Part III go into greater depth about marketing, so I will keep this section brief.

Reach out to folks and let them know you have a great product or service (what is available through your affiliate link and on to the merchant). To do so, keep this list in mind:

✔ **You can email folks you know.** If you know that people you know would benefit from the product or service, you can email them the link. Of course, keep building a list so you don't only rely on folks you know personally.

✔ **You can post the link through your activities.** Focus on places such as LinkedIn (www.linkedin.com), Meet Up (www.meetup.com), Yahoo! Groups (www.groups.yahoo.com), and other venues.

✔ **You can set up a website.** A website can help establish your business presence on the Internet. See Chapter 4 for more details.

✔ **You can set up a blog.** A blog can be a free way to post product reviews on what you are interested in (as an affiliate). Refer to Chapter 4 on how to set up a blog.

✔ **You can write articles on your topic and include your affiliate your link.** Doing so can generate an audience of readers who have an interest in the topic related to your affiliate product. Refer to Chapter 18 for more information.

✔ **You can use solo ads.** You can pay to have an advertisement about your offering (complete with link to the product) in an ezine that has many subscribers. Chapter 16 has more on marketing through ezines.

✔ **You can market through advertising programs, such as Google's AdWords and pay-per-click (PPC) advertising.** Chapter 12 covers both.

Step 5: Focus and be persistent

This step may be the most important step of all. Too often, affiliate marketers (especially many beginners that start a business) forget that real success doesn't come easily. A good affiliate marketer sticks to a good product and plan and persists by learning along the way. You can tweak your approach to affiliate marketing, but the bottom line is you to want to stay focused and stick to it, even when you face obstacles.

There is no fast and easy path toward success. You may be tempted to try affiliate marketing because of the numerous encouraging testimonies from merchants and affiliate marketers alike who have benefited from it, but it entails a great deal of hard work and persistence. Likewise, you need to be creative and flexible, and willing to embrace new ideas to market your partners' products until you find the perfect strategy that works for a specific market that you're targeting. Signing up for an affiliate program or copying ads and leading others toward the merchants' sites doesn't guarantee success.

Many affiliate marketers fail to understand the importance of persistence and focus, so when they don't make sales, they quit, look for other programs, and repeat the same mistake. In the end, they conclude that affiliate marketing is just one of those scams or dead ends on the Internet. Make sure you don't travel down that same road. These traits can teach you to carry on no matter how tough the job is. Check what's working and what's not and then make the necessary changes.

Spotlighting the Top Affiliate Sites

The best way to discover the most popular and successful affiliate sites is to visit them before you to start your career as an affiliate. Literally thousands of merchants are available with whom you can team up with as an affiliate, but a few do stand out. The following are some of the better affiliate sites. Check them out and see what makes them so successful.

Clickbank

Clickbank is an ideal place to start for any beginning affiliate marketer. In the world of affiliate marketing, Clickbank (www.clickbank.com) is the 800–pound digital gorilla — and for good reason. It's arguably the largest and most successful affiliate marketing website. Furthermore anyone can join and make his way to success. It was started in 1998 and has more one million affiliate marketers (and growing) and nearly 150,000 merchants (and growing), offering a diverse array of downloadable digital offerings.

Clickbank provides you a large and increasing network of publishers or affiliates to tap into. In fact, Clickbank has more than 100,000 affiliates who are experts in finding potential customers for your affiliate program. The reason why more and more affiliates are joining Clickbank is obvious — the process of gaining commissions in this network is absolutely fair and transparent.

On Clickbank, you can do three things:

- ✔ **You can promote products.** You can find products that you can promote and get paid to do so. The following sections provide more specific details about doing so.

- ✔ **You can sell products.** If you're a merchant, you can find affiliates at Clickbank to help you sell your products. If you self-publish digital products such as ebooks, digital audio programs, and other published products, you can use Clickbank. To find out more about how to create digital products, go to Chapter 10.

- ✔ **You can buy products.** Clickbank has literally thousands of products in all sorts of categories, ranging from self-improvement and wellness to business start-up and Internet marketing programs. Micro-entrepreneurs can find many good Internet marketing offerings on Clickbank (with a 60-day, money-back guarantee).

The following sections provide more information about Clickbank, including how to get started and how to succeed as an affiliate.

Getting started on Clickbank

If you're a Clickbank affiliate wannabe, being a part of this network isn't hard. To begin your affiliate marketing at Clickbank, you can follow these three steps. Doing so really couldn't be easier:

Step one: Set up your Clickbank account

Signing up as an affiliate is easy. From the home page (www.clickbank.com), go to the "Sign Up" tab at the top, which directs you to the page where you input the standard information (name, email, mailing address, and so on). Account registration is free. You can then choose a nickname, which acts as your account user ID. In the event that you generate earnings of $600 or more, you'll be asked for either your Social Security number if you're doing business as an individual or your business tax ID number (if payment is being made to your business). After you register, the site will email your user ID (the nickname) and your assigned eight-digit password.

As you generate commissions, the site mails you your first two checks. You can then opt to have payments submitted electronically to your bank account. Part of the reason why initial checks are mailed to you via regular postal service is for security: The site can verify that your address is real.

Some affiliate marketers open up more than one account for marketing and accounting purposes. Maybe they want to market in two or more niches, and they want to track the effectiveness and profitability separately of each market.

Step two: Find a product to start promoting

From the homepage, click on the "Marketplace" tab at the top of the page. You can do a keyword search for products that are in your chosen niche. The commissions can be up to 75 percent. You can also find products that have residual commissions. Make sure the product is in your specialty and a good fit for your target market. Clickbank has lots of articles, blogs, and forums to help you choose your product and acceptable marketing practices.

Although you don't need to buy the product to start promoting it, it may be a good idea. I personally like the 60-day, money-back guarantee, and I like to buy products before I market them so that I'm comfortable with both the product and the vendor. You can also pick up some good ideas for marketing purposes.

Here are some questions to ask yourself when you're considering a product to promote:

- **What is the product's gravity?** The *gravity* gives you an indication of the product's sales and popularity. It can also tell you to what extent the competition is with others who may also be promoting the product. A gravity of 100 or more means that there are many competitors and it may be too crowded for you to get your share of the sales. A gravity under 40 may indicate that the product is too new (untested?) or not as popular.

- **Is the product getting good reviews on the Internet?** Put the product's name in your search engine and review the results. Gauge whether customers and affiliates are generally happy with the product. Identify any complaints.

- **What do Clickbank's statistics say about this product?** When you look at the product, Clickbank offers key information about it and the results being generated. You can find out metrics, such as *average commission amounts per sale*, to see how profitable it may be to you and see how well the product ranks in terms of total sales, in its category, and so on. Clickbank offers videos that give you a tour of all the ways a product is tracked and how sales and commission results are measured. You can also read product reviews and opinions in Clickbank's blogs and forums from affiliate's experience with various products and vendors.

- **What sales assistance does the vendor provide?** Some of the most successful vendors provide extensive guidance to help affiliates succeed. If I see a product I like at Clickbank, I like to go to the vendor's website and see their affiliate's page (you can typically find a link at the bottom or top of the homepage). This way I can see to what extent the vendor provides advice and sales tools, such as sample landing pages and sales copy that I can freely copy and include in my emails and other venues (such as websites and blogs). It also tells me to what extent the vendor is committed to the affiliate's success; the more tools and guidance it provides, the better for you.

Step three: Get your hoplink and start marketing

After you decide on a product, you can click on the button provided that says "Promote". In the next window, you enter your nickname and a tracking ID. This field is optional, but it's good to use. A *tracking ID* helps you keep updated on how well a particular marketing campaign is doing. For example, if you promote the same Clickbank product in your blog and in a separate email campaign, with a tracking ID, you can put one for the blog (such as "myblog") and another for the email campaign (such as "email"). That way you can track each approach and see which one had better sales results.

When you finish putting in your nickname and the optional tracking code, Clickbank will instantly generate a *hoplink,* which is a unique link that you can use in your marketing efforts. When anyone clicks on this hoplink, Clickbank tracks it and provides you with full credit for any sale that occurs.

You can place the hoplink as easily as you can place any other link. You can put hoplinks on a website (although a website isn't necessary for Clickbank promotions), blog, Facebook page, or in your article marketing efforts.

Step four: Know what happens after the sale

Clickbank tracks the sales and any commissions generated by your promotional efforts. You can log in and check your account and what results you produced. If you have any commissions, Clickbank typically issues payment every two weeks for affiliates.

At this point you can decide on what else do you want to do. You can continue with promoting the product you chose, or you can find other products and vendors. Many affiliates like to promote multiple products in the same niche to enhance the sales opportunities. Going forward, keep testing your marketing efforts and measure the results. If you find products and marketing approaches that work well, then do it again. Successful affiliate marketers keep improving their efforts and continue testing, tweaking, and repeating their approaches to generate long-term success.

Being successful on Clickbank

Being a Clickbank affiliate is no minor achievement. It means you need to possess the ability to sell lots of affiliate products. You also need to have expertise in *search engine optimization (SEO)* (SEO refers to the entire range of strategies that you can employ to increase your site's ranking and visibility in search engines used by your customers; refer to Chapter 15 for more information), email marketing, newsletter marketing, *reciprocal linkage* (the act of exchanging links with other sites for mutual marketing benefit), *link exchanges* (websites that help you exchange links with other sites), and other methods of promoting your merchant's goods and services.

Among the secrets to become successful in affiliate marketing is to create a good content-based website and put your affiliate links in your content. For example, if you enjoy the dog training niche, place good content about dog training and include some affiliate links to dog training programs on your website. Your main purpose is to give your visitors good quality content about the things they're interested in. You provide the content along with some affiliate links. Don't bother trying to do any selling; you can sell at the sales pages (also called *landing pages*) when customers click on your affiliate link.

Discovering more about Clickbank

If you're interested in finding out more about Clickbank, you have several places that can give you great information. Here are the best places for the beginner:

✔ **Clickbank itself (who knew!):** Go directly to the site (`www.clickbank.com`) and see forums, blogs, and tutorials.

✔ **Clickbank Directory:** This site (`www.cbdir.com`) offers news and tracks the latest offerings at Clickbank.

✔ **Affiliate X files:** This site (`www.affiliatexfiles.com`) provides news, views, and tips on Clickbank and other affiliate sites and venues.

Commission Junction

Commission Junction (`www.cj.com`) is another major affiliate program for advertisers and publishers of websites and blogs. If you (the publisher) participate (you must be approved before you can), then you can put links of participating merchants on your website and blog.

Every time someone clicks on the link and buys something, you get a percentage of the sale. If someone clicks on the link and fills out a form, you get a commission for attracting a sales lead. If that person comes back to the site and purchases something or fills out the form, you can still get a commission. Many vendors put a tracking code (referred to as a *cookie*) on your computer to help track sales and identify you as the source of the referral. The cookie can be on as long as 90 days, which means than if anyone buys through your referral link for up to 90 days, you can still get paid.

If you want to make money as affiliates with large, big-name companies such as JP Morgan, Home Depot, and hundreds of other familiar companies, then Commission Junction is for you.

Even though these companies would love to have you help them get prospects and customers, you're not automatically approved when you sign up. Merchants (advertisers) on Commission Junction expect you to have a website or blog to prove that you aren't a fly-by-night company before you can be accepted. Make sure you first find out the requirements necessary for approval before you participate.

If and when you do get approved, you can choose from more than 1,000 advertisers (many are famous names). You can browse by category to see which would be a fit for the audience your blog or website is targeting. Make sure that you visit the company's website to make sure that its offerings are good for your audience.

Follow these steps on Commission Junction to start marketing:

1. **Look for an advertiser that interests you.**

   After you find an advertiser that interests you, click on the "Join program" button.

2. **Agree to the terms and conditions after reading them carefully.**

   Some programs approve you automatically, and some approve you manually, which takes time. After you're approved for a program, Commission Junction adds it to a "link relationship list," which is a list of all the advertisers that approved you to post their links on your website or blog.

3. **To get the link for the advertiser that approved you, click on the "Get links" tab from the home page of Commission Junction.**

   If you choose to post a link from an advertiser that isn't active or hasn't approved you yet, you don't collect a commission on the sales or leads.

4. **Choose a link or banner.**

   When you click on "View links," a list pops up for all the links that you can post on your site or blog. When you find a link you like, click on it, and from there you can copy HTML or Java for that link and paste it to your website or blog.

5. **Click "Publish" and the link appears.**

   That's it; you're done. Now your site can make money with Commission Junction.

Amazon

Becoming an affiliate for Amazon is a fast and easy way to allow your customers to order products from Amazon.com and for you to receive a referral fee.

You can be an Amazon affiliate without needing a functional website or blog, but it certainly helps. Some prefer to market an Amazon affiliate link through other venues such as email, their Facebook page, or through an ezine (which is usually sent via email). You can find out more about Facebook and other social media in Chapter 17 and marketing through ezines in Chapter 16.

Being an affiliate with Amazon opens up opportunities for sales that can generate commissions for you that can be from either digital products (such as Kindle ebooks) or from physical products (ranging from actual books to the universe of products that are sold through the Amazon site).

To become an affiliate on Amazon, follow these steps:

1. **Go to Amazon and sign in to your Amazon account if you have one.**

   If you don't already have an Amazon account, you can create one for free.

2. **Click on "Join Associates" on the left side of the home page.**

3. **Fill out the electronic application.**

   Provide your site address, site purpose, contact name, and so on. If you don't have a site (such as a website or blog), you can skip this item. However, Amazon can generate links with your affiliate code for you so that you can place it in your emails, Facebook page, and so on.

4. **After reading the contract terms and conditions, click the button to signify that you agree and submit your application.**

   Amazon will respond usually within 24 hours, either confirming or denying your request. If your request is approved, Amazon will provide you with the necessary links to place on your site so that your customers can order books. Approval is usually automatic (unless Amazon has had trouble with you before).

5. **Choose from Amazon's inventory the books (including Kindle books), CDs, and a wide variety of consumer products that you want to offer your customers.**

   You'll see a bar appear at the top of your computer screen every time that you're on the Amazon website that can allow you to link to different products. You can choose text or picture links.

6. **Submit this information to Amazon, place the `Amazon.com` link on your website, and you're ready to start making some affiliate cash.**

Amazon will send you regular reports of activity from your site. Retain these e-mails to track your affiliate earnings. Amazon doesn't pay as much as some other programs, but using Amazon as part of your earning plans has many advantages, including that it's a well respected site, online shoppers trust it, and it offers a wide range of products that make it a great site.

Use my experience for your affiliate adventure

Even though I have my own full-time business and I already have my own offerings, I have been an affiliate and marketed affiliate offers to folks on my email database list. I have made good money with the affiliate program on Clickbank. Just to show you how easy it was for me, here is what I did (feel free to copy and revise as appropriate for your business):

1. I opened an account with Clickbank (you can refer to the section on Clickbank in this chapter). Doing so was free.

2. I scanned Clickbank's marketplace for merchants that have offerings that appeal to you.

3. I chose one that I thought would be good for my subscribers (I write an ezine called Prosperity Alert . . . catchy, right?).

4. I registered for the affiliate program through Clickbank by getting the hoplink.

5. I went to the merchant's website to get ad copy that I used in my email message. Both the message and my hoplink are what I present to my ezine subscribers.

6. I sent an email describing the offer along with the link where interested folks could go for more details.

7. I then checked my Clickbank account and saw that sales were generated and I earned some commissions. Cool!

This entire process literally took me about a half hour to find the offer, register, and then send off an email to my list of interested folks. The first commission check was just under $200, and several more checks came later on for a total of about $400, which is a great result from work that took less than 30 minutes.

Chapter 12

Cashing In on Advertising

● ●

In This Chapter

▶ Focusing on making money directly with AdSense

▶ Making money with pay-per-click advertising

● ●

*W*hen you do a website or a blog, you're considered a publisher, and for good reason. You provide content and build an audience — folks who you hope to make money from. You can sell all sorts of things (ebooks, affiliate offers, and so on), but sometimes it makes sense to make money by allowing advertising at your site.

You can make money either directly or indirectly. Making money from advertising directly isn't that difficult. *Direct advertising* means you advertise your business directly to your customers; you're making direct attempts to market to them. An example of direct advertising is when you directly send an email to a customer's inbox. You get paid from advertisers directly because you put (or allow to be put) an advertisement at your site. Doing so isn't a problem, although some people may be uncomfortable or unsure about doing this type of advertising. In that case, you can try indirect advertising.

On the other hand, *indirect advertising* is when a middle man, or *reseller*, markets your business to your consumers on your behalf. In indirect advertising, you allow an agency to put ads on your site. The agency places the ads, and you get a percentage of the advertising revenue generated.

In this chapter, I take a two-faced approach by looking at Internet advertising. Here I cover advertising both from how you make money and get cash and also how you make money with it by buying it. Plenty of opportunities exist online that allow you to get paid some good money from advertising. In addition, if you want to do advertising, you can find just about as many opportunities. This chapter explains how you can go about doing it the right way.

Generating Cash from Advertising: Spotlight on AdSense

Google's AdSense (www.google.com/adsense) is considered the premier advertising revenue-sharing program on the Internet (especially for many small businesses running websites and blogs). AdSense is so popular because it's one of the easiest ways to start earning money on your site.

Google sends you a line of unique code, and you simply paste this code into your website. It automatically displays ads that Google chooses (based off the information that you provide and that its search technology can glean from the site). Each visitor to your site that clicks on these ads can earn you cash. The more visitors to your site means the more potential revenue you can generate (some folks have earned as much as $50,000 in a single month!). (By the way, for advertisers, the flip side of this program is Google AdWords, which I cover later in this chapter.)

If you use AdSense, you can get paid in two ways:

- **Impressions:** *Impressions* means that you get paid when visitors just view the ad when the page loads in their browser.

- **Clicks:** Being paid from *clicks* means you get paid when visitors actually click on an AdSense ad.

Additionally, you can also earn money by including a Google search box in your website's code. If visitors to your site use it, you'll earn a percentage of the revenue that is relevant to their search terms.

The following sections explain some of the things you'll need to do with your site so that you can be successful with AdSense. They can help in guiding your progress as your website starts to get more visitors.

Content is king

AdSense is a simple program. When you register for AdSense and allow space on your website or blog to carry AdSense advertising, you're allowing Google to place ads that it believes are most appropriate for the content that you're publishing. As a result, your website or blog's content is essential. The best AdSense results are typically generated on pages that provide great content on a very specific topic. For example, if you love gardening and you have a gardening blog, Google will place ads relevant to gardening.

Because you get paid per click in the AdSense program, the great temptation for site owners is to find a way to click on the ads that are present at the site to artificially boost income from the pay-per-click aspect of the program. Be forewarned; doing so will kick you out of the program. In addition, you could jeopardize any revenue you may have earned from AdSense. Therefore, avoid that temptation because Google technology is very sophisticated, and the penalty (and lost current and future revenue) can be severe.

Keywords are queen

When you use AdSense, you want to also become proficient with *keywords*, which are words or phrases that your potential customers type into the search engines when they're looking for products or services. The goal for you in terms of making money with AdSense is simple: Just keep posting fresh and original content (strategically including important keywords) at your site to keep attracting visitors, and a certain percentage of them will click on the AdSense ads.

When visitors to your blog or website do click on the ad, you'll get a percentage of the amount the advertiser pays per click. For example, if the click costs the advertiser a dollar, Google may pay you 20 cents. Google doesn't have a set percentage paid to those participating; it's generally a secret formula that Google sets. To grasp how keywords work, refer to the later section, "Keywords 101: Just the basics" for more how-to information.

Search engine optimization (SEO) isn't just a method for finding keywords. It's also a comprehensive strategy meant to rank your web page(s) higher on the search engine. Finding the keywords is only a part of the entire strategy.

Make sure you become proficient with keywords so you can succeed in the world of advertising, whether it's with generating revenue (with programs like AdSense) or when you're paying for advertising (as in pay-per-click advertising in programs like AdWords). Keywords are critical because you want your prospective customers to be able to find you. They may not be necessarily searching for you, but they most certainly will be searching for what you may be offering (be it content, products, or services).

Here are some additional resources to help you become more proficient with key words and search engine optimization:

- ✔ **Google Keyword Tool Box** (www.googlekeywordtool.com)
- ✔ **Market Samurai** (www.marketsamurai.com)
- ✔ **Word Tracker** (www.wordtracker.com)

✔ The latest edition of *Search Engine Optimization For Dummies* by Peter Kent (John Wiley & Sons, Inc.)

Generate more targeted traffic to your sites means generating more clicks, which in turn will mean more revenue from AdSense.

Ad placement is the third consideration

To achieve AdSense success, you ultimately need to consider where you place the ads. Whether you're using the site yourself (you can easily do your own blog at www.blogger.com) or you have someone technically helping you with a website, you need to decide where to place the ads. (Refer to Chapter 4 about setting up your own blog or website, or getting help.)

Ads come in *blocks* (definable segments in square or rectangular shapes on a web page that contain AdSense ads) and can either be horizontal (rectangular shaped) or vertical (square or rectangular). (See Figure 12-1 shows an example of a horizontal ad, whereas Figure 12-2 demonstrates a vertical ad.)

Figure 12-1:
You can choose a horizontal ad.

Illustration courtesy of William Donato

Advertising professionals have differing views on placement, but the latest thinking is that vertical placement and to the top right area is optimal. Many folks like to test out various methods of placement and analyze over time which placement strategies have worked best. No matter how sophisticated or cool the technology, some tried-and-true wisdom keeps coming back. In this case, testing and testing again is as good now as ever.

Additionally, many have had great results by placing relevant images near the ads. Make sure that you're also analyzing what others are doing to keep your strategies fresh and effective.

The most typical ad sizes you can choose from include the following:

✔ 336 *x* 280 large rectangle; horizontal, almost square (see Figure 12-3)

✔ 300 *x* 250 medium rectangle; horizontal, almost square

✔ 160 *x* 600 wide skyscraper; vertical

Skyscrapers are large vertical banners you typically see on the right side of a web page. They're long and usually appear in the top fold (or top section of a web page that is immediately viewable in the visitor's screen). If you think of a web page as a newspaper, the top fold is the top part of the web page you see without scrolling.

Figure 12-2: You can also choose a vertical ad.

Illustration courtesy of William Donato

Figure 12-3: An example of a large rectangle ad.

Illustration courtesy of William Donato

In addition, keep these points in mind about ad presentation:

✔ Some ads can be in image link format, whereas other ads are in word link format. *Image link format* means that the advertisement is an actual picture that you can click on. The most popular image links formats are .jpg and .png files that are basically simple static image files. *Word links* (also called *text links*) are simply the word or text appearing for the link. If you have ever seen the words *click here* underlined in blue on a web page, then you have seen a word or text link. In other words, an ad can be a clickable picture or the ad can be in a text format where the words are clickable. See which works better for your particular site.

✔ If you're using an ad block, think about the most suitable color or color palette for an appearance that more closely matches the overall look for your site. Some like to have a large contrasting color to help the ad stand out.

✔ Some like to break up the ad blocks and do two (or more) strategically placed small ad blocks. Some prefer to use a single large ad block that goes vertically and be adjacent to the content.

Make sure you test and test some more to figure out what works best for you and your site.

Tracking and changing your approach

Following the advice in these sections is only part of the picture. Don't assume that having ads on AdSense as a set-it-and-forget-it approach. Monitor what is going on so that you can keep tweaking the approach to maximize your income potential.

Keep the click-through rate (CTR) in mind as you establish and manage your ad. *CTR* is measured when you see how many visitors have come to your website or blog and how many of them have actually clicked on the AdSense ads. In other words, it's the percentage of people who viewed an ad and actually clicked on it.

For example, if you have 100 visitors, and 5 of them actually click on the ads, the CTR is 5 percent (5 clicks from 100 visitors is 5 percent). You'll get paid from those five clicks, but look to see if you can improve it. At the same time, look to see what you can do to avoid getting worse.

Making your text ad or banner ad more appealing can increase your CTR. Higher-positioned ads can also have a higher CTR because people see them first. Search engines consider CTR when ranking ads, so if you increase your CTR, you may be rewarded by the search engine with lower bids.

If you have lots of visitors and fewer and fewer clicks, look to see what is happening. If your CTR drops from 5 percent to less than 1 percent, you need to change your approach. Maybe the content you're providing and the ads that are shown are diverging. You may not be able to control what ads Google is putting on, but you can certainly see whether you need to modify your content, your keywords, or the ad placement. Sometimes just a single element or a single change can make all the difference. The point is to continue monitoring.

AdSense (and the other advertising revenue programs; refer to the next section for other options you have) do provide tools to help you monitor how well you're doing. They have tools to help any webmaster or publisher figure out results by site, or by page or key word.

You can find instructions on how to improve the efficiency of your AdSense approach and continue your education (and I hope your profitability):

- **The AdSense Blog** (`http://adsense.blogspot.com/`)
- **The AdSense Publishers group** (`www.linkedin.com`)
- **AdSense Resources** (`www.google.com/adsense/adsense-resources`)
- **More info on AdSense** (`www.support.google.com/adsense`)

Identifying other advertising sources that pay you

I usually hate it when one entity has too great a grasp on a marketplace. I like competition because it keeps both prices and services at a higher level. Don't assume that AdSense is necessarily the best; look at competitors because they'll frequently run deals so that you can try them out.

In addition to Google's AdSense, you have many other options online for making money with advertising. Here are the other major advertising networks that have revenue-sharing programs for publishers:

✔ **Adbrite** (www.adbrite.com)

✔ **Bidvertiser** (www.bidvertiser.com)

✔ **Chitika** (www.chitika.com)

✔ **Clicksor** (www.clicksor.com)

✔ **Kontera** (www.kontera.com)

✔ **Linkshare** (www.linkshare.com)

✔ **Project Wonderful** (www.projectwonderful.com)

✔ **Tradedoubler** (www.tradedoubler.com)

✔ **Tribal Fusion** (www.tribalfusion.com)

The same way you comparison-shop so many things in this world, consider doing the same with advertising-revenue sharing programs. AdSense may be the 800-pound gorilla in this slice of the Internet world, but competitors can give you a better deal sometimes.

Getting Customers and Sales with Pay-Per-Click: AdWords or AdCenter

Pay-per-click means you buy advertising space from website owners and other search engines. *Pay-per-click (PPC)* gives your micro-entrepreneurial enterprise the opportunity to compete with other larger businesses like very few other forms of advertising. You can literally get your ad in front of millions of people in less than 30 minutes — the fastest way to get people to your website.

Micro-entrepreneurs all over the world use PPC to generate sales, test launch new products and services, gain exposure, and get new potential clients. Your micro business would be at a huge disadvantage if you ignore PPC.

These sections give you a brief introduction on how you can start to sell your product to the masses via PPC. After reading these sections, you should have the skills and resources you'll need to confidently launch a successful PPC advertising campaign in less than an hour and get targeted prospects to your site.

Here are two places to get started if you're interested in PPC advertising:

✔ **Microsoft's Bing AdCenter:** This site (www.adcenter.microsoft. com) includes the search engines Bing (www.bing.com) and Yahoo! (www.yahoo.com). It also includes more than 100,000 websites associated with AdCenter.

✔ **Google AdWords:** This site (www.adwords.google.com) includes Google and its search partner sites. With by far the most volume, in 2011 Google raked in more than 33.3 billion in revenue from people using its ad network for PPC. Folks wouldn't spend that kind of money unless they were getting profitable results.

The lowdown on PPC and how it works

PPC is an advertising model where you, the advertiser, pay only when your ad is clicked. When your ad is clicked, prospects are directed to your website or sales page. With search engines like Google, you select the keywords you want your ad to appear for and you pay each time your ad is clicked.

However before I explain how PPC sites like AdWords function, allow me to explain some benefits and downsides of PPC marketing.

The benefits of PPC marketing

The following are the benefits of a PPC campaign:

✔ **Speed:** You can generate sales and acquire new customers within minutes of opening an account. PPC gives your ad the ability to appear on the top of Google or Yahoo almost instantly.

✔ **Targeted marketing:** You can target your ads to a specific country, state, town, or zip code. You can even target your ads to run in certain languages, at specific times, or even in specific time zones. Targeting a specific market is easier with PPC versus many other forms of advertising.

✔ **Right person at the right time:** PPC generates prospects that are searching for your service at that exact moment, which is a complete shift in approach of other types of advertising in the past. You have the advantage of showing ads only to people who are searching for what you sell. For example, if you bid for the keyword "buy frozen duck," only when someone searches this exact phrase will your ad will appear, meaning you're paying for prospects searching for frozen duck at that specific moment.

✔ **Trackable:** Unlike other forms of marketing, such as magazines and billboards that can take weeks or months to track progress and change, you can track and edit PPC campaigns up to the minute. You can track progress of your ad with click-through rates. (The click-through rate [CTR] is the percentage of visitors to a page that actually click the ad on the page; see the earlier section "Tracking and changing your approach" for more details on CTR.). You can also track effectiveness of your website or landing page with bounce rates and conversion rates.

The *bounce rate* is the percentage of visitors who visited your page and left (*bounced*) without viewing any other pages. A high bounce rate can be bad; it can mean people are clicking on your ad and then leaving your site because they believe that the site wasn't relevant to them.

To lower your bounce rate, focus on improving your web page or offer. You can find a good resource at Kissmetrics (www.blog.kiss metrics.com/landing-page-design-infogrpahic).

Meanwhile the *conversion rate* is the percentage of people who visited your web page and performed a certain action. This action can include buying a product, filling out a form, or some other goal. When you pay for traffic using PPC, you need to know what your conversion rate is at all times. For example, if 100 visitors clicked on your ad and came to your website, and 6 of them bought your product, then you have a 6 percent conversion rate.

If your average CPC is $1.16, then your overall cost is $116 (100 × $1.16). If your product sells for $67, then your sales are $402 ($67.00 × 6 = $402) and your net profit is $286 ($402 − $116 = $286).

As you can see from this example, if your CPC remains constant at $1.16, then you would need to have a conversion rate of at least 2 percent to be profitable. You should always be determined to increase your conversion rate. To do so, here are some tips to help you:

- **Test.** Testing ensures your program is always progressing. Testing will result in lower advertising costs and higher conversion rates (more people responding to your offers). *A/B split testing* is a method of testing similar web pages or offers against each other, by doing so you can see what converts better. Check out *Smashing Magazine*'s guide to A/B split testing at www.smashing magazine.com.

- **Upsell your ads.** *Upselling* means introducing new items to the customer during the sales process to increase the size of the order. The customer may visit your page to buy weight loss pills, for example, but you may want to upsell the customer other health products to increase the amount they purchase. For example, you sold your product for $67, but what if you offered customers extra add-on items? This is a sure way to increase your bottom line.

- **Add multiple forms of payment.** The more convenient ways your customers can pay, the more overall sales you will have.

- **Strive for duplicate success.** Big companies spend big money to increase conversion rates, visit their pages, and see what attracts you about their offer.

- **Make good impressions.** Also known as *ad views, impressions* are the number of times an ad is loaded onto a website. The more traffic you send to a page, the more page views or impressions you generate.

- **Quality score.** Basically, Google uses this way to rate your overall marketing campaign in terms of effectiveness. Having a high score indicates that Google thinks your ad, keyword, landing page, and so on are all relevant and useful to visitors. You can find out more about this at `http://support.google.com/adwords/bin/answer.py?hl=en&answer=2454010`.

✔ **Control:** You have complete control of your PPC campaigns. You can set a daily budget or a monthly budget, along with setting spending limits and maximum bids you're willing to pay for each click. You can turn your advertising on or off whenever you wish.

✔ **Inexpensive:** You can use PPC to get new visitors to your website for less than $0.15! Your results are far better than any $400 ad in the phonebook can deliver.

Downsides

On the flip side, PPC does have its disadvantages. Here are the downsides:

✔ **Expensive keywords:** Bidding wars with Fortune 500 companies can inflate the price of keywords. In 2011, the price for the keyword "insurance" hit the nose-bleed level of $54 per click! Fortunately for you, you can get around this cost. I discuss a strategy you can implement in the "Keywords 101: Just the basics" section later in this chapter.

✔ **Scalability:** As your traffic increases, your ad spending increases (assuming your cost-per-click remains the same). PPC advertising doesn't *scale* well, which means if you want to increase the amount of traffic you receive, you'll have to scale up (increase) your ad-spend.

Compare it to SEO where you pay a fixed amount of time/or money and can scale your return. If you want more traffic, be ready to pay for it.

✔ **Maintenance:** Successful PPC campaigns require tweaking to maximize your ad spending. Unlike buying a magazine ad and forgetting about it, with PPC you have to keep an eye on what keywords are producing. You can maintain your ads with weekly reviews.

Selecting where your PPC ads appear

If you're new to PPC marketing, you may be wondering where you ads will appear. You can choose for your ads to run in three basic areas when you're setting up your ads. The three are very different and produce varying traffic:

✔ **Search engine:** Your ad will appear only on the search engines. This selection will produce less traffic for your ads at a higher price per click compared to the other two options; however, it will produce top quality traffic.

✔ **Search partners:** Your ad will appear in partner sites associated with the search engine. For example, if you select your ad to appear for Google's search partners, it will include Google search sites, such as Google Gmail, Google Shopping, Google Maps, Google Images, and Google Groups.

✔ **Content network:** The content network is composed of tens of thousands of users running Google AdSense on their sites (refer to the first section in this chapter for a refresher on AdSense). You're basically paying them to run your ad on their website, and Google is the middleman. This selection produces larger amounts of traffic but it's cheaper than the other two options.

The content network is cheaper for a reason. It requires a lot of attention because of click fraud. If it's your first time using PPC with AdWords or Microsoft's AdCenter, I suggest you select only search and search partners when setting up your campaign. Avoid the content network until you become more experienced.

Creating your first PPC ad

Before you can create your ad, you need to know exactly what you want to promote: a product, service, or brand. You want to be as specific as you can about what you're offering because the deeper you target your niche, the less money you will spend on your ad and the more targeted your customers will be — all in all, a win-win approach!

As you begin to create your ad, ask yourself these questions:

✔ Who will buy your product or service?

✔ Where are these customers located?

✔ What words do they use to describe your product or service?

The answers to these questions can help you better target your prospective buyers in terms of what and where they will buy along with what potential keywords they may use. Because you can use many tools to pinpoint both the words and the buyers (see resources throughout this chapter), you can have any easier time generating responses and subsequent sales.

After you have a better idea about what you want your ad to say and how you want it to look, you can choose from two popular types of ads to promote your business through PPC.

Type No. 1: Text ads

Text ads are very popular for PPC; they're used on sites like Google, Facebook, LinkedIn, and Bing. Text ads usually have a bold headline with a short snippet of text. The text ad is clickable and leads to your web page or sales page. The best part about text ads is that you select where you would like them to appear.

When you're creating a PPC text ad, keep these important points in mind:

- ✓ **Title:** The *title,* also known as the *heading,* is usually bold blue. It's usually the first thing potential customers will see, so you want to create an attention-grabbing, thoughtful targeted title. Use words like "SALE" or numbers like "50 percent off" to grab their attention. (Refer to Chapter 14 for more information about writing good sales copy.)

- ✓ **Simplicity:** Don't overcomplicate your ad; keep it simple because you'll have a limit to how many characters you can have in your ad (a 25-character limit is typical).

- ✓ **Description:** The two description lines are limited to 35 characters each. Use this space to insert at least two of your keywords because it will help your ad establish relevance and help lower your bidding. Having a quality text ad can lead users to a relevant website and you'll be rewarded by the search engines with lower ad spend. Keep the words in your text ads relevant to your web page, and your ads will receive higher quality scores. By doing so, it can reduce your clicks.

- ✓ **Telephone contact:** You can also add your phone number to your text ad. Doing so works especially well if you're targeting mobile devices because the number appears as a *click-to-call* feature (readers can click directly on the phone number from their smartphone, and their phone makes the call) on your ad. Some advertisers allow you to include your phone number to your ad if you pay a premium. If you include your phone number on your ad and you're advertising toward mobile sites, then your number will have a click-to-call function. URLs get included automatically; emails generally aren't necessary. Google reports that AdWords advertisers have experienced a 6 to 8 percent average increase in click-through rates, simply by activating call extensions.

Type No. 2: Banner ads

Banner ads are great for building your brand. Banner advertising is very cheap, whether you select pay per click or CPM. You can have your banner showing on hundreds of websites for just a few dollars every month. If you heed the following advice, you can create a great banner ad and may only have to pay a few cents for every visitor that clicks on your banner.

You have two options to pick from when you choose to pay for your banner ads to show:

- ✔ **Clicks:** This method works the same as the text ad; see the preceding section.
- ✔ **Cost per Millie (CPM):** CPM is measured by 1000 impressions. Meaning each time your ad is seen 1,000 times, you are charged. However, some CPM rates are as low as 15 cents. This means that potentially 1,000 people can see your ad for as little as 15 cents.

Keep these pointers in mind when creating a banner ad:

- ✔ **Size:** When creating a banner ad, you want to create multiple sizes to be sure it fits into all websites. I suggest you choose from the most popular banner ad sizes:
  - Medium rectangle 300 × 250
  - Square popup 250 × 250 (see Figure 12-4)
  - Leaderboard banner 728 × 90
  - Full banner 428×60
  - Wide skyscraper 160 × 600

Figure 12-4: An example of a square popup ad.

Illustration courtesy of William Donato

✔ **File size and formats:** As a general rule, try to keep your file sizes smaller than 50KB and save your file as .png, .jpg, or .gif , which are the most popular image formats. These standards can ensure your banner ad gets approved.

✔ **Research design:** Examine what hot item or hot topic you can display in your banner ad. Maybe you can visually express an idea that can grab attention. For example, coupon sites like Groupon have found people show more interest in banner ads with images of great-looking food. If your micro-business sells balloons, for instance, maybe you can have a banner ad with unusual shaped balloons to grab interest. The key is to grab interest visually from targeted prospects.

Another popular design option is to create a flash banner. A *flash banner* has moving images. They grab more attention. For resources on flash banners, keep reading.

✔ **Follow-through:** Great banners should lead to great offers and great websites. When people click your ad, make sure your offer or website is consistent in both style and content. Track your banner's performance and tweak until more and more of your clicks turn into profitable results.

✔ **Remarketing:** (or re-targeting prior prospects) is a strategy in which you re-market to people who have previously visited your site. This works because people may leave your site without buying anything; however remarketing gives you the opportunity to get them back to your website.

According to a recent report released by SeeWhy (www.seewhy.com), 48 percent of shoppers who abandoned shopping carts after online shopping more than once in the previous 28 days returned to the site and purchased items after a remarketing.

Remarketing is a bit tricky to set-up. Do some research about it at these sites:

- **Google's remarketing page** (www.google.com/ads/innovations/remarketing.html)

- **Remarketing** (www.remarketing.com)

✔ Remarketing is a popular topic on major marketing sites, such as www.marketingpower.com and www.webmarketingtoday.com, so do a search there for current articles.

To help you with preceding list, check out these resources:

✔ **123-Banner:** This site (www.123-banner.com) is a good place to create a free flash banner for your advertising efforts.

> ✔ **Tucows:** Here (`www.tucows.com`) you can get free software (or get free usage of software for 30 days or longer) that can help you create banners and image files.
>
> ✔ **Odesk:** This site (`www.odesk.com`) is a great place to hire a designer for creating your banners; you're sure to get a great return on your investment. To get more help from others, check out Chapter 19 on outsourcing.

Keywords 101: Just the basics

Selecting the right keywords is the most important step in setting up a PPC campaign (It is also important for other venues such as AdSense and for Search engine optimization strategies). Selecting your keywords is the last step before you launch your PPC campaign. Start by creating a list of keywords. Keywords on your list need to be relevant to your target audience. You'll need to make a list of keywords you're willing to pay for so your ad appears when your target audience makes a query for that word. For more on keyword strategies with AdSense that also apply with AdWords and AdCenter, go to the section "Keywords are queen" earlier in this chapter.

Find keywords with large amounts of search queries that have a low cost-per-click. For example, having your ad show on Google for the keyword "buy balloon" may cost you $3.28 per click, however, the keyword "Buy party balloon" may cost you as little as $1.59 per click. The right keywords can save you a lot of money.

The following is a simple three-step strategy to help you start so you can select the best keywords for your ads.

Step 1: Find keywords for your list

Start by researching words that are common in your industry. A great tool to search for keywords is Google's keyword tool. Type a word or phrase into the tool, and Google will generate hundreds of similar keywords for you. Look through the words the tool provides and make a list of keywords relevant to your micro-business. Look for terms with high global search volume and aim to gather at least 100 keywords into your list to start. You can find Google's tool at `https://adwords.google.com/o/KeywordTool`.

Searching for more help

If you want additional help, these resources can help you not only with PPC strategies but also figure out keyword search and what your competitors are doing, too. You can actually find out what your competitors are bidding for, how much money they are spending on PPC marketing, some top-performing text ads, and more.

- ✔ **iSpionage** (www.ispionage.com)
- ✔ **Spy Fu** (www.spyfu.com)
- ✔ **Word Tracker** (www.wordtracker.com)

Step 2: Estimate traffic for your new keywords

After you narrow down your list of selected keywords, alter the keywords so you can reduce estimated prices per click. The best way to do this is to make slight variations to expensive keywords. For example, from the preceding example, you can add a word, such as the word *party* to "buy party balloons," which reduced the price per click by roughly 50 percent and still attracted the same customer base. You can find Google's traffic estimator tool at https://adwords.google.com/o/TrafficEstimator.

Step 3: Set up your AdWords account

You can utilize this information to set up your AdWords account to start your advertising campaign. Go to Google's AdWords page at www.adwords.google.com to do so. Make sure you first view the tutorials on creating your ads, deciding how they will appear, and on attracting your customers.

Part III
Marketing and Selling Your Micro-Business

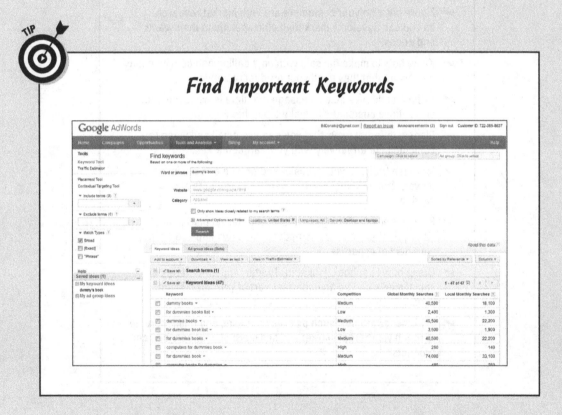

Find Important Keywords

Visit www.dummies.com/extras/microentrepreneurship for more information on how you can create a marketing plan, if you need one, and how you can use it to sell your products or services.

In this part . . .

- ✔ Figure out who your customers are with market research so you can develop a marketing plan specific to their wants and needs.

- ✔ Know how to make the sale with cold calling and convince new customers that they need your product or service.

- ✔ Write an effective sales message that details what you offer and entices customers to make a purchase.

- ✔ Identify different ways that you can use email and video to communicate effectively with your target market.

- ✔ Increase traffic to your website and/or blog and tap into the power of search engines to market your products and services.

- ✔ Rely on ezines and blogs to inform your target market about what you offer and provide updates on news and events in your field of expertise.

- ✔ Grasp how Facebook, LinkedIn, Twitter, and other forms of social media can be an important part of your marketing plan.

- ✔ Try other strategies, such as press releases and online forums, to reach your target market and sell more of your services and products.

Chapter 13

Understanding Your Marketing Approach

*W*hen you're ready to sell a product or service (which is after you figure out what you're going to sell), then you have stepped across the line in the vast and murky world of marketing. You have to choose the best person or group of people (your market) to approach to make money.

In addition, doing your marketing plan, which acts like a road map to get you from where you are (a person offering something for money) to where you want to be (a person who just got money for what he offered!) is important.

If you're ready to start marketing, you've come to the right place. This chapter covers market research. Here I explain how to understand your target market and competitors and how to create your marketing plan.

Identifying Your Target Market

I always smile when I say the words "target market" because I can't help thinking about an archer with a bow and arrow, but maybe this picture is more appropriate than I think. A *target market* is actually the name given to those folks that best benefit from what you have to offer.

Figuring out who your target market is the first question you must ask in your marketing plan (refer to the later section, "Doing Your Marketing Plan" for more specifics). For now, the question to ask isn't "Who is my target audience?" You first should ask, "Who best benefits from what I have to offer?" This question focuses your mind in the same way that an archer needs to zero in on his target.

The following sections examine why you need to know who your target market is and how you can select your target market.

Understanding the importance of having a target market

You can't sell to the world. Okay, maybe you could try, but doing so would cost a fortune. You'd lose a lot of money because you would end up spending lots of time, effort, and money trying to reach folks that either can't or won't buy the product or service that you offer. When you're offering a product, service, or both, and you have limited funds, you need to be efficient in your approach. (Everyone has limited funds, except maybe Bill Gates or Oprah Winfrey, but they're not micro-entrepreneurs.) Hence, you need to know what individuals or group of individuals on whom you can focus your attention.

Just remember: Even the richest businesses on the planet don't try to sell to everyone; they make choices about where they can get the most for their money for their marketing and advertising dollars.

Although you may be tempted to sell to everyone — if 7 billion people would only buy your stuff — having some focus on who to sell to is more practical and doable. Don't spend your time trying to reach 100 percent of the market. Spend 100 percent of your time trying to get to that ideal 1 percent of the market — those people who are willing and able to buy from you. You just need to figure out who they are.

Choosing your target market: The how-to

Your target market is the people whom you specifically choose to communicate to about what you have to offer. You spend time analyzing what that group of people would want or need, and whether your product or service best fills that want or need. To start figuring out who your target market is, first look at what you have to offer, and ask what need or want your product or service will fill.

You can approach a target market from two different angles: You have a product/service first and then you seek a target market, or you find a target market first and then find suitable a suitable product or service to offer to it. This section focuses on those who have something to offer and then need to find a target market.

A good tool to help you deal with these questions and find your target market is an approach called the grid of possibilities. Years ago, I came across the grid of possibilities. It's a great tool to use your creative and analytical abilities for business problem-solving. Table 13-1 shows an example of a grid.

Table 13-1	The Grid of Possibilities for Selling Gift Baskets			
Event	*Married Couples*	*Engaged Male*	*Existing Client*	*Additional Identified Client*
Valentine's Day		Do advertising at a male-oriented website in late January		And so on
Anniversary	Market at wedding-related sites	Not applicable	Not applicable	And so on
Birthday			Send client a gift basket on his birthday	And so on
Christmas	Advertise about sending a gift to mother-in-law		Contact small businesses in November about sending a basket to their best customers	And so on

The following walks through this table to help you understand how you can use it in your attempt to identify your target market. In this example, say that you sell gift baskets. You need to figure out who wants the gift baskets and why. Look to see what the reasons are for someone to buy gift baskets. Follow these steps to use the grid of possibilities:

1. **At the top of the grid, put in each box a particular type of client who would want your product.**

   For instance, in the first box, you can add married couples. In the second box, you can add an engaged male. In the third box, you can put in another type of client, and so on.

2. **In the side boxes, add the reasons why someone would buy your product or service.**

    In this example, in the first box, add "Valentine's Day"; in the second box, add "Anniversary"; in the third box, add "Birthday"; and so on.

3. **Wherever those boxes intersect, add a statement that explains the rationale that type of customer would have for buying your product or service.**

    Examine why a certain customer would buy the product. For this example, would a married couple buy a gift basket for Valentine's Day? Which type of customer would buy a gift basket for someone on an anniversary or birthday or for someone at Christmas?

4. **Fill in all the boxes and wherever you find the most compelling case for a particular customer along with a compelling reason for buying, make that a marketing campaign you will implement.**

    Find ways to make the marketing connection in that situation. Do a search for those websites, groups, forums, and so on where the potential buyer (your target market) is and see how you can get them to view your message or advertisement.

Researching and focusing on your target market

As you zoom in on your target market, you want to research and discover as much as you can about them. To do so, ask yourself some important questions about your potential target market, such as the following:

- ✔ Is my target market a specific demographic?
- ✔ What are my target market's biggest concerns?
- ✔ Is my target market a specific age, sex, ethnicity, and so on?
- ✔ Does my target market neatly fit a particular occupation or industry?
- ✔ Is your target market in a particular venue, such as a political or cultural affinity?
- ✔ What qualities or interests does my target market have?
- ✔ Does my target market celebrate a particular event or date?
- ✔ Does my target market dwell in a specific location or even online or offline?
- ✔ What are the actual buying habits of my potential customers?
- ✔ Does my target market view videos (YouTube advertising and so on)?

Asking these questions boils down to market research. The more specific you get, the better your subsequent marketing efforts. After you know who your target market is, researching them and finding out as much as you can about them is important. You can also look on LinkedIn (www.linkedin.com) to see if you can easily find your group there. If so, you can then spend your time and effort, communicating with that group.

You can also use Google's keyword tool (www.googlekeywordtool.com), which is a free tool that helps you identify what people are searching for (what keywords are being used). You can see exact phrases for what people are looking for (and presumably ready to buy). This tool also tells you how many searches are being done on that word or phrase, the location (United States and so on), and even trends. Refer to Chapter 15 for more info.

Knowing where your target market is

After you know your target market, you need to know where to find your target market. To do so, ask yourself these questions:

- ✔ Is my target market easily found with a search engine?
- ✔ Is my target market found offline, such as a local club meeting, church gathering, social or civic group, chamber of commerce, or other area of affinity?
- ✔ Does my target market congregate at LinkedIn or other Internet venues?
- ✔ Does my target market show up at conferences, trade shows, or other large industry gatherings?
- ✔ Who reaches my target market but doesn't compete with me?

After you answer these questions, you can start to formulate your marketing plan. If part of your target market is offline, find out where it meets so you can attend its events. If members of your market are in a formal association, you can go to your library's reference section and look up the *Encyclopedia of Associations* for details. You can also find groups at places such as Meetup (www.meetup.com). If the group is at LinkedIn (http://www.linkedin.com), go there, join, and actively participate in the group.

The question "Who reaches my target market but doesn't compete with me?" is a zero-cost marketing question because it opens up your creativity (and many possibilities) to do joint ventures with marketers that do reach your target market. (*Zero-cost marketing* is actually a reference to my book, but it generally means performing marketing strategies without paying any money up-front for them.)

For example, a videographer client of mine who specializes in wedding videos called me for some advice on marketing. He performed his wedding videos in northern New Jersey. He told me that he spent a small fortune advertising his business in bridal magazines and wedding directories. I told him to join and get active in photography associations in northern New Jersey. He hesitated because he said he wasn't a photographer.

In his case, the point was clear. Videographers and photographers reach the same target market but don't compete with each other. He joined and became active with the photographers' association and improved his bottom line. He received several business referrals from those photographers. As a matter of fact, one photographer sent him business worth more than $150,000 in revenue during the past six years!

Identifying Your Competitors

Your customers will either buy from you or from someone else. Customers represent demand (consumption), and you (and your competitors) represent supply (production). The customer (consumer) makes a choice — either you or someone else.

"Someone is eating your lunch" and it's not your uncle Boris. Of course, that phrase is a reference to your competitors that muscle in on your turf. Consumers consider a wide array of producers of goods and services, and if you don't serve your customers well, they'll turn elsewhere. As a result, you need to understand your competitors.

You have a lot to find out from your competitors, both good and bad. When you're running a business, no matter how small, you have competitors; your customers always have choices. As you figure out who your competitors are and what makes them tick, keep in mind these points about them:

- **Take heed of your competitors' marketing.** You can identify what their product or service is, so look to see how your product or service compares. Look to see how and where (Facebook, YouTube, Twitter) your competitors market. Study their advertising efforts so you can select the right advertising channels for you.

- **Know who your top three competitors are.** With this information in mind, determine why your customers would choose them over you.

- **Recognize your competitors' strengths and weaknesses.** Figure out how you stack up against them. You can then figure out how you can offer the similar product or service better. You can also see if you can add any additional value to your product or service that your customers can't.

These sections help you examine more closely who your competition is so you can position yourself better against them. With the information you discover, you can also figure out how you're going to compete against them and how you can potentially work with them.

Positioning yourself versus your competitors

As a micro-entrepreneur and owner of a small business working from home, you want to keep down your costs and overhead, which translates into cost savings to your customers, which in turn means you have an advantage when you position yourself against your larger competitors.

To better position yourself versus your competitors, get on the mailing and/or email list of all your competitors. By doing so, you can watch and learn how they market to their prospects and customers. With that information, you can see which strategies and tactics you want to embrace and emulate, and which strategies and tactics you want to reject. Of course, your learning process becomes obvious. The successful competitors are doing many things right, and the unsuccessful or mediocre competitors aren't.

Keep in mind that as you pick up one customer and then another, these customers (no matter how few) are valuable feedback for you. When people are actually spending money on what you offer, find out why. You may pick up reasons that may have not occurred to you. If even one customer gives you some good reasons as to why he chose you, more than likely others are doing the same. Incorporate those reasons and information in your marketing and communication.

Staying updated on your customers' actions with competitive analysis

Competitive analysis is just a fancy way of saying that you should know what your competitor is doing. The Internet can help you do so. In addition, here are some other things you can do to stay up-to-date with your competitors:

- ✔ **Set up a Google Alert.** Google Alert is a free service that will alert you based on keywords you choose and when web pages with those keywords become publicly available and viewable. For example, say that you sell gift baskets and you set up a Google Alert for the term "gift baskets". Any time a new incident of that word shows up on a web page at a website or blog, you get alerted via email. You can then go to the site and see what's happening.

✔ **Check on press releases.** Many companies issue press releases to announce new developments and events. Regularly check their websites and also active publicity directories such as `www.prnewswire.com` and `www.marketwire.com` to stay updated on their activities.

✔ **Track competitors for complaints or praise on popular consumer sites.** You can check at consumer sites, such as `www.yelp.com`, to find out about any complaints (or praise) about your competitors. You can change or improve your business practices to take advantage of these comments.

✔ **Use social media.** Use Facebook (`www.facebook.com`) and Twitter (`www.twitter.com`) to see how your competitors are doing and learn from their successes and failures. Check out Chapter 17 for additional ways to utilize social media.

✔ **Use competitive intelligence websites.** These websites track what your competitors are doing and provide you with data, such as sales and what keywords they're using. Utilize sites such as iSpionage (`www.ispionage.com`), Keyword Spy (`www.keywordspy.com`), and AdGooroo (`www.adgooroo.com`).

Turning competitors into partners

The old saying, "If you can't beat them, join them" may apply for you in your relationship with your competitors. Sometimes competitors are better off being turned into partners. If you find that your competitor has a good product or service and that its superior marketing would be too difficult for you to overcome, then reconsider what you're doing.

Ask yourself these questions to spur a possible partnering relationship with your competitors:

✔ If my competitor has a great product or service, could I be better off simply selling its product or service and making a commission?

✔ Could I sell my product or service in conjunction with my competitor in some way? (For example, if I want sell books and Amazon is my competition, why not sell my books on Amazon?)

✔ Could my product or service be a good follow-up offering that could easily dovetail with my competitor's offering? (My product could be good enough to use as a follow-up (or bounce-back) offer.)

✔ Does my competitor's offering have gaps or shortcomings that I can fill in with what I offer? (Every product has strengths and weaknesses, so look for a fit.)

Think seriously and creatively about these questions because joint ventures and other types of partnerships can result in greater success for your business in due course. Make sure you know as much possible about your competition through competitive analysis.

Doing Your Marketing Plan

Identifying your customers and your competitors is part of your marketing plan. Chapter 2 covers the creation of your overall business plan, but I consider this segment of the business plan — the marketing plan — to be the most important part.

The *marketing plan* tackles the entire approach that you're undertaking to find and sell to folks that will be your customers. This plan is the whole point of being in business — making sales and netting a profit. These sections cover the actual component and concerns of your marketing plan to remove the mystery about how you should proceed.

Uncovering your marketing strategy

You have a goal with your business to make it profitable by increasing sales (while you're keeping costs down), and your marketing plan is giving you a comprehensive approach to accomplishing this goal.

Your *marketing strategy* is what you want to accomplish with your marketing and how you will actually accomplish these business goals. The marketing strategy goes into the *what* of your marketing approach, while the rest of the marketing plan goes into detail about the *how* of your marketing approach. For example, do you want to get a certain number of more customers in a time frame? Do you want to reach a certain amount of money in monthly sales during a time frame?

Remembering your mission statement

A mission statement may sound a bit pretentious, but crystallizing what you aim to do in your business is important. What are your marketing efforts going to do for your business? The *mission statement* is typically part of your business plan. It acts as a guiding principle, and it can remind you to maintain integrity and consistency in your marketing efforts. Check out Chapter 2 for how to create a mission statement.

Knowing your target market

Being able to identify your target market is at the heart of your marketing plan. I discuss how you can figure out this information in the earlier section, "Identifying Your Target Market," in this chapter. It bears repeating here as you go over all the important elements of a good marketing plan. Just remember: Who is your ideal customer?

Analyzing your competition

You need to know exactly how you stack up to your competition. Doing a thorough analysis of your competitors can help you immeasurably with your marketing efforts. I discuss how to analyze your competitors earlier in this chapter in the "Identifying Your Competitors" section. I mention this action here to make sure you investigate your competition in your marketing plan.

Identifying what makes you unique

Determine what makes your business or what you offer that's different and unique from other businesses or products/services. Doing so answers the *Unique Selling Proposition (USP),* a reference that has been a part of the marketing world for what seems like forever.

This proposition allows you to see how you're different, better, unique (and more desirable) in the eyes of your potential customers when they compare you to others who are offering similar products and services. If you're not sure, check out how others handle that point or get examples of USPs (go to the marketing websites in this chapter and do a search of "unique selling proposition"). For instance, if you're a home-based freelance editor and writer, what sets you apart from other home-based freelance editors and writers?

Many useful tutorials and how-to videos can help you do what it takes to create a good USP (or become more proficient on any marketing point or topic covered in this book). You can find some of these tutorials (video and otherwise) at

  ✔ **How Stuff Works** (www.howstuffworks.com)

  ✔ **Instructables** (www.instructables.com)

  ✔ **YouTube** (www.youtube.com)

Developing a pricing strategy

Part of what makes people decide to buy either your product or someone else's is the price. Think about how you behave when you're the customer. Price matters to you, and it usually matters to your potential customers, so take the time to create a pricing strategy for your products and services you offer.

To develop a pricing strategy, do the following:

1. **Analyze what your competitors are doing in terms of pricing.**

   Your customers are also comparing your price with your competitors'. If you're pricing lower or higher, have a reason why and give you customer justification for the difference.

2. **If you're charging more than your competitors, clearly communicate why in your advertising (or whatever your communication venue is) before you lose price-conscious customers.**

   Presenting to your customers why you charge less than your competition is easy. If you charge more, make sure you project to your customers how your higher price is saving them money through higher value or quality. (Customers are more price-conscious during difficult economic times.)

To find more great information on pricing strategy, refer to the sidebar later in this chapter. Search those sites for "pricing strategy" articles.

Some people may want to give very low prices, whereas others charge much higher prices, but provide the justification through emphasizing quality and so on.

Others pack their offering with lots of content, value, and so forth and charge higher prices, whereas still others seek a low-price strategy but in the process offer less content or value. You have to decide what's right for you. Refer to the sidebar, "Tapping into additional marketing resources for additional help" in this chapter for more in-depth pricing help.

Promoting your marketing activities

Some folks call this part of the marketing plan the *promotional plan* or the *promotional component*, or they use the term *advertising and promotion*. When you hit the ground running with your marketing activities, what do they encompass? What are you actually doing?

This section may encompass every attempt or opportunity you have (or make) to communicate to prospects and customers. Think of everything that potential customers see or experience about you. You want to know how they will find out about you and what you have to offer.

- **Advertising:** Buying advertising (either offline or online) is paying to send a marketing message to the audience of that particular magazine, website, blog, or media outlet. The costs can vary. Advertising can get expensive, so do your research about the costs and benefits. Refer to the resources in the sidebar, "Tapping into additional marketing resources for additional help."

- **Packaging:** Believe it or not, everything about you, your business, and your product is a marketing message about you and what you offer. Packaging can make a product more (or less) desirable for the customer. In this case, we are talking about packaging for your product. Find out more about how packaging can enhance your marketing efforts (there's lots of great information on packaging using the resources at the end of this chapter).

- **Public relations:** Doing press releases and creating newsworthy events are great ways to inform your target market or to get prospects and customers engaged in a venue that ultimately highlights your business or your offering.

- **Direct sales:** When you call someone on the phone or make a sales visit (the *cold call*), you're making an attempt at direct selling. Examine to see whether your product or service is conducive to this approach. Would you need to hire sales staff or find a way to do outbound telemarketing? *Outbound telemarketing* is suited to higher-ticket items that may be complex and need explaining. Live support and communication can boost sales with products that aren't easily explained on a website or a mailing piece.

- **Internet marketing:** People will see your website, blog, or other Internet presence. Every word and image is all about marketing. Make sure you are projecting the right image and message.

- **Sales promotions:** Determine whether you'll run contests and other promotions to help bring exposure to your business. Businesses of all types run events and promotions in their marketing approaches. Find out what works within your industry or niche.

- **Marketing materials:** Your brochures, flyers, business cards, and so on are all part of your marketing. Make sure they look professional. Some great sites can help you produce good-looking materials. Shop around at places such as Vistaprint (www.vistaprint.com), Printing for Less (www.printingforless.com), and PS Print (www.psprint.com).

- **Email marketing:** Every email you do is a form of marketing. Add a signature at the end of your emails with a clickable link to your website, blog, and so on. Make email marketing a part of all your communications to some degree. Consider doing a free ezine or broadcast announcements about you, your business, and what you offer. Check out Chapter 16 on how you can use ezines.

✔ **Social media marketing:** Facebook, Twitter, YouTube, Pinterest, Squidoo, and so on are forms of social media you can use to market your business and your offerings. You usually don't have to spend any money to use social media marketing, although it does take some time and effort. Check out Chapter 17 for how to use social media in your marketing plan.

Tracking with a marketing worksheet

You should regularly measure your marketing for both total cost and total effectiveness. Different types of marketing activity are measured differently. For example, when you do online activity, you can track the activity in various ways, such as with (www.google.com/analytics), which is free and can help to track clicks and other behavior by Internet users. You need to know how well people are responding to your efforts.

One thing I tell my students is that whenever they make any specific effort in the marketplace to generate sales, they should do a marketing worksheet to track the effectiveness of the effort. Figure 13-1 provides an example of a marketing analysis worksheet.

SAMPLE   Date: __/__/__

Part 1:

Details:
Name of campaign: **Key:**
Venue:
Category: **Promotion Type:**
Offline or online: Paid ad:
Niche: Affiliate:
Type of product/service: PPC:
Other: CPA:
Other: PPV:
                                                                           Article:
Total cost of promotion: Traffic:
                                                                           JV:
Comments on marketing: Other:

Part 2:

Results:
# of views:
# of clicks:
# of sales:
Total sales revenue:
Profit per order:
Profit from campaign:

Comments

Figure 13-1:
A sample marketing analysis worksheet.

The marketing analysis worksheet is a tool to help you analyze the costs and benefits of a particular marketing approach. You can model a worksheet after my example and model it to your needs. Here are some of the important elements of a good marketing analysis worksheet:

✓ **Description:** Describe the advertising, publicity, or marketing venue. Keep detailed accounts of which one you used, whether it was online or offline, and in what venue (website, blog, and so on) you used it.

✓ **Tracking Key**. Use a key or tracking code in your marketing efforts so that you can easily trace where responses are coming from and how effective a marketing approach is.

✓ **Responses:** Track how many people responded to your ad or offer.

✓ **Date:** Have a space where you can record when the responses came in. This element tracks how many responses on day one, day two, and so on.

✓ **Orders:** Evaluate how many of these responses resulted in orders.

Do a marketing analysis worksheet for each individual marketing effort. After every week or month take time to review these worksheets. Continue doing what works. If something worked really well, do much more of it. If something doesn't work or give you the results you seek, either change the approach or drop it.

Tracking your marketing costs

Determining how you you're spending on marketing efforts and what the breakdown is for these costs is straightforward. Some things have a definable cost, such as when you pay for advertising and other costs that are generally easy to track. Some activities are more of a gray area because the cost isn't financial but measured in time. The bottom line: Track your costs — both financial and nonfinancial — so you can make better judgments about what is an effective (and profitable) use of your time.

To track, consider opening separate bank accounts, one for business use and one for personal use. I personally prefer credit union accounts because they're usually easier and cheaper to maintain than a regular bank checking account. Try to pay for your business costs with either checks or a debit card (which usually comes along with the bank or credit union checking account). Most banks and credit unions now have expense tracking software at their websites to help you analyze where your money goes and for what expense. It's easy to categorize expenses. At the end of each month, ask yourself about the expenses you paid for in that month. Refer to Chapter 2 for more about accounting issues.

Creating an action plan

As you finish developing your marketing plan, you need to determine who will implement the different aspects of your plan. (This is called an *action plan*.) If you're a one-person micro-entrepreneurship, then you may have to do most of the tasks yourself. No matter who does what, your marketing plan must get done. You need to assign responsibility. If you have no one to help you, then you need to prioritize and learn to manage your time and become more efficient. You may also be able to hire outsourced workers for some of the tasks. (Chapter 19 can help you find workers who may be able to help.)

Keep these points in mind as you're actively working your marketing plan:

- **Have a due date for each action item.** Create a timeline for both big and small tasks.

- **Work your marketing plan daily or weekly.** The best marketing action plans are worked regularly and tweaked and improved along the way. Keep it as a dynamic document that you can change as needed rather than a plan you create once and forget about it.

- **Be patient and persistent.** Don't expect great success to come immediately. Professional marketers are patient and keep testing, improving, and applying their strategies until they get positive results.

- **Get regular feedback from others about the value of what you're offering and the ongoing tactics and strategies in your marketing efforts.** Successful marketers share information and feedback with other marketers to keep improving their marketing efforts.

- **Choose several steps that you're comfortable doing and start implementing.** Don't try to do 50 different things to see what works or doesn't work. Most successful entrepreneurs do a few things very well. You can outsource the tasks you don't do well.

 Regularly ask others about strategies and tactics. You can interact with other marketers in different marketing forums, such as at Linked In (www.linkedin.com), Yahoo! Groups (www.groups.yahoo.com), and forums such as the Warrior Forum (www.warriorforum.com).

Ensuring you offer a quality product or service

All the marketing, sales, and advertising in the world are meaningless and worthless if your product or service isn't based on quality and integrity. Getting customers is hard; losing customers is easy . . . very easy. Excellent marketing begins and ends with something of value that truly helps people in some way.

Many businesses succeed at marketing without going crazy doing expensive and time-consuming marketing because their product or service is so good that it nearly sells itself. In fact, word-of-mouth marketing is among the best type of marketing out there (and it's free). You want customers to be so happy with your product or service that they're effortlessly referring others to you because of what you offer. If you offer a shoddy product or service and lose customers as a result, you've wasted all the money you've spent on marketing. I do seminars across the country, and I feel good when I walk into a classroom to do a seminar and find out that some of the participants in the room came because they were referred by others that took a seminar of mine. That's free marketing! Your product or service has to have quality and value, which will make getting new customers, repeat customers, and referred customers that much easier.

TIP

Tapping into additional marketing resources

Marketing is a heady and important topic, and it's the cornerstone of your business success. Therefore, no matter what product or service you offer, and no matter how big or small (or really small) your business is, marketing is your path to financial success.

These helpful resources address the topics that I've discussed in this chapter (and other related marketing issues) and go into much greater depth. Here you can find plenty of great articles and information on the world of marketing. Most of these sites have a searchable feature to easily find information on your most pressing marketing concerns. Here are the sites:

✔ **American Marketing Association** (www.marketingpower.com)

✔ **The eMarketing Association** (www.emarketingassociation.com)

✔ **eMarketing and Commerce** (www.emarketingandcommerce.com)

✔ **HubSpot** (www.hubspot.com)

✔ **Marketing Best Practices** (www.marketingbestpractices.com)

✔ **Marketing Profs** (www.marketingprofs.com)

✔ **National Mail Order Association** (www.nmoa.org)

✔ **SiteProNews** (www.sitepronews.com)

✔ **Target Marketing Magazine** (www.targetmarketingmag.com)

✔ **Wilson Web** (www.wilsonweb.com)

Many of these organizations do have active groups on Linked In (www.linkedin.com) that you can join for free. In addition, they have a presence on Facebook and Twitter. Many of them have free or low-cost ezines with good articles and news on marketing topics. Don't forget that you can get sample business plans and marketing plans from places such as the Small Business Administration (www.sba.gov) and the Service Corps of Retired Executives (www.score.org).

Chapter 14

Communicating with Prospective Customers

....

....

After all is said and done, your business boils down to selling. Whether you're a one-person operation working from your kitchen table or a huge Fortune 500 company with operations sprawling across the globe, you gain your revenue from the gentle art of salesmanship.

At the heart of salesmanship is the art of persuasion. Whether you're selling over the phone, in person, through writing, or in any other form of communication, you have to persuade someone else to exchange what you offer (products or services) for their money.

This obligation to persuade belongs to entrepreneurs. You have to earn your customers' money if you want it. In order to persuade them, you need to make the initiative to contact someone. If you already have a product or service, you need to get customers. This chapter focuses on the act of selling and the different forms that it can take, such as spoken, written, or multimedia (videos and podcasts).

Recognizing Your Role: You're Already a Salesperson

Thinking of yourself as a salesperson may seem like an odd thought. You may think that if you were put in a selling situation that it would be a dreadful experience where you would only utter, not knowing what to say, before scooting out the door terrified. As a micro-entrepreneur, no matter the type of business you have or the type of product or service you offer, you are a salesperson — you want people to purchase what you offer.

I can prove to you that you're a great salesperson and give you the secret of great salesmanship! No, I'm not kidding. Did you ever have a moment in your life where you said something like this to someone else?

- ✔ "What a great restaurant I was at last night! My wife and I had an excellent meal! The food and ambience were great. You really should go this weekend."

- ✔ "What a horrible movie we saw last night! Don't bother going; it was boring, violent, and stupid. Don't waste your money!"

- ✔ "Come with us to the county fair this Saturday. We had a blast last year. It was lots of family fun. We really enjoyed some great food and drinks, and the kids loved the rides and games!"

Perhaps you didn't have those exact conversations, but you've probably had plenty of similar conversations. My point here is that selling is merely a form of persuasion, and you have had numerous moments when you persuaded someone to do something. It may not have occurred to you at that moment that you were performing an act of salesmanship, but you were.

What's the common thread in these examples? You were passionate about what you were communicating. More than likely, you were also persuasive, maybe not to everyone, but certainly to someone. That's selling in a nutshell. The following sections take a closer look at the art of selling. Here I examine what makes a good salesperson and how you improve your cold-calling skills.

Letting you in on the big secret to salesmanship: Be convincing

If you aren't excited about what you're offering, how can you make someone else excited about it? In other words, you're trying to get the prospect to part with his money, but that can't happen until he is convinced of the value and goodness of what you're offering. He won't be convinced if you aren't convinced!

As a micro-entrepreneur, you aren't just the lead salesperson. You are, in fact, the entire sales force. As a result, whether you're a micro-entrepreneur or a salesperson for anything else, make sure you're convinced of the value that you offer and excited about sharing your product or service with your prospect.

That word *sharing* is a critical one. Successful salespersons don't see themselves as "selling" something; they believe that they are sharing information on something great to help someone else.

Many novice salespeople take seminars, classes, and other educational venues on better selling. They're hearing great tips and techniques for approaching and persuading people to buy their stuff. Many of them still won't be great salespeople because they're not passionate about what they're selling. They won't become great salespeople because they aren't excited about sharing their products or services with prospective customers.

Breaking the ice — the cold call

Until you get to know your prospective customers, you need to break the ice with a *cold call,* which refers to the initial call to a new potential client. If you plan on growing your business, the moment will come when you may need to talk to a total stranger to see what the possibilities are (in terms of gaining revenue from him).

The cold call may be the most dreaded call that you have to make, but it doesn't have to be. Studies have revealed that some people get physically ill when calling up a total stranger. (If they had to call my uncle from Bratislava, getting sick would be justified.) You need to look at the cold call in an entirely different light.

The essence of cold calling is that you're approaching someone with the intent of making a meaningful and appropriate proposal. It doesn't always mean a sale of a product or service; it could be to propose a mutually beneficial arrangement, such as a joint venture or something that could benefit their customers or contacts.

Your attitude toward cold calling goes a long way to making it either a positive or a negative pursuit. You can view it negatively as a bother and as a numbers game — the idea that you have to call a bunch of people and hope that someone ultimately says yes to your proposal. Or you can think of it positively where you quickly get to the decision-maker to discuss your proposal in a relatively fast manner. Cold calling is the purest form of direct marketing.

How you look at cold calling determines how successful you'll be. Refer to the nearby sidebar for an example from my life to see how my view of cold calling affected my success.

My personal experience in selling and cold calling

In 1985, I earned my certified financial planner (CFP) designation. At that time, people told me the best way to make money as a CFP was to sell products — insurance, investments, and so on. With that advice, I got my licenses to sell financial products.

I passed all the exams, got the licenses, and found a broker-dealer to work with. I took the training and — poof! — I was ready to tackle the world and sell investments. I remember some of my colleagues telling me, "Paul, you would be natural for selling investments. You have a sense of humor and an outgoing style; you will do well!" How well do you think I did?

In my first six months of selling, the total sales I generated were a whopping zero. Nothing! Every time I had the opportunity to sell someone on buying insurance or investments, I choked. I just couldn't get out the words. I felt that I couldn't sell a life preserver to a drowning man.

I failed at selling. The amazing thing is that some of these prospects were people I personally knew. My failure in selling was with two groups of people: those who didn't know me and those who did.

I was trying to sell something that I wasn't convinced about. I wasn't happy or confident in my approach, and at some level my prospects saw that. If I wasn't convinced that buying my stuff was good, why should they be convinced?

My real happiness wasn't in selling financial products; it was in selling my knowledge and information. I started doing seminars on investing in 1986 and on home business start-ups in 1987. In 1991, I started teaching seminars in mail order, and I found some success with cold calling.

The first book that I wrote during the pre–Internet and pre–PayPal era was a self-published work entitled *How to Achieve Credit Card Merchant Status*. It focused on how home businesses and mail order companies can get the ability to accept credit cards in their business (at the time it was very difficult). I sold the book in my seminars and even through radio interviews.

I was very excited knowing that I wrote a book that solved a big problem for micro-entrepreneurs during that time. I remember calling a mail-order catalog that specialized in home business books to suggest they put my book in its catalogue.

During that phone call, I excitedly shared how my book would benefit the catalogue's clients and that it would sell well. I even said that the catalogue didn't have to even buy a large quantity of the book; it could be drop-shipped. In other words, the catalogue company could put the book in its catalogue and solicit for orders without buying books. In drop-shipping, the company takes the order from the customer and then sends me my portion of the order (typically the split was 50 percent of the purchase price) along with shipping information for where to send the book.

As I finished the call and hung up the phone, I was happy that I made a sale — I got a customer for my book. It hit me that I had called a total stranger and made a sale! I didn't even realize that I was making a cold call; I was just calling someone who I thought was a perfect prospect for what I was offering, and I excitedly and confidently shared in that phone call the benefits of what I offered. I was able to handle any objections with an equally enthusiastic response.

For me, this moment was transformational. All the sales skills and training in the world don't have the power of helping you sell unless you're firmly convinced that you're offering something of great value to those you're communicating with.

Tackling the cold call: Helpful tips to make it successful

Cold calling is more than a call to a stranger. It's also called *canvassing and prospecting*, and it may entail face-to-face selling, too. Cold calling has taken several forms over the years, including door-to-door and face-to-face at events, such as trade shows and conferences. No matter the form it takes, these tips can help you have greater success when cold calling.

Understand your prospects before you call

Before you call or email any prospects, you need to know who you're calling and why what you offer is right for them. The more you know about who you're calling, the greater your chances of a successful call. Even basic information, such as their occupation, their demographics (Millenial, Gen X, Baby Boomer), and their interests can help. The more you can craft your message to them and what is likely to interest them, the better for you.

Set up the call before you call

Breaking the ice before you call can help. You can send a brochure, catalogue, sales information, or other form of communication via direct mail or email before the call. Doing so can help set up the call and make it a little less . . . cold.

Get the prospect's attention during the first 15 seconds

You have approximately 15 seconds to get the prospect to decide whether to continue the call or not. In that short amount of time, you need to communicate a strong benefit to them personally of what you offer and excite the prospect with value and/or savings.

For example, you can focus on the product's value: "For struggling homeowners, this could lower payments, avoid bankruptcy, and give you more income by at least $500 per month." Or you can focus on what the prospect can save: "This program can save you $2,000 over what you're currently doing."

Be like your prospect

Studies have shown (along with your own experience, I am sure) that most people are comfortable with dealing with like-minded folks. If you're a single mom, you're more likely to have a conducive conversation with another single mom than if you're a retired gentleman. Of course, if you aren't a single mom, then at the very least you should become familiar with words, phrases, and topics that resonate with a prospect who is a single mom. Sharing the same language isn't just a linguistic thing; when you communicate like your prospect (with the same style and content, you'll have an easier time making a connection during the conversation). Focus on using the same language and approach that your prospect uses to enhance your chances of success.

Ask for an action

When talking with your prospect, keep moving forward toward a sale, even if a buying decision isn't rendered at that moment. Ask if you can call back at a later time or if you can email him further information. Many times a prospect isn't really saying "no thanks," Many times he's saying "no thanks . . . for now." You may be able to be successful at a later point when you become more familiar.

Don't wing it; use a script

Make sure you write out a script so you know what you'll say and where to go in the conversation. You don't want to leave the conversation to chance until you're very proficient with cold calling.

In your script, identify the main points (such as benefits and features) and have them ready. List the benefits in order of how powerful and relevant they are to the prospect. If you're talking to a prospect who is an auto mechanic, be ready with a benefit that would resonate immediately. For example, you could say, "This would save your business 100 man-hours of work per month, which can easily save you more than $7,400 in production costs per year in your garage."

The script should also list answers to the most common objections that prospects usually bring up. If the prospect says your product or service is too expensive, be ready to explain how your product or service can actually save money over the long haul.

Besides listing benefits and responses to common objections, have all the necessary details of the product/service available at your finger tips. Finally, have paper nearby so you can jot down points the prospect makes. What you learn from one call (either good or bad) can help you succeed in the next call.

When someone calls you on the phone to sell you something, pay attention to how she started the call. What did she say and how did she say it? Be aware of how you're sold to and take note of what you thought was effective and what turned you off.

When you get better at cold calling, you can potentially make a business out of it. Many businesses pay for cold calling. Telephone sales positions are some of the most resilient jobs in any market-based economy, no matter how good or bad the economy is.

Getting additional help

The ability to use persuasion to initiate the sale of a product, service, or even a business relationship will always be a powerful and profitable skill whether you're working for yourself or others. The prime reason is clear: Generating new customers is the lifeblood of any ongoing business, and those who possess these skills have a very bright future.

After reading these sections, if you want additional help to improve your selling, check out these general selling resources:

- **Dale Carnegie** (www.dalecarnegie.com)
- **Erik Luhrs** (www.guruselling.com)
- **Harvey Mackay** (www.harveymackay.com)
- **Jeffrey Gitomer** (www.gitomer.com)
- **Just Sell** (www.justsell.com)
- **Rain Today** (www.raintoday.com)
- **SalesPro Central** (www.salesprocentral.com)
- **Sales Resources** (www.salesresources.com)
- **Sales and Sales Strategies** (www.sales.about.com)
- **Sales Training Advice** (www.salestrainingadvice.com)
- **Tom Hopkins:** Tom Hopkins is a well-known sales expert and trainer, and he is also the author of *Selling For Dummies* (John Wiley & Sons, Inc.). You can find more information at www.tomhopkins.com.

You can also look up some of my favorite sales educators. Reading what the experts have to say on a given activity can pay off. In the world of successful salesmanship, these are my favorites:

- **Joe Girard:** Joe earned the title of "World's Greatest Salesperson" in the Guinness Book of Records. Check him out at www.joegirard.com.
- **Brian Tracy:** Brian has been a sales trainer and educator for many years. Go to www.briantracy.com.
- **Zig Ziglar:** I love Zig's style, and his great quotes on sales and success are indeed very motivational. Go to www.ziglar.com.

Although technology may change, human nature and the art of selling and persuasive communication will always be an ongoing skill. These books offer some timeless guidance and strategies:

- ✔ *Cold Calling Techniques that Really Work* by Stephen Schiffman (Adams Media)
- ✔ *The Greatest Salesman in the World* by Og Mandino (Bantam)
- ✔ *Telephone Sales For Dummies* by Dirk Zeller (John Wiley & Sons, Inc.) (www.dummies.com)
- ✔ *Smart Calling: Eliminating the Fear, Failure, and Rejection of Cold Calling* by Art Sobczak (John Wiley & Sons, Inc.)
- ✔ *Supremely Successful Selling* by Jerold Panas (John Wiley & Sons, Inc.) (www.wiley.com)
- ✔ *Take the Cold out of Cold Calling* by Sam Richter (Beaver's Pond Press) (www.takethecold.com)

In addition, you may look for more help from professional associations. They pride themselves on having the best information regarding their specialty. These organizations (and their sites) offer great tips and guidance on the world of selling:

- ✔ **National Association of Sales Professionals** (www.nasp.com)
- ✔ **The Sales Association** (www.salesassociation.org)
- ✔ **Sales Lead Management Association** (www.salesleadmgmtassn.com)

Getting referrals

One of the best ways to get in with sales prospects is to have a third party, who is a business contact or friend, refer you. The old "tell 'em Bob sent ya" is as good a referral today as it was 50 years ago (provided that Bob is reputable).

Fortunately, getting referrals is more than just a pursuit that you cultivate among your family, friends, and business associates. It has become its own specialized form of sales and marketing.

To cultivate referral marketing, go to these resources for help:

- ✔ **Bridgeline Digital** (www.bridgelinedigital.com)
- ✔ **Business Networking International** (www.bni.com)

🖝 **Le Tip International** (www.letip.com)

🖝 **The Referral Institute** (www.referralinstitute.com)

Focusing on Your Sales Message — Your Cold Call in Print

Writing a message to your prospect isn't that difficult, and you don't have to worry about him hanging up the phone on you (unless you mind him deleting your email or tossing your hard-copy sales letter in the bin). The sales message is like a cold call in print — it works like a salesperson on behalf of your company.

When I refer to a sales page or a sales email, I'm talking about a detailed sales message that seeks to persuade. Where this page appears depends on you. It may appear as an email that you send a prospect, an ad that you paid for that appears in someone's newsletter or ezine (refer to Chapter 16 for more information on ezines), or a listing on an auction site, such as eBay (check out Chapter 7). Inevitably what makes a sales page a sales page isn't necessarily the venue — it's the message and intent to make the sale. In these sections, I help you write effective sales messages.

Communicating benefits versus features

When you're communicating with your prospective client through the written word, you need to make sure that you understand the difference between benefits and features. *Benefits* are about what the product or service offers the customers, while *features* are about the product itself. As a micro-entrepreneur, knowing the difference is crucial, much like the difference between making money and not.

For example, identify the benefits and features of eggs. The benefits are that eggs are nutritious and can boost your health with valuable protein that helps build strong bones and muscles. Eggs' features are that they're oval-shaped, with a white (or brown) brittle shell, and with gooey insides with a yellow mushy ball called the yolk.

When your prospect is reading what you're offering, you stress the *benefits* above all, which is why they'll buy from you. When writing your copy (or talking with the potential client), you lead with the benefits. You keep stressing benefits so your prospect can see how your product or service can help her in her everyday life. The features come afterward. You discuss features when she shows interest. The features mainly tell her how the benefits will materialize.

Knowing the AIDA formula

In the world of sales copy writing, the AIDA formula is probably the equivalent of $E=MC_2$ in science (yes, it's that important). The *AIDA formula* is the foundation of sales copy writing, and copy writers still use it today. Although it was originally used in print venues, such as magazine advertising and direct mail pieces, today it's also used on web pages and in sales emails. You will even see it in action in eBay listings, ezine ads, and even YouTube videos (refer to the later section, "Cold Calling with a Video: Use YouTube to Your Advantage" for more info on using it in videos). The vehicle may have changed, but the principles have endured. Here are the details:

A=Attention

The *A* stands for attention. Step one is getting your reader's attention. If you don't get the reader's attention, it doesn't matter how fantastic your message is. You can get his attention in a variety of ways, depending on the venue:

✔ In email, it is the subject line. The *subject line* is the first thing your prospect sees in her inbox (the attention-grabbing headline).

✔ In an eBay (or other auction site) listing, it's the listing heading. This *listing heading* is your opportunity to draw in prospects (eBay calls them *bidders*) and let your full listing do the selling for you.

✔ In articles, a sales letter, or an advertisement, it's the headline. The *headline* features that compelling *why* she should read the rest of the piece.

For example, look at the following headlines and figure out which is more effective if you were trying to convince gardeners to go to your website or blog from an article you wrote at a different site. Your intent is to have visitors see what you offer at your site.

Headline A: "Some Important Points about Gardening"

Headline B: "Three Powerful Ways to Double the Yield from Your Garden"

Headline A is a little lackluster. Headline B has some good sizzle to it. This headline promises a strong benefit for readers. If you were a gardener, which would you find more enticing?

The most successful copywriters spend the most amount of time (relatively speaking) on the headline than on any other single element of the article, sales letter, or advertisement they're creating. Push your creativity and work to improve your headline writing skills. Before you write the article, write at least 20 headlines for it.

When writing your sales message, remember the five-second test. This test says that someone should be able to look at your webpage, sales letter, or email and know exactly what it's about in five seconds or less. You can easily achieve it with your catchy heading, supplemented by functional images.

Successful copywriters will do a swipe file of all the great stuff they see. A *swipe file* is like an informal collection of articles and ads that act like a treasury of ideas. Start your own swipe file so that you can accumulate articles and ads that have great headlines and other important elements that you can adapt to your needs. Don't confuse a swipe file with stealing and using other people's content without their permission. A swipe file is solely meant as a creativity booster to spur on our unique writing.

I=Interest

The *I* stands for interest. After you have the prospect's interest with your attention-grabbing headline, you have to hold his interest. To do so, you put in some compelling copy about his problem(s) (which, of course, will be addressed by what you're offering).

Say that you're marketing a weight-loss product. The interest part is how you suffered with your weight problem, how your friends joked about it, and how you were too embarrassed to go to the beach. After you started using the product, things started to change. Your prospect can identify with some of this. She can feel as if you're talking to her and describing what she has gone through. She is now interested in how this product can resolve this issue (her issue too).

D=Desire

The *D* stands for desire. You can build desire for your product or service. Instead of just listing benefits, you can tell your prospects what they'll gain from what you have to offer. Provide testimonials and examples of successful use of the product or service. You can save the biggest benefits for this section and make them drool.

I continue with the weight-loss example from the previous section. You generated interest because the reader (the prospect) identified with the problem. Now you build desire in your offering. You can continue with the following:

> "Things started to change when I started to use the product. Slowly I started to lose the pounds and gain confidence! The product helped me fit into my old clothes again. I had more energy and I didn't change my eating habits! The product was inexpensive, but what I gained was priceless! I didn't just get thinner; I also got healthier!"

With that copy, you were able to generate desire for the product. You alluded to a good price, weight loss benefits, and improved health.

A=Action

The second *A* stands for action. At this point of your sales message, you don't want to leave your prospect hanging. Ask him to do something — in other words, direct some action.

To get your prospects to take action, communicate with urgency. You can ask them to order now or click the button below. Don't leave it to chance; tell them exactly what you want them to do so that they can enjoy the benefits of your offering as soon as possible.

Communicating effectively via email

The way you communicate with prospects and clients can make or break your business. You need strong communication to gain your prospects' trust and their business, but make a careless comment or send a poorly written email, and you can lose them.

Keep these points in mind when communicating with any prospects or clients.

Read your message

Before you send an email, especially if it's a sensitive message, read it and then read it again to make sure that your message is clear and compelling and has the A-I-D-A elements (refer to the earlier section). If you're writing something negative, have a trusted person read it and give you feedback. Make sure that the email is accurate and that it isn't communicating anything improper or inflammatory that could get you into trouble (legal or otherwise).

Remember that email is forever

Whenever I send an email (particularly a sensitive one), I make it second nature to ask myself, "If someone read this back to me in five years, would it bother me?" Today people can indefinitely save data (such as emails). Before you send it, ask yourself whether this email could come back to haunt you. If so, make the appropriate changes to the text and save it in your archive with explanatory remarks so that you know the full details of the email, if necessary.

Know that writing doesn't equal talking

Before you send an email, read it to ensure that the tone is appropriate. An email can come off much differently than if the same message were spoken. When humans speak, they get the opportunity to intone their voice to add or subtract meaning, whereas doing the same in written communication can be more difficult to communication nuance. Think about how many times you've received an email and thought, "Gee, that was a snarky response," and the writer had a different purpose.

Keep it simple and clear

Keep your message as focused as possible without any unnecessary words. Use bullet points and short sentences. I like to number my points if I do a long email. Make your message easier to read, especially because people are reading emails and using more mobile modes, such as laptops, phones, tablets, and smartphones.

Respond quickly

Where possible, get back to folks as soon as you can. People like a quick reply, so respond in a timely fashion. If you feel you'll be away for more than a day or so, consider doing an *auto reply* that lets your prospects and customers know that you won't get a chance to reply immediately.

Make sure your email looks professional

In business emails, being professional in both content and style is important. Remember that your email is all about the look. Double-check your grammar, spelling, and punctuation. Don't use all caps because it looks like you're shouting. These things don't convey to your prospect or business contact a strong or positive image of you as a professional, so be extra careful. If grammar and punctuation aren't your strong points, have a trusted friend read an email before you send it.

Don't share inappropriate content

You don't want to offend your prospects or business clients, so make sure your emails don't include any offensive or off-the-wall text. Keep the emails professional. You don't want to worth the risk of losing any business for sending them a belly laugh about something they may find in bad taste.

Say please and thank you

Courtesy goes a long way, both in speaking and in writing. Use it every chance you get in your emails by frequently expressing your appreciation and gratitude. The good will it builds can be priceless and maybe even come in handy later on if a problem or difficulty arises.

Compose yourself: Never send an email if you're angry or upset

Often, people wish they could have called a sent email back after it's too late because they've said something they later regret. Whenever you're angry or upset, or if you suspect the other person is and you're about to send an email, write and save it in your draft folder and wait to send it. Allow the conversation or email points to circulate in your mind until you're less upset and have a greater grasp over your thoughts (and emotions).

Use the Send fields correctly

Make sure you know how to use the Send fields in an email. Here is a brief lowdown of the fields:

- ✔ **TO:** This field directs the email to the person or people whose attention or action you're seeking.

- ✔ **CC:** Use this field primarily as an FYI. Send copies of emails to people who you want to keep in the loop about something.

- ✔ **BCC:** Use this field at your discretion. If you're sending an email to a large group of people, and you want to respect their privacy, use this field. You can also use this field if you want to keep someone in the loop, but you don't want the other recipients to know.

Turning to additional resources for help in writing sales copy

Writing an email or a letter to someone is certainly easier (at least from a psychological standpoint) to picking up a phone and calling someone you may or may not know well. In the age of social medial, email, and texting, this is truer than ever. But how you write the copy is key, and picking up sales copy skills is just as important in writing a Twitter message as it is in a multipage sales letter.

You can find out a lot of valuable tips by reading the best. Here are some of my favorite experts:

- ✔ **Ted Nicholas:** Ted Nicholas is considered by many as the legend of copywriting. He has written sales copy that resulted in literally billions of dollars of sales for himself and his clients. He has lots of free reports and articles on the art of sales copy writing at his site: www.tednicholas.com.

- ✔ **Bob Bly:** Bob Bly is easily one of the most recognizable pros in the world of sales copy writing. He keeps an archive of his writing tips and pointers at www.bly.com.

- ✔ **Jeff Dobkin:** When it comes to nuts and bolts of sales copy writing for selling products and services, Jeff is a nonpareil. Find out more at www.dobkin.com.

- ✔ **Clayton Makepeace:** Clayton is another legendary name who literally has helped his clients generate millions in sales from writing great ad copy. He has a free newsletter at his site: www.makepeacetotalpackage.com.

- ✔ **Michel Fortin:** He's another hot writer who has developed a following from copy writers due to his talented writing sales. He has a blog at www.michelfortin.com.

If you want to see some great examples of copy writing, you can follow a blog or regularly visit a website. Writing sales copy is an ongoing pursuit. Here are some great suggestions to help you keep in the know and to keep growing. Successful copy writers make six figures, so it can be a good business for you, too.

- ✔ **Copyblogger** (www.copyblogger.com)
- ✔ **Freelance Copywriter's Blog** (www.freelancecopywritersblog.com)
- ✔ **Men With Pens** (www.menwithpens.ca)
- ✔ **Top Copywriting Sites** (www.topcopywritingsites.com)

Furthermore, if you want to rub elbows with professional copy writers, you can consider joining or visiting a professional association. Here are some places where you can find good copy writers (these places also do conferences and educational events):

- ✔ **LinkedIn Groups:** You can find plenty of writers' groups on LinkedIn (www.linkedin.com). Some of the groups to join are Advertising Copywriting and Marketing Communication.
- ✔ **The Professional Writers Alliance:** This subgroup of American Writers and Artists, Inc. (www.awaionline.com) is a professional association just for direct response and sales copy writers.
- ✔ *Target Marketing* **magazine:** This site (www.targetmarketing.com) offers lots of articles and how-to information on the topic of writing advertising, direct marketing, and sales copy.

Cold Calling with a Video: Use YouTube to Your Advantage

Before the Internet, the main tool for selling was the telephone. Fortunately, today you can take full advantage of the Internet, and video selling messages make your life so much easier (easy in the sense that you won't feel the personal pain of rejection).

Your prospects either view your video or not. They either see it all the way through or not. But in any case, creating a video is easier than doing a live sales presentation or a cold call. You can't talk about video marketing and selling without mentioning YouTube (www.youtube.com). If you properly create a video and post it on YouTube, you can reach potential customers. Using YouTube is a great way to sell.

Anyone with a digital video recorder or flip camera and a point of view can create a video and post it on YouTube. If some guy in a gorilla suit walking and falling off his roof can get a huge viewership, then you can, too. Explore creating your own video and consider doing a search for "video marketing" to see tons of videos done by others.

You can embrace YouTube as a sales tool and make your own video sales message. Here are some tips for doing it:

- **Make it easy to find you.** Remember that prospects (millions of them) go to YouTube every day to find videos of interest. Use YouTube's ability to add keywords and a complete description to accompany the video.

- **Look at lots of videos.** You don't have to start from scratch. No matter what you're selling, you can probably find a ton of videos about that niche or category. Look at many videos to see how others are doing it and ask yourself how applicable it is to what you want to sell. See how others are doing it well and not so well.

- **Do the A-I-D-A formula.** The AIDA formula also works well for creating a sales video. Refer to the earlier section, "Knowing the AIDA formula" for the specifics. When you view other videos that are selling products or services, examine to see the extent they successfully apply the formula. Then, figure out how you can apply it to your sales videos.

- **Be short and to the point.** Videos don't have to be a major motion production. They should be definitely less than ten minutes long, preferably less than five minutes. Today is the age of the short attention span, so keep your videos interesting and succinct to avoid losing your prospective customers' interest.

- **Get feedback from others.** Have some trusted folks view your videos before they go public and get feedback on the quality of the video. YouTube gives you the ability to do private videos, which you can make public when you're ready.

- **Provide good content.** Give your prospects good information to justify them viewing it. If you don't give compelling content, they'll quickly start viewing something else. For example, if you're selling skin cream, give some good tips on skin health.

- **Integrate social media.** Use Facebook (www.facebook.com) and Twitter (www.twitter.com) to help you gain viewers. When I do a video at my YouTube channel, I set my channel to automatically send a message to my Twitter followers to alert them about my latest videos. Chapter 17 provides some helpful advice about marketing with social media.

✔ **Place ads in your videos.** You can add HTML links in the video. Prospects can link back to your sales page or website if they're interested in finding out more information or purchasing something.

✔ **Add a call to action.** The last step of the AIDA formula is action. When viewers are finished viewing your video, prompt them to do something, such as click to something else, like your sales page, blog, or website. For example, if you did a sales video on gardening, tell them they can find more information by either subscribing to your YouTube channel or clicking on the link in your description (to go to your sales page on a gardening product or service).

Doing sales videos is a great form of selling in today's marketing environment. In addition to YouTube, you can check out the following resources to help with our video cold calling:

✔ **Reel SEO** (www.reelseo.com)

✔ **Vimeo** (www.vimeo.com)

✔ **Web Pro News Videos** (www.videos.webpronews.com)

✔ **The Web Video Marketing Council** (www.webvideomarketing.org)

For more on video publishing, check out Chapter 10.

Chapter 15

Utilizing Search Engine Strategies to Market Your Business

*N*o matter what service or product you're selling, you would love it if people that were searching for your service or product could find you and buy from you. Literally millions of people are constantly looking for something on the Internet, every second of every day. The main question is how you get them to find you — the little needle in the huge haystack of the Internet. The answer is search engines. This chapter delves deeper into the world of search engines, including the lowdown on search engine optimization (SEO) and what you can do to help your prospective customers find you.

Grasping How Search Engines Work and Where You Can Search

With billions and billions of web pages on the Internet (approximately 13.5 billion as of 2013), you may be a bit overwhelmed about how you can find what you want and how any of your potential customers can find you. You certainly can't start working your way through that amount of pages! Thankfully search engines can help. Search engines dramatically reduce the amount of time needed to find something.

Search engines are basically data collectors. They use sophisticated, high-speed technology (automated software known as *spiders* and *bots*) to digitally sift through and index at lightning speed this huge (and growing) collection of web pages. These spiders are speedy little devils; four of them can collect information from about 100 pages per second. The spiders generally start the searches from the most heavily trafficked pages. The exact methodology and technology used by search engines are actually closely guarded trade secrets.

Spiders generally only crawl through your site if you have added something new. But if you see that no spider has been to your site for a while, you should ask yourself why. Check to see if you've updated your content and ensure that your site map is updated (a *site map* is a map of your site's pages that makes it easy for a search engine to crawl).

Search engines do have some differences. Make sure you're aware of them because these differences affect how the information is collected and what results searchers see. For instance Google looks at the position of the words on the page and filters out insignificant words such as *a, an,* and *the*. Other search engines, such as Alta Vista, index every word, including words like *a, an,* and *the,* to get a more complete picture. Other search engines index hidden pieces of code called *meta tags*. The methodology used by all the major search engines continues to change.

Google today has approximately 70 percent of the search market, and their share in recent years has continued to grow, so it makes sense to tailor your site to the search engine that potentially will deliver the most customers to your site. As Google continues to tweak its search engine algorithm, the distance between the information Google values and other search engines value may continue to grow.

As a micro-entrepreneur, don't focus so much on how search engines work but on what you need to do to make sure that your website and web pages attract search engines and help the right people, such as customers and prospects, find you when they search.

Refer to the following for the top search engines:

- ✔ **All the Web** (www.alltheweb.com)
- ✔ **Ask.com** (www.ask.com)
- ✔ **Bing** (www.bing.com)
- ✔ **Duck Duck Go** (www.duckduckgo.com)
- ✔ **Google** (www.google.com)
- ✔ **Yahoo!** (www.yahoo.com)

In addition, you can check out *meta-search engines,* which are effectively web-sites that do a simultaneous search on multiple search engines. I prefer using meta-search engines because every regular search engine performs their searches a little bit differently (so why not use a batch of them at the same time?). Here are some of the top meta-search engines:

- **Dogpile** (www.dogpile.com)
- **Ixquick** (www.ixquick.com)
- **Mamma.com** (www.mamma.com)
- **Metasearchengine.com** (www.metasearchengine.com)
- **Search.com** (www.search.com)

If you want a more comprehensive look at the different search engines available, you may want to check out these search engine directories:

- **Beaucoup** (www.beaucoup.com)
- **List of Search Engines** (www.listofsearchengines.info)
- **Search Engine Colossus** (www.searchenginecolossus.com)
- **Search Engine Directory** (www.searchenginedirectory.net)
- **Search Engine Guide** (www.searchengineguide.com)

Some of the search engine directories list specialized search engines as well as search engines for some specific industries or topics. Say, for example, that your business is in real estate and you want an easier time connecting with (or being found by) real estate agents and investors. Then consider getting into search engines and directories that specialize in real estate. Refer to the section, "Making Yourself Findable" later in this chapter.

Getting the Lowdown on Search Engine Optimization (SEO)

When micro-entrepreneurs hear about search engine optimization (SEO), they're often a little confused. They often wonder how they can optimize gigantic search engines like Google, Yahoo!, and Bing.

When I talk about *optimizing,* as in SEO, I refer to the design of your web pages and web content to present your website in such a manner that search engines see that your site deserves to have the natural traffic their search users generate funneled to your site rather than another site.

You aren't really optimizing the search engine, but instead you're using the information that search engines can provide to optimize your website, get more prospects and customers, get more orders, and make more money. SEO isn't just a technical process, but it's also the content, strategy, and direction you want to go in.

A lot of companies will try to convince you that you need to hire them to do your SEO. However, the truth is that by following some of the simple information and tools you find in the following sections and in this chapter, you can do your own SEO. Here I explain in greater depth what SEO can give your new micro business.

Feeding the "hungry crowd"

If substituting imagination, creativity, and ingenuity for the large wads of cash that large companies have is one of the hallmarks of the micro-entrepreneur, then Gary Halbert should be considered one of history's best.

He would come up with brilliant, low-cost strategies that would beat the pants off competitors even though he used less money.

Gary once asked an audience of potential entrepreneurs this question: If you could only have one thing that would make your business a success, what would it be? Hands in the audience went up. One person gave the standard real estate and business answer of location. Another person said a large advertising budget. A third said an expensive print ad campaign. As each answer was given, Gary responded, "No." As the answers petered out and the hands went down, Gary continued.

"If I could only have one thing that would make my business a success, it would be (drum roll please), a hungry crowd."

That's all micro-entrepreneurs need for their business — a hungry crowd — a crowd of customers who are looking for what micro-entrepreneurs can provide. A crowd of ready, willing, and able customers hungering for the

solution you can provide. If you were selling hamburgers, it wouldn't matter if you had the best location, wads of cash for marketing, or a great advertising budget. The micro-entrepreneur with a hungry crowd starving for the food he could provide would be raking in the cash. If you were a large corporation, you could form a focus group, do some polling, or spend large amounts of cash on advertising.

That's what search engine optimization (SEO) gives you — the keys to a hungry crowd that wants what you're providing. SEO gives you the secrets on where the hungry crowd is and what you can do to most effectively appeal to its needs and generate sales. It allows you to spy on your competition and find out what they've learned about the customers you want. It leverages and shortcuts your learning curve and boosts you into the top ranks where you'll earn money — if you figure out how to crack the SEO code and master its secrets. And best of all, you don't need large wads of cash or focus groups.

You can discover these secrets for free. In fact, you'll have some of the largest companies as your partners, such as Google, who will willingly give you these secrets to enable your business to profit for free.

Before you start your own SEO research

Prior to being able to implement any SEO, you first need a firm grasp on what your business is about. Using SEO can help you answer the questions you need to ask yourself when you're deciding on a business venture. Chapter 3 discusses some important questions to ask yourself as you start to figure out what business venture is right for you.

In relation to this discussion, you need to ask yourself specifically these three questions:

- ✔ Are there enough potential customers for the item or service I will be offering to make this venture a profitable business?

- ✔ Will the potential customers or clients be willing to pay enough for the item or service I am offering to make this a profitable business?

- ✔ Who are my potential competitors, and is there enough potential opportunity to make this a viable business?

You may have a great idea, but if you'll be competing head to head with large and well-funded rivals for the same customers, perhaps you should look for a field that offers you more opportunity where the competition isn't as fierce and the market has openings for you to compete effectively.

Using SEO can help you answer these questions before you have invested a lot of time in a venture that will prove to be unprofitable either because the competition is too entrenched or there aren't enough customers looking for the item or service you're offering. Check out the next section for how SEO can specifically help you.

Beginning your research: Google can help

You can start your SEO research using some completely free tools. Although some SEO tools will cost you some money, they merely make your job quicker and easier. The best place to start is with Google.

Google's keyword search tool (www.googlekeywordtool.com) is now part of its Webmasters Toolbox. (Chapter 12 discusses keywords and keyword search tools in greater depth.) When you're at this site, consider browsing because it has other powerful tools to help you, such as Google Analytics (which can help you measure activity and search performance at your site) and services such as Google+ for business. Here I discuss this specific keyword tool.

After you're at www.googlekeywordtool.com, click on the blue highlighted "Google Keyword Tool" in the upper part of the page. When you click on it, you should go to the keyword tool page, as shown in Figure 15-1, which is also used in the AdWords section.

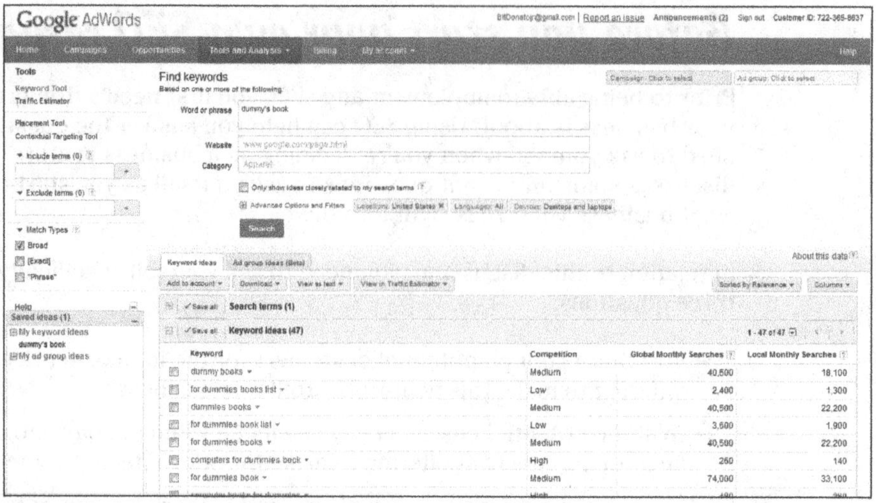

Figure 15-1:
Google's
Keyword
Toolbox
page.

From this page, you'll go to the AdWords Keyword Tool page at `https://adwords.google.com/o/Targeting/Explorer?__c=1000000000&__u=1000000000&ideaRequestType=KEYWORD_IDEAS` (see Figure 15-2):

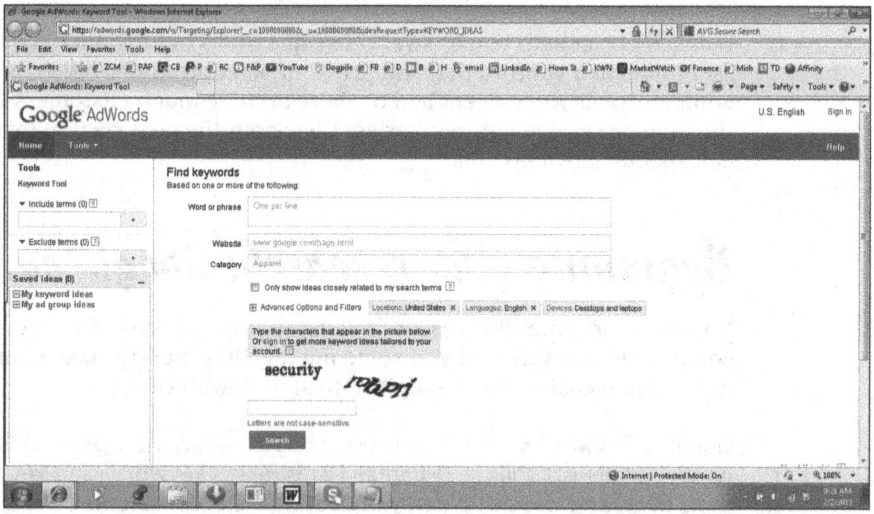

Figure 15-2:
Google's
AdWords
Keyword
Tool page.

The following sections walk you through how to use this keyword tool to your advantage.

Figuring out the keyword fields

You'll see several fields for you to fill out as well as some terms that you may not understand. You have a column on the left with a heading that says Keyword Tool and several fields to fill out.

The first field is terms you want to include. For example, say that you have what you thought was a terrific new business idea for big hunting knives, but you have no idea whether any people searched for that term or whether they would be willing to pay money for it. So in that first box of terms, you can enter "big hunting knives." If you didn't want any term specifically included, you enter it in the second field. So if for instance many people were searching for "Johnnie's big hunting knives" and adding the "Johnnie" to the phrase made the search refer to something unrelated, you can eliminate those results.

Choosing the match types

You next have to figure out which matches to choose. By choosing the right match type, you can fine-tune the results to exclude results that don't apply to your potential product and may give misleading results. You need to be aware of the three following potential matches:

- **Broad match:** This type of keyword match returns the greatest number of searches. But it's misleading because it also includes searches that aren't relevant to people you want to reach and that aren't for what you're offering. So in sticking with the same example as the previous section, it will find "big hunting knives," "big game needs big hunting knives," "hunting for big knives," and so on. In other words, it adds up all the searches that include these words in any order. The search terms may even be separated from each other by minor words.

- **Exact match:** The second type of search match is *exact,* which means the keyword tool only comes up with exactly your search terms in the exact order you specified: "big hunting knives." This search results in the fewest found items of these three types of matches.

- **Phrase match:** This third type finds only your search term phrase, although the words may be in a different order. So this match adds the searches for "hunting big knives," "big knives hunting," "knives hunting big," and so on — you get the idea — basically your search phrase term in any order. This match may give you a misleading impression of the commercial potential; it gives you more matches because it includes results that aren't your topic or relevant to your market.

Of these three types, gaining the most search results (such as the broad match) isn't necessarily better because it adds related searches.

Below where you designate the match is a help area. You can either search for something you're unsure of in the search box or click on one of the questions.

Working on the right-hand side

On the right-hand side of the page under the Find Keywords heading, you can enter keywords and specify whether you want to search for a term or search a specific website. These fields can also give you a category search so you can further focus your search.

In this example, search for a term and enter "big hunting knives" in the word or phrase box and hit the search button. Your search will result in related keyword ideas and their search volume. If you want to see what keywords a particular website is targeting, you can enter a website selection and hit enter. Google provides information on competition, trends, and how much AdWords advertisers were paying (which gave you an indication of commerciality), although Google has moved a lot of this information to its AdWords keyword tool (`https://adwords.google.com/o/KeywordTool`).

Logging in for all the information

To get the full range of information, you need to log in to your account. Your username and password is the same information you use to log in to other Google accounts (such as an email account at `www.gmail.com`). If you don't have an account at Google, you can set one up for free.

This AdWords page follows the same scheme as the keywords tool with one difference. You want to go down to the middle-right of the page where it says Columns and Click on All Columns. Doing so brings up additional information on competition, ad share, Google search network, search share, and approximate cost per click (CPC; the amount of money AdWords advertisers would have to pay per click; refer to Chapter 12 for more information on CPC). This process with CPC gives you a rough indication of commerciality. It can also give you an idea of local search trends and show you the web page if the information was extracted from a web page.

The difference between keywords when you're designing your website promotion is that you're trying to find what keywords people are searching for and what they're willing to whip out their wallets and spend money on. When discussing keywords in the sense of AdWords, you're basically looking at the same thing from the other side. How much are you, as an advertiser, willing to pay for someone who is using that search to come to your site? The more money an advertiser is willing to pay, the higher the advertising position and the more likely people will be to come to your site. (Refer to Chapter 12 for more info on AdWords.)

As a website owner and micro-entrepreneur, you need to know this difference because it can give you a very rough indication of what Google AdSense might pay you if you allow its advertising to be placed on you website. It's only a rough indication because Google doesn't divulge how it calculates the numbers. You do your best, take the check Google sends, cash it, and monitor your site.

Using other SEO tools

If you choose not to use Google, other SEO tools and software are available. You can check with the following sites, which have tools to help you do keyword checking and strategy, link popularity, and link checking and have ways to help you increase your ranking at major search engines.

- ✔ **Market Samurai** (`www.marketsamurai.com`)

- ✔ **SE Nuke** (`www.senuke.com`)

- ✔ **SEO Book Tools** (`http://tools.seobook.com`)

- ✔ **Self SEO** (`www.selfseo.com`)

- ✔ **Submit Express** (`www.submitexpress.com`)

- ✔ **Traffic Travis** (`www.traffictravis.com`)

- ✔ **UpCity SEO** (`www.upcity.com`)

- ✔ **Webconfs SEO** (`www.webconfs.com`)

- ✔ **Wordtracker:** This site (`https://freekeywords.wordtracker.com`) is free. You do have to sign up for a free account to use this free tool, and it will try to get you to sign up for a monthly subscription service.

Personally, I don't like subscription services because the cost can end up being far more than the use you make of it. You can get all you need from the free tools in this list. It just may take some more time and effort.

Hiring an SEO consultant

Although doing your own SEO is easier than ever, you may just not have the time to really pursue how implementing a strong SEO plan in your web presence can build your business. If so, you may want to hire the services of an SEO expert.

Finding an expert to help you perform your SEO strategies isn't difficult. Furthermore, it may be some of the best money you'll ever spend. If you do want to hire an SEO expert, you may want to search for one in the following places:

- ✔ **Search Engine Marketing Professionals Organization** (`www.sempo.org/`)

- ✔ **SEO** (`www.seo.com`)

- ✔ **LinkedIn** (`www.linkedin.com`). You can find an active group of professional SEO experts available for hire called "SEO Expert" (go figure!).

- ✔ **Elance** (`www.elance.com`) and **Odesk** (`www.odesk.com`)

If all you need is a quick SEO optimization for your website or blog, you may be able to find someone who can inexpensively do it on micro-task sites, such as Fiverr (`www.fiverr.com`) and Gigzon (`www.gigzon.com`). Check out Chapter 19 for how you can outsource this task.

Making Yourself Findable

After you set up your website or blog, you want to make sure people can find you when they're searching for a service or product that's in line with what you offer. These sections explore the use of keywords and links to help people find you. You can also use listing services and the search engines themselves to get listed.

Using keywords

When people search for a product or service, they will type keywords in their favorite search engine. *Keywords* are the search terms (such as words or phrases) that people will enter in their search efforts. I discuss keywords in this chapter and also in Chapter 12.

Take the time and find out what people search for because it will definitely pay off for you. You can adjust your site(s) so that your prospective customers can more easily find you.

You can make sure that your keywords are present in the following ways to increase your prospects finding you:

- ✔ **Meta tags:** *Meta tags* are keywords that are embedded in the coding of web pages. They're technically not the same as keywords that are in the visible text of the web page. Your web page designer or your web page software can place meta tag words of your choice in the coding. Many search engines use them in their search criteria. You can actually view the meta tags when you use the "View Source" feature in your browser software (such as Windows Explorer) and even edit the words (only do it if you're familiar with web page creation and design).

- ✔ **Headlines:** Make sure your page headings (and/or subheadings) have keywords.

- ✔ **In your content:** Make sure you have keywords strategically placed throughout your content.

- ✔ **Domain name:** Keywords in the domain name itself are helpful toward your SEO efforts.

- ✔ **Images:** Even images can be keyword optimized. Make sure that the image file name has keywords as well. For example, if your site has a picture of an umbrella and you want people to find it when they do a search for "umbrella," then make sure the image file name is "umbrella.jpg" or "umbrella.gif" depending on the image file format.

Making your website and/or blog easy to be found on search engines (getting them *optimized*) is certainly a priority, but you also want to keep in mind that any presence you post on any site (even if the site isn't your own) will help you to be found. Here are some other forms of web presence that you should optimize:

- ✔ **Your articles:** If you write articles and get them published at article database sites, such as www.ezinearticles.com, optimize them. Make sure that you have enough keywords strategically placed in your content.

- ✔ **Blog posts:** If you're writing posts for others (such as when you do guest blogging), remember those keywords so that you are easily found. If your prospective customers find you in the blog post (and, of course, you have a link to your site), then it boosts your marketing.

- ✔ **Your video channel:** People can easily find videos on YouTube and other video sites on the major search engines, so make sure that your videos and your video channel have the appropriate keywords in the title, description, and so on.

Try to include keywords in your content naturally, but don't overdo it because doing so can harm your site. The search engines will drop you like a hot potato if you do practices such as *keyword stuffing*, where you find devious ways to add lots of keywords in an attempt to elevate your site's exposure with the search engines and get your site ranked higher. Keyword stuffing is a big no-no, and it will harm your SEO efforts.

Increasing links to your site or blog

Another aspect of SEO is getting more links aimed at your site or blog. A *link* (also called *hyperlink* or *hypertext*) is specially coded text that users can click on to navigate to the web page or element of a web page associated with that link's code. A site that has 100 other sites linking to it (called *back links* because they link back to the desired web page or site) will have much more success than a site that has no other sites linking to it (all things being equal). Search engines that detect with their technology that more and more other sites are linking to you will rank you higher.

Even if several back links don't get you ranked higher on search engines, you still want lots of back links because the cumulative effects of those back links mean more traffic for your site.

Increasing links back to your page doesn't automatically happen. A website needs to make it happen. Either you can contact other websites to exchange links ("you link to me and I link to you"), or you can get various services that can perform this function for you. There are ample strategies for either approach (most will try to do both approaches). See the resources in the nearby sidebar, "Tapping into more general SEO resources," to find out more about how to do it.

To find out more about linking strategies, check out these resources:

- ✔ **Link Exchange** (www.link2me.com/)
- ✔ **Linking Matters** (www.linkingmatters.com)
- ✔ **Link Strategies** (www.linkstrategies.com)
- ✔ **Link Wheels** (www.linkwheels.net)

Getting your business listed on search engines and directories

Your website and/or your blog should be listed on the major search engines, and you should also make sure your business is listed and easily found on search engines.

If your business is in a public venue (such as in a mall or downtown), go to sites, such as GetListed.com (www.getlisted.com) and enter your business name and zip code so people can directly find your business. It tells you whether you're listed on the major search engines such as Google, Bing, Yahoo!, and so on.

If you aren't listed, you can go to any of the major search engine sites and use their own search engine to do a search for "how to list a business on (insert your topic)." It's relatively easy to do.

In addition, these sites have both free and paid services to submit your website to major search engines:

- ✔ **Add Me** (www.addme.com)
- ✔ **Add Pro** (www.addpro.com)
- ✔ **World Submit** (www.worldsubmit.biz/)

You can also do a search for others and compare services.

Keep in mind that you can boost your SEO with business directories too. Manta (www.manta.com) is a large and popular directory, and you can create a free searchable listing for your business.

Tapping into more general SEO resources

If you want to keep up-to-date on the happenings of what's going on in the world of search engine optimization, you can look up these sites. These resources are primarily about informing you with the latest news, views, and strategies to improve your search engine marketing efforts:

✔ **Search Engine Journal** (www.searchenginejournal.com)

✔ **Search Engine Land** (www.searchengineland.com)

✔ **Search Engine News** (www.searchenginenews.com)

✔ **Search Engine Roundtable** (www.seroundtable.com)

✔ **Search Engine Watch** (www.searchenginewatch.com)

✔ **SEO Logic** (www.seologic.com)

✔ **SEO Moz** (www.seomoz.com)

✔ **SEO by the Sea** (www.seobythesea.com)

✔ **Webmaster World** (www.webmasterworld.com)

Many excellent blogs cover the world of search engine marketing and SEO strategies. One of them is TopRank Online Marketing Blog (www.toprankblog.com). They actually maintain an extensive listing of marketing blogs. You can find their list of blogs on search engines and SEO strategies at www.toprankblog.com.

If you're more of a book person, here are some great books on SEO optimization:

✔ *Search Engine Optimization All-in-One For Dummies,* 2nd Edition, by Bruce Clay and Susan Esparza (John Wiley & Sons, Inc.) (www.dummies.com)

✔ *Seo Fast Start* by Dan Thies. This is a free ebook on SEO strategies that you can find at (www.seofaststart.com).

✔ *Search Engine Optimization (SEO) Secrets* by Danny Dover and Erik Dafforn (www.wiley.com)

Chapter 16

Using Blogs and Ezines in Your Marketing Plan

....

In This Chapter

▶ Marketing with a blog

▶ Incorporating ezines in your plan

....

S etting up a website or blog is just the beginning to having a web presence and beginning your micro-business. Check out Chapter 4 for details on setting up a blog. Creating a blog or website though is only half the battle. The other half — the more important half — is all about marketing and how you can use your blog in that battle. This chapter is all about using your blog to market your business and your service or product.

Blogs and ezines are a great part of your arsenal, even if your business is essentially off-line. For example, say that you're a landscaper. You can use blogs and/or ezines to stay in touch with customers and prospects all year round. Marketing is more than a sales pitch or other obvious attempt to generate or increase revenue. It is also about cultivating business relationships with the idea that you're building the potential for revenue down the road.

In this chapter, I explain how you can use a regular blog, a video blog (both with a YouTube channel and at your regular blog), and an ezine to market your business. I use my own pursuits with these three to show you how to do it.

Choosing Whether You Want a Blog, Ezine, or Both

Before you start any type of marketing with a blog or ezine, you seriously need to think before you start one. A *blog* (a site that acts like an online journal with the writer's comments, views, and other content) and an *ezine* (an online newsletter) are typically ongoing entities, which mean that you're committed to growing them for more opportunities for selling more products and services.

Blogs and ezines are both forms of *content sharing,* which means you regularly offer content to your audience to keep them coming back (and hopefully grow your audience too). However, the main difference between the two is that a blog is basically stationary — people visit it at that fixed Internet location. The ezine is an opposite delivery method — the content visits the subscriber at his or her email address.

Sometimes the line between a blog and ezine gets blurred because many folks put their ezine content on their blog (or website) and simply send an email telling folks that their current issue is ready to read. The email has an active link that the subscriber just clicks, whisking them away to the blog. Here are more differences:

- **Blog:** Many blog hosts give you the ability to have subscribers. In other words, the blog has a subscription vehicle (maybe a button that says "subscribe to my blog now"), and the subscriber is automatically alerted when there is a new post at the blog.

- **Ezine:** Many ezine subscribers prefer that the content is actually sent as an email message so that the subscriber can simply and quickly read the issue or message right there in the inbox.

   Many ezines like to take a middle course. They directly send an abbreviated version of the content to the subscriber's email inbox but include a link back to the blog or website where the subscriber can see the full content ("click here to read the full article").

To determine whether to do a blog or ezine, choose by doing a two-step approach.

1. **Analyze your personal needs and decide on what you actually want to do.**

   If an important part of your strategy is developing a list of prospects, then go the ezine route. If an important part of your strategy is more ad revenue (like AdSense), then go the blog route.

2. **Research what others are doing in your niche.**

   Regularly visit your competitors' blogs and sign up for your competitors' ezines. Analyze what they do in terms of content and marketing. Sooner or later, you'll see the benefits and choose your path.

Using Your Blog to Make Money

Your primary goal with your blog is to market your business and product or service. When you have a blog, you need to know what your blog marketing strategy is. You basically can directly make money with your blog or indirectly use it as a stepping stone to other venues that can make you money. These sections examine how you can implement these two strategies.

Making money directly

As a micro-entrepreneur, you're offering goods and services, and your blog can strategically help you do so. Although some people write blogs for the love of the topic, in this case, you're writing and doing your blog because you love the topic and want to make money.

To make money with your blog, you basically package or self-publish your knowledge, information, experience, research, and so on as information products (ebooks, audios, videos, and such; Chapter 10 tells you how to do so) or if you're creative, you make your products (in the form of arts and crafts; flip to Chapter 6). You can have either products or services that you already offer, or you can create products and services. You can then use your blog to promote your offerings so prospective customers will buy them.

Consider these examples that show how you can use your blog to make money:

- A corporate security expert does a blog to cover the world of security and may include articles and news items related to the world of security. Doing so draws an audience so that he can raise his profile and his brand and find customers.

- An interior designer does a blog to showcase both good and bad examples of interior design. The blog showcases (pardon the pun) her knowledge and good taste in a public venue.

- Your humble author writes, speaks, and consults about business and financial matters. I package my knowledge as ebooks and audio programs for sale, both online and offline. If I write a blog post on investing (www.mladjenovic.blogspot.com), for example, I place links from that post to an appropriate audio seminar at my ecommerce site www.ravingcapitalist.com.

Packaging or self-publishing your knowledge, information, experience, research, and so on as information products (ebooks, audios, videos, and such) isn't that difficult (find out more in Chapter 10). If you're creative, you have the ability to do a variety of arts and crafts that are fun to make and profitable.

Making money indirectly

You can certainly make money without offering your own products or services. In fact, you can earn great money by selling what others offer. Plenty of sources also offer commissions when you place their affiliate links on your blog posts. Check out Chapter 11 for sources that can post on your blog as affiliates.

Doing both

Just because you offer your own stuff doesn't mean you should limit your ability to make money with other people's stuff too. Consider doing both direct and indirect marketing on your blog to expand your ability to make money. I do a blog on investing and home business start-up. I have my own products, but I'm also comfortable working with many other great merchants that offer products and services in my niche.

For example, if you sell nutritional supplements and you see a merchant that you trust that offers exercise equipment or a weight-loss program, the merchant's offering can be a good fit with your nutritional supplement. Just check out the merchant to see if it offers any other items that may compete with you. Then when you do a blog post on nutrition (along with links to your sales page for your offering), you can offer that merchant's stuff in several possible ways.

You can also use the merchant's affiliate program in co-marketing or in follow-up marketing. Co-marketing means that you include the link to the merchant's product or service with your product. When folks buy your product, they can see a sales page (say, for the exercise equipment or weight-loss program) with the affiliate link. In follow-up marketing you can send a "thank you for your purchase" message along with a sales page with the merchant's affiliate link. This all flowed from your initial blog post on your topic.

Promoting Your Blog

Your blog doesn't exist in a vacuum. If you have gone to the trouble to display your knowledge and the value of what you have to offer, you want to let the world know about it and market with your blog. Marketing with your blog takes an overall strategy, and you need to regularly upkeep it so people know who you are and you can build your audience. These sections cover some immediate blog marketing strategies that can build your audience relatively quickly.

What better way to figure out how to use your blog as a marketing vehicle than to regularly check out those blogs that are doing marketing successfully:

- ✔ **Blogging Basics 101** (www.bloggingbasics101.com)
- ✔ **Blogging Bits** (www.bloggingbits.com)
- ✔ **Blogging Tips** (www.bloggingtips.com)
- ✔ **DailyBlogTips** (www.dailyblogtips.com)
- ✔ **Lorelle on Word Press** (www.lorelle.wordpress.com)
- ✔ **Pro Blogger** (www.problogger.net)
- ✔ **Successful Blog** (www.successful-blog.com)

Getting listed in search engines and blog databases

When marketing with your blog, make sure that your blog is listed in the major search engines. Initially, people, beyond the ones that you directly invite, won't visit your blog just because it's online; the rest will find you only because they've done an online search, usually for information on a given topic. You want your blog (or website) to show up in the search results when they're looking for your topic and their search engine finds you. You just have to make it happen.

Your blog needs to be prepped for the search engines. Your blog will need the right keywords, tag lines, and so on. Chapter 15 goes into greater detail about how you can make sure you show up in search engines.

In addition, you want to make sure you blog shows up in various blog databases. The following are three great blog databases that can help your blog be found. They'll all generally ask for information, such as your blog's title, web address, category, and so on.

- ✔ **Blog Roll** (www.blogroll.com)
- ✔ **Blog Digger** (www.blogdigger.com)
- ✔ **Blogarama** (www.blogarama.com)
- ✔ **Blogbuzzer** (www.blogbuzzer.com)
- ✔ **Feed Shark** (www.feedshark.brainbliss.com)
- ✔ **Pingates** (www.pingates.com)
- ✔ **Pingler** (www.pingler.com)
- ✔ **Ping-o-matic** (www.pingomatic.com)
- ✔ **Sphere** (www.sphere.com)
- ✔ **Technorati** (www.technorati.com)

Doing a micro-tasking blast

You can also utilize micro-tasking websites, such as Fiverr (www.fiverr.com), to market your blog. When you go to these types of sites, you can find all sorts of offerings for only five dollars (or another small amount of money) that can be a good test for your marketing purposes. After you acquire the gig, the boost to your traffic can be immediate. Because these service providers already have their audience (Twitter followers, ezine subscribers, or Facebook fans), you quickly can tap into their audience.

For example, you can find where folks are offering the following:

- ✔ "I will tweet your message or link to my 3,000 followers."
- ✔ "I will tell my 5,000 fans and friends on Facebook about your new product, service, or blog post."
- ✔ "I will get you 2,000 views to your YouTube video within 48 hours."

You can find many more gigs like this. Some may have value and some don't, but for five bucks, what do you have to lose? Using a micro-tasking site may be worth a try, but if you do so, make sure you monitor the results by choosing those gigs that provide verification. For example, if it's a tweet to their Twitter followers, you can also be a follower on their list (be anonymous if possible or get a second account and be a follower) and check if the tweet was sent. In the event that you aren't satisfied, Fiverr can withhold payment (in the worst-case scenario, you lost five bucks, but you won't use that source again).

Some marketers have used micro-tasking sites with worthwhile results and have purchased again from the same source. Others kept trying until they found decent results. It can vary, so investigate the potential. You can find more information about micro-tasking sites and other forms of outsourcing in Chapter 19.

Using multiple blogs

Some marketers may have several blogs that market the same offering but do so in several entirely different ways. Maybe they do a primary blog that they regularly update, but maybe they also do a second blog that is more static (doesn't change much) but has different key words, different content, and so on that leads visitors to the same sales page for the same product. Some do three very different blogs, but they all send traffic to the same offer.

Utilizing more than one blog in this manner is a perfect example of the funnel principle to leverage your ability to get results. You may have one blog that sells informational products on losing weight. You may consider creating another blog that does product reviews on various weight loss programs (along with affiliate links where appropriate). Creating and running another blog is low cost (even free). You can then monitor the results to see which approach works best. Chapter 4 provides some insight for setting up a blog.

Guest blogging

The practice of *guest blogging* is where you can write an article (the *post*) at someone else's already established and well-trafficked blog. This is like piggybacking on someone else's successful blog and can be a great way to market your offerings. It can simultaneously help you get visitors to your blog (or subscribers to your ezine sign-up page) as well as elevate your reputation (or brand). In fact, consider guest blogging a must in your overall marketing action plan . . . regardless of what you're offering.

Guest blogging isn't that difficult. If you want to guest blog, keep these points to keep in mind:

- ✔ **Get familiar with the blog that you want to write for before you make any inquiry about writing.** Read it thoroughly and regularly. Get to know it inside and out. Make it a point of reading any guest blogs you come across and analyze their content. Look at what and how they utilize their guest posts from a marketing point of view.

- ✔ **If possible, go to the blog and regularly make comments on blog posts and regularly email the writers in a positive and professional manner.** Doing this can elevate your exposure at the blog and build rapport with both the blog's audience and participants.

- ✔ **After some time has passed (a few weeks of activity or longer) and you have developed some rapport, inquire about what the blog's guidelines and needs are regarding guest posting.** Many successful blogs welcome guest posts, especially if they believe that their blog and/or audience can benefit from that person's content.

- ✔ **After you review the blog's requirements, submit a blog post that comes as close as possible to what the blog's stated desires are.** Write your post so it's similar in look and feel to the blog's other posts. Ask a trusted friend to proofread or edit it. Make sure the post is in-line with your marketing purpose. Avoid any hard sell when you guest blog (or you may not be invited back). Use the platform to build awareness of you and your blog. If links are allowed (usually at least one link is), then link to your blog (no affiliate link in your initial blog). Any link may be to a free offer at your blog. Most guest blogging is done for free (you give them content and they give you exposure).

In addition to this list, find out as much as you can about guest blogging. These resources offer lots of information about effective guest blogging:

- ✔ **Blog Guests** (www.blogguests.com)

- ✔ **Guest Blog It** (www.guestblogit.com)

- ✔ **Guest Blogging Guide** (www.guestbloggingguide.com)

- ✔ **My Blog Guest** (www.myblogguest.com)

Doing some video blogging

You can create a video, post it to YouTube (www.youtube.com), and then share it with others right through your blog. A *video blog* allows you to express yourself visually to your audience. Whether you're sharing opinions, information, or a sales message, a video can be a powerful way to communicate. When you do it at YouTube, you can add a title and text in the description (and links to any sites or sales pages). At YouTube, you can share your video with others in two ways:

- ✔ **A link:** You can place the link for your video on your blog, ezine, social media, or in a simple email message.

- ✔ **An embedded HTML code:** You can incorporate this code in your website or blog. (You can also include it in other venues, such as Google+ and Facebook). If you use this approach, be sure to indicate at your YouTube channel (where all your YouTube videos reside) not to "show suggested videos when the video finishes" because it may show competitors videos when your video ends.

I do a financial and business blog at www.mladjenovic.blogspot.com, but I don't always write something. Sometimes instead I post a video. I use my YouTube channel (feel free to view it at www.youtube.com/paulmlad). In my case, I can take that embedded HTML code and place it into my blog post (at YouTube, the coding can easily be cut and pasted from there straight into your blog post). Then visitors can view the YouTube video right on my blog. I could have the video either in place of text or in addition to text. I like to title my blog post and then provide introductory text just before the video with some added text afterwards that encourages the viewer/reader to click on a link to an appropriate offer or other consideration (such as opt-in to my list).

You can then integrate your YouTube channel, blog, and ezine (refer to the next section for more about ezines) with Facebook, Twitter, and other social media, which expands your potential as both a publisher and marketer. Refer to Chapter 17 for more on using social media in your marketing plan.

Doing an Ezine

An *ezine* (an *email magazine,* also known as an *electronic newsletter* or simply an *email newsletter*) is a form of communication where you email your subscribers a periodic publication on a particular topic.

In these sections you can see how an ezine can be an important component of your marketing strategy. You can discover what to write about and who to send it to by building your list of prospects.

Thousands of ezines are online that you can read to improve yours. One of the best ways to educate yourself is to carefully watch others. You can see what to do and what not to do. Ezines cover almost every topic you can think of, and some that make you think. Here are some ezine directories to help your search:

- **Best Ezines** (www.bestezines.com)
- **Email Universe** (www.emailuniverse.com)
- **The Ezine Directory** (www.ezine-dir.com)
- **New List** (www.new-list.com)

If after reading these sections you want more detailed information about the world of ezines, I suggest you check out these resources for additional help:

- **Alexandria Brown:** For many years she has been known as the "Ezine Queen" and offers great guidance on launching and maintaining an ezine at www.alexandriabrown.wordpress.com.

- **Charlie Page:** Charlie Page is an ezine expert and maintains an extensive directory of ezines at www.charliepage.com. He has written about ezine publishing since the late 1990s.

- **ebook Crossroads:** This site (www.ebookcrossroads.com) has a great section on email newsletter publishing.

- **National Association of Independent Writers and Editors:** This site (www.naiwe.com) has loads of great guidance on writing and editing.

- **Self-Publishing Resources:** This site (www.self-publishing resources.com) has lots of great self-publishing resources applicable to ezine publishing.

- **The Site Wizard:** This site (www.thesitewizard.com) has an extensive section on ezine publishing.

Don't forget to check out the writing resources and strategies in Chapter 9 and the publishing resources in Chapter 10 because they go so well with publishing blogs and ezines.

Knowing what to write about in your ezine

To start sending out an ezine, you have to choose a topic — one that you have a passionate interest in. Focus on your niche — what your product and service or business are about. Writing an ezine, even one where the text for a partial issue is brief, is an ongoing undertaking. Doing so takes a lot of patience and perseverance to create a successful ezine. Whether you're writing and sending it out daily, weekly, monthly, or even quarterly, you need to have an ongoing replenishment of content.

Creating fresh, interesting content isn't always easy, but many publishers find other ways to satisfy the need for content. Some get content at article database sites (refer to the later section on article databases for some specific resources).

If you use your creativity, you can come up with plenty of ideas for content. For example, I subscribe to a newsletter that regularly provides great quotes on liberty. Another ezine I get has great tips and quotes on the world of business. Other ezines do a joke of the day or a recipe of the month. Some others do headlines from the general news that may apply to their particular niche along with commentary tying the headline to how the item affects the niche.

Subscribe to as many ezines as you can that are tied to your topic. Doing so can give you plenty of material and ideas. I don't suggest that you use other people's material; reading these other ezines can spur on your creativity and thinking for fresh content in your ezine.

If you do see an article that you find compelling enough to share with your audience, contact the ezine's publisher and ask for permission to reprint it. Most ezine publishers would probably react favorably to such an inquiry. More than likely, they'll allow you to reprint it as long as you properly attribute it.

In fact, I've reprinted articles on my Prosperity Alert newsletter. When I'm drawing a blank about what to write, I check some of my favorite financial websites and blogs, find a good article on investing or a related matter, get permission to reprint it, and voila, I have content. You can always find good content, and writers and editors are usually happy to oblige reprinting it, especially when they receive good exposure from doing so.

Building a list

Creating a list of people interested in what you have to offer and then and cultivating it is critical to the success of an ezine. In fact, getting a list to grow is essential for a successful ezine. For good reason, after all, if you have no list of readers, then you have no point in spending time doing an ezine. Building a list means more money in due course for your business. Just remember this simple calculation:

More readers = more subscribers = more opportunities for revenue

These sections focus on the ways most successful ezine publishers build their lists:

Offer something free that your target market would like

Take a look at how other ezine publishers market their ezine. The odds are good that they give away some freebies to boost subscriptions. The most typical give-aways are digital reports or ebooks that offer content that is perceived as valuable to new subscribers.

Use a subscription box

The easier you make it for folks to subscribe to your ezine, the bigger your subscriber list. The *subscription box* (where your customers subscribe) can be as simple as a button that your visitors click, which then takes them to a page where they can easily sign up for a subscription to your ezine. Figure 16-1 shows an example — the subscription box I currently use.

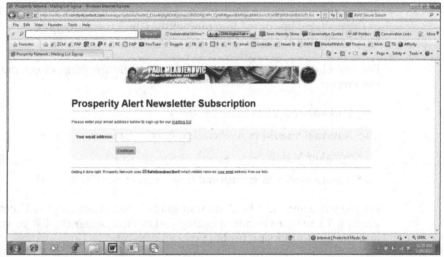

Figure 16-1:
My subscription box for ezine signups.

Illustration courtesy of Paul Mladjenovic

My bulk email service provider supplied this sign-up page. You can find these firms in the "Using bulk email service providers" section later in this chapter.

Do public speaking

For micro-entrepreneurs, doing public speaking is a great way to make money directly, but it's also a fantastic way to meet prospects and customers, gain exposure, build a list of ezine subscribers, and so on. In public speaking, your opportunities are only limited to your time, effort, and creativity.

Investigate the world of public speaking; you may be surprised at how many great ways you can build both your business and your subscriber list. First, look to your local board of education. Most of them have adult education programs so inquire with them. In addition, you can find adult education (and other forms of public speaking) in venues as varied as association meetings and conferences, corporate events, trade shows, local club meetings, public libraries, and so on.

I love to speak in public and teach, and I've been doing my seminars and classes nationally since 1986. In some of these events, I get crowds of 30, 40, or more. In others, I get smaller crowds. Regardless of the size, I'm in a room sharing my knowledge and information with folks that paid to be there. Just don't do a hard sell; they're already interested in your product. Just share your knowledge and what you offer.

Invariably, some of the students become clients for what I offer, and many of them signed up for my free newsletter (the Prosperity Alert — the ezine I make available at my blog and websites).

For more information about the world of public speaking, check out these resources:

- ✔ **LinkedIn** (www.linkedin.com)
- ✔ **National Speakers Association** (www.nsaspeaker.org)
- ✔ **Speaker Match** (www.speakermatch.com)
- ✔ **Toastmasters International** (www.toastmasters.org)

I could write an entire book on this single topic. (I actually do a seminar about it.) The more public speaking you do, the bigger the list you can create and the more sales and profits you can generate.

Swap ads

Ezine publishers commonly swap ads to build their subscriber lists. You offer to let another ezine publisher put a free ad in your ezine if it allows you to do the same. Doing so can be a little tricky because you have to work out a fair arrangement if the two ezines have a significant difference in their subscriber list sizes. If so, be creative when making an ad swap.

For example, if your list is 3,000 subscribers and the other ezine's list is 6,000 subscribers, you may work out an arrangement where you offer to run its ad twice in place of allowing you to run your ad once.

In addition, consider doing a *solo ad,* which is an advertisement that you pay the ezine publisher to send to their list and you are the only ad in that email blast. This will cost you but it is not that expensive and it is a great way to get your message to a targeted audience. If, for example, you sell software that is perfect for webmasters consider getting a solo ad to an ezine specifically for webmasters.

Trade subscription lists with other ezines

To build your subscription list, you may consider negotiating a trade with another ezine publisher. Offer to allow the other ezine publisher to email your subscribers in exchange for you emailing its subscribers. This type of deal is actually more common than you think. Just make sure that the other ezine is in a comparable niche.

If you let other ezines email to your list, make sure that you seed your list with some names of people that you personally know. *Seeding* is the act of putting anonymous names of people in the list for verification and security purposes. In other words, seeding the list is a good way to know if users of your list are acting according to the agreement that you negotiated. You don't want anyone abusing your list, which can damage your relationship with your subscribers (not to mention any potential fraud that may occur).

Join forums and discussion boards

Many forums have thousands of people who are interested in a particular niche or topic. If you spend time and regularly post at a particular forum, you can easily get noticed by many potential subscribers. Chapter 18 explains how you can use forums in your marketing plan.

Guest blogging

Guest blogging, which is good for both blogs and ezines, is one of the best ways to market yourself and what you offer. If you have something to offer, but you don't have an audience, then you can go to a source that has an audience, but doesn't have your particular offering. In the case of ezines, you can use guest blogging to build your subscriber list. When you do your guest blog, you can use a link to your ezine subscription (or opt-in) page. Refer to the earlier section, "Guest blogging" for more information.

Morph your articles' content into different formats

Many successful marketers take the same (even the exact) content and morph it into a variety of forms to multiply its usability and reach. They may do a blog post entitled "19 Ways to Look Younger" (for a health and beauty niche blog) and then turn it into an ezine article to email to their list and then do a YouTube video (and so on).

Of course, they don't haphazardly do it. The content may appear in a variety of formats, but it all has (or should have) the same focus — sending traffic to the right spot, which is a sign-up page for your ezine or a landing page for what you're offering.

For example, say you're doing a video version of your article and posting it at YouTube. At YouTube, you can have a description adjacent to the video. You can place a link in the description to have the viewers go to where they need to go if they're interested in what you're offering.

In addition to videos, you can also do audio blogging (or *audio podcasting*). With a simple digital recorder, you have the ability to create an audio that can be heard at your blog. Many folks create podcasts, and many venues can help. Find out more in Chapter 10.

Distribute press releases

Whenever you're doing any initiative or activity with your business, including something with your blog (such as a speaking program), it has publicity value. In other words, you can make an announcement about what you're doing in the form of a press release. If it gets published, it will give you (and what you offer, such as your ezine) added exposure, which can mean more traffic to your blog or website and a potential boost to your ezine subscriber list.

A *press release* is structured as if it were a news item, but in reality it's a form of marketing so that people can find out about you, your company, and/or your product or service. Media sources, who are always seeking appropriate information for their readers, listeners, and viewers, can receive your press release and choose to run it as news. Refer to Chapter 18 for how to draft a press release.

Market with articles

When you're writing an ezine, you're writing different articles that combined form the ezine. You should also consider writing articles for business-building and increasing your subscriber list for your ezine.

I remember one time I wrote an article about the economy and about some forecasts I was making. I had that article published in a couple of financial-oriented sites. Guess what? Within two weeks, more than 500 people emailed me, asking me about my ezine and my other offerings.

At the time, I didn't have a bulk email service to quickly and conveniently process those inquiries. A bulk email service can create an email list in a jiffy. Refer to the later section, "Using bulk email service providers" for more help.

Check out the next section for some great resources on how others do article marketing. You can see how to get your articles found in article databases (see the list in the next section).

Rely on article directories

Many places on the Internet serve as massive databases of articles. Writers contribute these articles to the directories' databases, and publishers are allowed to use the articles as posts in their websites, blogs, and/or ezines. The writers seek to use the articles for marketing purposes. The publishers use the articles as content. It's a win-win.

If you publish an ezine, consider being on both sides of the equation. As the publisher, consider writing articles that you can contribute to the article database so that others can run them in their venues. You can build your list with zero-cost marketing (When I say "zero-cost," I refer to actual costs involved. It will still mean some time and effort on your part.)

In addition, you can use some of the articles in the database that others have written when you have an occasional mental block and need a good fill-in article to satisfy your readers.

Here are some of the most active article databases that you can use:

- **Article City** (www.articlecity.com)
- **Articles Factory** (www.articlesfactory.com)
- **Ezine Articles** (www.ezinearticles.com)
- **Go Articles** (www.goarticles.com)
- **Ignite Point** (www.ignitepoint.com)
- **isnare** (www.isnare.com)

Flippa strategy for gaining subscribers

Flippa (www.flippa.com) is a site where domain names and entire websites are bought and sold. You can find those sites that have subscribers or a list of customers, which gives you the opportunity to buy a site for a relatively low amount and pick up possibly a valuable database of prospects.

For example, say that you're a wellness site, and you find a nutritional website being sold on Flippa for $150. If you knew that this site had 5,000 names, and your niche and the website's niche were close enough, then buying it could be a good deal.

In addition to Flippa, other websites that basically do the same are Website Broker (www.websitebroker.com) and Deal a Site (www.dealasite.com).

Attend conferences and trade shows

To build your ezine subscriber list, you can also be in a room of potentially hundreds or even thousands of potential subscribers at conferences or trade shows that focus on your niche. A good resource to find appropriate trade shows is the website Trade Show News Network (www.tsnn.com).

Mingle at LinkedIn and other groups

Publishers of blogs and ezines (and other self-publishers) have an active presence at LinkedIn (www.linkedin.com). You can also look up the groups on blog publishing and ezines. Maybe more importantly, search for those groups tied to your content. For example, if you have an ezine on sports memorabilia, find a LinkedIn group on that topic. Head to Chapter 17 for more information.

Ask current subscribers for referrals

What better source of growing your subscriber list than on your current list! Every now and then, ask your subscribers to forward an issue to their friends. Maybe you can give them an incentive, such as a free report or ebook. Most of the bulk email service providers do have a feature to help take advantage of referring a friend.

Create a viral report or ebook

You can also compile a report or write an ebook that you give away and then encourage the individuals who received it to also give it away. Make sure the report or ebook has plenty of links back to your email newsletter sign-up page. For more information on how to do an ebook, check out Chapter 10.

Turn to social media

Using Facebook, Twitter, and others is a powerful part of any micro-entrepreneur's marketing plan. They're free, and they can be very effective for any ezine publisher to get more subscribers. Refer to Chapter 17 for how to use social media to your advantage.

Market with your mobile device

With the advent of smart phones, tablets, and other mobile devices, a whole new world has opened as more and more people are able to view web pages and emails on their handheld devices. Check with your bulk email service provider about how to take advantage of mobile devices.

Using bulk email service providers

When you start doing your ezine, I suggest that you use a bulk email service provider because they have plenty of guidance and information on how to properly create and distribute an ezine. Here are the main ones to check out:

- **AWeber** (www.aweber.com)
- **Constant Contact** (www.constantcontact.com)

> ✔ **Get Response** (www.getresponse.com)
>
> ✔ **iContact** (www.icontact.com)
>
> ✔ **Mail Chimp** (www.mailchimp.com)

Most of these providers give you plenty of services besides merely blasting out your ezine to a group of readers on your list. In addition, they can do the following:

> ✔ They can integrate with Facebook and Twitter so that the world of social media can see your ezine and ideally provide a viral boost when others receive and forward it to their contacts.
>
> ✔ They can provide valuable information such as *open rates* (how many of those people receiving the email you sent actually opened it) and *click-through rates* (how many clicked on the links provided in that email).

Don't forget the legal side of ezines. There is a big difference between sending off an ezine to a group of people and spamming. *Spamming* is sending unwanted email, which can be illegal. An ezine is a wanted item in a subscriber's inbox; subscribers opt in and acknowledge that they're subscribing.

Make sure you find out about any legal obligations you may have. You obviously don't want to spam, but you also have to consider other points.

> ✔ Make sure you provide an easy way to *opt out* (request to be removed from the subscriber list and cease receiving emails).
>
> ✔ Include a privacy statement and policy explicitly at the blog site (or at the end of the email message) that tells the reader or visitor how you officially regard issues of privacy with any information you have or receive at your site. Assure readers that you won't spam them or make illegal solicitations. Look at the privacy statements at your competitors' sites and then place your own unique official statement at your site too.

Fortunately bulk email service providers are very familiar with laws pertaining to conducting large email campaigns and avoiding the incidence of spamming.

Advertising with your ezine

After you build an audience, keep in mind that others will pay to gain access to your list. In the same way you advertised to gain exposure to your target market, they will seek to do the same. You can be able to offer advertising in your ezine.

Find out how others are doing advertising. You can find these ezines in places like Best Ezines (www.best-ezines.com) Sign up to some ezines that are similar in size and content to yours. See how they do an advertising program with advertisers. You can even email them or go to their websites for advertising rates and information. Doing so can help you formulate your policy, pricing, and so on. You can offer advertising directly or indirectly:

✔ **Direct ezine advertising:** Advertisers can run ads in your ezine at a cost of $25 for a four-line classified ad or $95 for solo ads.

✔ **Indirect ezine advertising:** You can also offer advertising in your ezine indirectly. You can sign up your ezine to ezine advertising networks. A large advertiser of a product that your ezine is about wants to advertise with that network. Assume that the network has ten ezines on the topic with a total combined readership of 50,000 subscribers, and you're one of the ezines in that group.

Through this network, the large advertiser decides to run an ad at a set cost. In this case, the ad would run in all ten ezines, and they would get a *pro-rata share* (based on size of ezine subscribers) of the advertising revenue for that ad (after the network deducts its share).

I know someone who does a free ezine. It has great content and readers love it. The ezine has a huge audience because they're happy with the content. Even though the ezine is free, the publisher makes six-figures in sales. Wow! How could that be? The publisher generates revenue from advertising fees and affiliate commissions. Money from free content? I like it!

Chapter 17

Marketing through Social Media

---

*I*f you're going to socialize, then do so with business-building in mind. Everyone you meet has the potential to either be a prospect for what you have to offer directly, or an *intermediary* (a go-between) who can refer you to a potential prospect.

As a micro-entrepreneur, you strive to have a positive impact on everyone you come across, both online and offline, because people like to buy from people they like. Social media, such as Facebook, LinkedIn, and Twitter, can help you meet people and build relationships that can in due course translate into sales.

Just make sure you remember how to use social media. Social media is social first and foremost. You don't just jump into social media and launch your sales pitch. You'll more than likely turn off your audience if you put on a hard pitch for your products and services. No matter what the social media venue is (any social media that I mention in this chapter and any other that you find), be social first — and sell later.

This chapter gives you not only some general rules for success but also some strategies and resources for success in whichever social media you choose. The world of social media is too big for a single chapter to do justice, and it's certainly fast-moving and constantly changing. To help you keep abreast of what's going on, particularly from a business and marketing perspective, refer to some of my favorite places:

- ✔ **Facebook marketing** (www.facebook.com/marketing)
- ✔ *Facebook Marketing For Dummies* by Paul Dunay and Richard Krueger (John Wiley & Sons, Inc.)
- ✔ **Center Networks** (www.centernetworks.com)
- ✔ **HubSpot** (www.hubspot.com)
- ✔ **Marketing Profs** (www.marketingprofs.com)
- ✔ **Mashable** (www.mashable.com)
- ✔ **Social Media Examiner** (www.socialmediaexaminer.com)
- ✔ **Social Media Explorer** (www.socialmediaexplorer.com)
- ✔ **Social Media Today** (www.socialmediatoday.com)
- ✔ **Social Times** (www.socialtimes.com)

Focusing on the Rule of 250

When delving into the world of social media (both online and offline too), remember the Rule of 250, from the great Joe Girard (also known as the world's greatest salesman, according to the Guinness Book of Records).

The Rule of 250 is simple: Whenever you make a positive (or negative) impression on someone, you have the potential of having that same impression on 250 other people. According to some studies, the average person knows (more or less) about 250 people. These people range from family and close friends to coworkers and people that they know to some extent in some venue such as clubs, civic organizations, sports activities, and so on.

Look for the impact of this rule in your own life. You have probably been doing it, but you should be more aware of it because it certainly applies

to your own business. If you're going to be a good entrepreneur, think about your experiences as a customer.

When you had a great experience with a business, look to see how you behave and how you communicated with others. For instance, say you received a really good deal from someone or that they really did a great service for you. Recognize what you did and you reacted.

When you crossed paths with others (those folks among your 250), more than likely, you wanted to share that good deal with them and share your good experience with them. You may have said something like, "Hi Bob, how are you doing? Say I have to tell you about a great deal I got from the XYZ Company. It was great; I saved 30 percent on something that I really needed. In fact, it was the best deal I got all year." That's right.

Succeeding on Social Media: Follow Some Golden Rules

I want you to succeed beyond your wildest wealth-building dreams. Social media is indeed a megatrend within the greater megatrend of the great Internet digital era. To help you succeed using social media, I suggest you follow a few golden rules that are worth emphasizing to help you start and stay on the right path.

- **Focus on the social aspect first and then the business aspect.** There is a time and place for everything, and social media is no different. There is a time for being social with friends and a time and place for sales and marketing. Social media first and foremost is a way to keep in touch with friends and family. Before you use it to market your business, find out whether business talk is appropriate. Relate to people and find out their needs, wants, interests, and so on. Market research comes before marketing.

  For example, I once received a message from a college buddy. "How nice!" I thought, but I soon discovered that it was some type of business deal. He immediately went into a sales pitch — how sour it made me! He was eager to use this Facebook connection to leverage his business (I don't blame him really. I would like to see him succeed.) and make money.

- **Discover how the ropes work.** Every social media venue has its own quirks, rules, and so on, so take the time to figure them out before you do any attempt at selling.

- **Be a lurker.** Lurking sounds bad only in the offline world. In the online world, it's okay. No matter what the social media site, you can view other peoples' posts. Find out what they say and how they say it. Make yourself knowledgeable online. In the same way your mother told you that you would learn more by listening than by talking, you should read all the posts that are relevant to your field or topic before you start participating.

- **Watch others.** Focus on the activities of others within that media. Take notes about how they market themselves. Ask yourself why they're successful. Determine what makes them interesting or compelling. Look for any tactics, techniques, and strategies they use that you can duplicate. Focus on what the leaders in your niche are doing to build their business.

- **Rinse and repeat.** If you think that a single effort by you will yield riches, think again. Watch what happens and then measure the results, make any revisions, and then try again. Successful people try again. Failing people give up after one effort doesn't work.

- **Tread carefully because the world is watching.** Think twice before you post anything negative, including attacking someone or accusing someone of anything. Assume that anything you post could (if you aren't careful) come back to haunt you. It can range from embarrassment to the loss of clients to potential legal problems. As micro-entrepreneur, err on the side of being positive or just not posting at all.

Maximizing Your Time on Facebook

Facebook (www.facebook.com) is a worldwide phenomenon with approximately one billion users (give or take 100 million) and growing as of early 2013. People and businesses of all stripes participate to some degree on Facebook. As a micro-entrepreneur, Facebook offers so many opportunities for you and your business, so make sure you don't ignore this macro audience.

To be on Facebook, all you need is a pulse (along with an Internet connection and an email account, of course). You don't have to pay any fee to sign up and participate. You're probably already on as are many of your family, friends, clients, prospects, and associates.

Getting active means that you connect with people you know and you exchange comments about what is going on in your life and vice-versa. In the world of Facebook, you quickly pick up the lingo of friends, fan, and likes. If you're going to be active on Facebook, then you first need to get up to speed with this site so you can (secondly) profit by it. These sections give you a brief overview of Facebook and how you can use it to your advantage in your marketing plan.

If possible, have two profiles on Facebook: one personal and one business. You can post your usual activity about your family or dog on your personal site. On your business presence (or fan page; see the later section, "Creating a Facebook fan page" for more information), you can keep it professional and stick to business. Just keep in mind that you can't keep them entirely apart. Your prospects may be at your business site and stumble on your personal page. Let the world know what you do in business (you should be doing things that make you proud of being a micro-entrepreneur), but think two or three times about what you put on your personal presence. It can hurt you or your business-building potential.

Getting started on Facebook

To move forward from just providing a snarky comment to your friend's picture, you focus on your business. You can mingle in several different groups, depending on your niche. Find groups that your target market is in and get active. Read what people post. Ask open-ended questions. As in any forum, don't do any aggressive or pushy sales pitch. Take the time to build your network and connections.

You can also start to make connections with friends and colleagues. With Facebook, you can easily find people at places such as

- Your high school
- Your college or university

✔ Your hometown

✔ Your former employers

✔ An affinity organization (such as sports, business, or civic organizations)

As you build your profile, keep in mind where you can find like-minded folks who may be predisposed to think fondly of you.

Using Facebook to build your business

Your business belongs on Facebook because many of your prospects and clients are there, and you want to be rubbing digital elbows with them, right? Utilizing Facebook to communicate the positive aspects in an interesting way without aggressive sales pitches can yield good results for your business.

For instance, I see many of my friends and colleagues posting all sorts of things. Some of it's interesting, and some of it will make you scratch your head. You'll find that people are willing to share all sorts of personal information. I am not that crazy about doing that.

If you ever look me up on Facebook (paulmlad), you can find that I generally post items relevant to my business and my professional pursuits. Posting all sorts of personal information can make you vulnerable to some negative developments. Identity theft is a major problem in society, and you aren't sure who is looking at your Facebook activity. Be very scrupulous about what you post. Make sure that you don't post anything that could hurt or embarrass yourself or the people you can are about.

I saw one news item where burglars would see who was on vacation and then rob their homes while they were away. In addition, you don't know what will professionally harm you. If you're a consultant, for example, you don't need your clients to know what wacky things you were doing on New Year's Eve.

Given all that, Facebook should be part of your overall business strategy. Keep in mind these things that you can do:

✔ In your personal page, post links to your website, blog, or video channel.

✔ Build your brand by regularly offering content, such as news and views on your specialty.

✔ Network with colleagues, business partners, vendors, and potential clients.

✔ Exchange business ideas with those in your industry.

✔ Become a fan of those that you approve of or admire in business. A *fan* is anyone on Facebook that likes a particular Facebook page.

- Keep tabs on what your competitors are doing.

- Invite those people who you're connected with to participate in events, surveys, contests, and other things that build awareness of you and your business.

- Get opinions from friends and colleagues on various products, services, and perhaps business resources that can help you.

Don't stop there! You're only limited by your imagination and creativity.

Creating a Facebook fan page

As a business, you have the opportunity to set up a fan page for free. This fan page serves like a mini website where you can post images, ad copy, links, and so on. It's a great way to build your presence. Go to `www.facebook.com/pages/create.php`.

You can build your brand by sending a message to customers, friends, and others to "like" your fan page. "Likes" are a big deal on Facebook, because they help create good will and elevate your brand.

Using Facebook advertising

Perhaps you want to take it up a notch and do advertising. With Facebook, you can pay to reach your target audience, and Facebook makes it generally easy to do it within your budget.

You can do some very precise target marketing. Facebook shares with its advertisers lots of valuable demographic information. Say you provide a service and that you feel that your ideal market is female home-based entrepreneurs that are older than 50 and live in California. Facebook can give you that specific demographic.

In addition, the advertising can fit your budget. If you can only afford to advertise at a cost of $10 per day, Facebook can customize it so that your ad campaign stays within your budget. The ads can be on a *pay-per-view (PPV)* basis (anytime someone views a page with PPV, the advertiser is charged) or on a *pay-per-click (PPC)* basis. (PPC means that anytime someone clicks on an ad, the advertiser is charged.) You can find out more about these types of advertising methods in Chapter 12.

Relying on other Facebook marketing resources

Because Facebook is a huge presence on the Internet, you can find plenty of resources to help you do business with it. Here are some places to go to:

- ✔ **The Facebook Marketing Guide:** This guide (www.facebook.com/business/fmc/guides) is all about Facebook marketing straight from Facebook.

- ✔ **B2B Bloggers:** You can find plenty of Facebook marketing information and guidance from experienced marketers at www.b2bbloggers.com/facebook.

- ✔ **Free Facebook Tutorials:** This site (www.freefacebooktutorials.com) has lots of how-to guidance and information for novice and intermediate participants at Facebook.

You can also check out *Facebook Marketing For Dummies* by John Haydon (John Wiley & Sons, Inc.) for more information.

Focusing Your Attention on LinkedIn

For micro-entrepreneurs, LinkedIn (www.linkedin.com) is a prime resource for your business-building activities. If you haven't noticed, I have sprinkled it throughout the book where appropriate. Here is where I give more detailed information about how it can really help you. You can also read *LinkedIn For Dummies* by Joel Elad (John Wiley & Sons, Inc.) for more in-depth information.

Setting up your profile

Signing on to a basic account is free, and the environment at LinkedIn is geared for serious professionals. In fact, the total users reached more than 100 million during 2012, and it's still growing.

At LinkedIn, you set up your profile, which acts like a résumé (if you are or would like to be someone's employee) or a bio (if you're an entrepreneur). Remember that your profile acts like a salesperson on your behalf. At your profile, you can upload a picture of yourself and list your accomplishments and credentials.

Making connections

LinkedIn allows you to make connections with folks, and they make connections with others. You have the chance to connect with so many others that you may not have considered. You can review your connections' connections. If you see someone whom you want to be connected, you can ask your connection for an introduction.

For instance, maybe you're a software salesperson and you see that your connection has a connection who is a purchasing manager for a large real estate property management firm. You have real estate management software that could be perfect for them. This opportunity would be great for you, so ask your connection for an introduction with the purchasing manager.

Joining LinkedIn groups

One of the greatest aspects of LinkedIn is in the power of affinity groups. (*Affinity groups* are groups formed around a shared interest or common goal.) You can find all sorts of groups, ranging from groups of like-minded entrepreneurs and employees to groups tied to political, cultural, economic, and other concerns. When looking for groups, keep the following in mind:

- ✔ Find groups to stay informed about your industry or niche.

- ✔ Find groups where your clients are.

- ✔ Find groups where they discuss sales and marketing strategies.

- ✔ Be active in discussions at least weekly to build your personal brand.

- ✔ Keep track of how others are marketing themselves and if you think they're doing it well (or not).

- ✔ Consider starting your own group. Many micro-entrepreneurs have done so to build their brand. You can invite others to participate (such as joint venture partners and/or potential clients).

Maximizing your experience on LinkedIn can benefit your business-building efforts. The more you educate yourself on using the site, the more value you can gain from your time and effort. LinkedIn has free training resources found at `http://learn.linkedin.com/training/` so that you can become proficient with its functions and benefits. While there, check out the links to "Guide" sites that have specific how-to information for different profiles. You will find guides for small business, entrepreneurs, consultants, and others.

Marketing with Twitter

Twitter has been all the rage in recent years. Everyone's tweeting from President Obama and the Pope (he started tweeting in late 2012) to every celebrity and media-minded CEO. Twitter is an abbreviated form of communication called *micro-blogging*.

The world of Twitter has followers and those that are followed. They communicate by tweeting. A *tweet* is a brief message (only 140 characters long) that contains a succinct message and may contain a link to an article, a picture, or a video.

In these sections, I provide you with a bit more basic information about using Twitter in your marketing plan. You can also check out *Twitter Marketing For Dummies* by Kyle Lacy (John Wiley & Sons, Inc.) for more in-depth information.

Implementing strategies

Because Twitter is a great tool for announcing events (with tweets), keep in mind how you can use it in tandem with other media. You can enhance venues, such as blogs, websites, and video channels with Twitter. Try and tweet five to seven times per day.

The goal for a micro-entrepreneur when using Twitter is really quite simple:

- Follow the trends in your niche and the market leaders that are in your products and services.
- Comment on others' tweets.
- Tweet short helpful tips relevant to your niche.
- Tweet marketing messages to those that follow you without being too pushy.

For example, I do a YouTube channel with subscribers. I can integrate it with Twitter. This way, when I do a video and upload it to my channel, Twitter automatically sends an alert to my followers.

Furthermore, many bulk email service providers integrate with Twitter. This means that when you send an ezine, it's integrated with Twitter, and a tweet is automatically sent to your followers. (Check out Chapter 16 for more on how bulk email service providers can help your business.)

Keep in mind that the name of the game for you, as a micro-entrepreneur and a marketer, is to build your list of followers on Twitter. The more followers you have, the more people you can communicate to about what you are doing (and what you are selling).

Twitter can also help you do joint ventures. Consider doing a search using the resources at the next section and even on Twitter at (`www.search.twitter.com`) for keywords.

For example, say that you're an interior designer looking for more clients. Do a search for words and phrases tied to interior design to find those conversations, Twitter groups, and companies that are discussing interior design, or you can follow those that need or use interior designers.

With some creativity (and the following Twitter resources), you can tremendously boost your business.

Relying on other Twitter resources

These resources can help you better utilize for marketing and for market research:

- **Social Brand Index** (`www.socialbrandindex.com`)
- **Twellow** (`www.twellow.com`)
- **Twibs** (`www.twibs.com`)
- **Twiends** (`www.twiends.com`)
- **Twitalyser** (`www.twitalyzer.com`)
- **Twit Town** (`www.twittown.com`)
- **Twitter Snipe** (`www.twittersnipe.com`)

To give yourself a boost with not only Twitter but also with other social media (such as Facebook and LinkedIn), consider outsourcing (flip to Chapter 19). You want to boost your marketing efforts and for a relatively small fee.

For example, I needed a boost to my total number of followers on Twitter. I went to Fiver (`www.fiverr.com`) and paid $5 to someone to boost my list of followers by 2,500 people. In addition, I was able to pay $5 to have my message tweeted to thousands of folks on that person's list of followers.

Considering Other Social Media Sites

You can also look into other social media sites that can provide a marketing boon to your micro-business. Here are a few more.

Squidoo

Squidoo (www.squidoo.com) is a social site that focuses on content-sharing. It's a great place to find some great articles on all sorts of how-to topics. Users can view an article (or other content such as an audio or video) through a *lens*.

For the marketer, Squidoo is a way to market your product or service and business by offering content. When participants at Squidoo like your content, they can be receptive to what you have to offer for sale. These sections give you an overview to using Squidoo.

Putting links in your content

One of the simplest ways to make money (or to do your marketing) is to put links in your articles. You can hyperlink text in your articles (for example) that the reader can click and be able to go to your website, blog, video, or your landing page that sells a product or service for which you're an affiliate.

Just keep in mind that whatever you sell or are connected to, make sure that it's closely matched to whatever content (such as your article) you're sharing. Some people view a product review and then include links to that product so that they can get an affiliate commission.

Advertising on Squidoo

Squidoo makes its money from advertising. But in the same way the folks share their content through lens; Squidoo shares its advertising revenue with those folks that provide the content. Half of Squidoo's advertising revenue goes into a pool of revenue that is divvied up among those providing the content. Find out more about how you can take advantage of it at Squidoo.

Pinterest

Pinterest (www.pinterest.com) burst out on the scene in 2011. It's a site where participants share pictures and other images with each other. For example, someone may love a particular book, so they "pin" (upload or provide a link to) a picture of it to share. Maybe someone really enjoyed a particular movie so he or she pins the movie poster or graphic.

You can participate on Pinterest by pinning pictures of products or providing videos of interest that are tied to what you offer.

Here are some resources to help you succeed on Pinterest:

- ✔ Pinterest marketing guide (`www.pinterest.com/marketingprofs/free-marketing-resources`
- ✔ Pin Forums (`www.pinforums.com`)
- ✔ Copy Blogger's Guide to Pinterest (`www.copyblogger.com/pinterest-marketing`)

Using other sites

Connecting with potential customers and building business relationships is the whole point of your business being on social media sites. Find out about all the major ones and make a plan to focus on a couple to see if their venues can help your business. Investigate these sites because sometimes they can prove to be useful to your business pursuits:

- ✔ **Bebo** (`www.bebo.com`)
- ✔ **Flickr** (`www.flickr.com`)
- ✔ **Google**+ (`http://plus.google.com`)
- ✔ **MySpace** (`www.myspace.com`)
- ✔ **Stumble Upon** (`www.stumbleupon.com`)
- ✔ **Tumblr** (`www.tumblr.com`)
- ✔ **Xing** (`www.xing.com`)

Chapter 18

Implementing Other Marketing Strategies

Consider this chapter a potpourri of marketing strategies that you can apply for your business. (By the way, if you're selling potpourri, then go to Chapter 6 on selling arts and crafts.)

This chapter focuses on the power of the written word in marketing your business. Here I discuss how you can incorporate several options, including articles, publicity and press releases, and forums, into your marketing plan.

Writing Articles to Market Your Business

Everyone has the ability to write interesting articles. Doing so isn't that difficult, even if you feel you can't put together a clear thought. The power you can get from even a single article can be amazing. Article marketing should definitely be a part of any business-building strategy.

I recall an article I wrote for several financial websites, and within a day or two I got more than 100 new subscribers to my email newsletter. I have also done an article and made a few hundred in sales of my products within 24 hours.

These sections discuss the nuts and bolts of this great strategy, including how you can implement article writing into your marketing plan, where you can send your articles, and how you can build profits.

Grasping how article writing works

An article can market almost anything (okay, don't go crazy). Whether you're looking to get visitors to a website, a blog, a video, or even an auction listing, as long as it has a link, it can work in the context of an article. In article marketing, the article you write is a way to get readers to begin a journey by linking to what you offer. (By the way, videos are all the rage, although article marketing is still strong. Check out Chapter 10 where I discuss how to create videos.)

Note: This type of article writing is different than what I discuss in Chapter 9. Those articles are the end product; you're making money from actually writing the article.

Even though the article's main purpose is to get people to link to your online platform, the content must still have value. You want potential customers to see some value in reading the article and linking to your platform. Be persistent and write a marketing article every week. Many businesses have been able to do this and add thousands to their bottom line. Your article marketing can take a couple different forms:

✔ **Paid article marketing:** Even if you're getting paid for the article, you can still do article marketing. Of course, you have to do it tactfully so that the site paying you for your article doesn't get annoyed that your purpose was purely marketing (when it should be 100 percent content). To find out more about writing articles (and other forms of writing) for payment, go to Chapter 9.

✔ **Free article marketing:** You can also build up your distribution list for your articles and spread your articles across cyberspace. As I pick up more websites that want to run my articles, I keep building my distribution list. Sometimes I have sent an article at 8 a.m., and the article has shown up on literally dozens of sites by lunchtime.

✔ Imagine if you had an article that gets published on 10, 20, or 30 sites. It can translate into thousands of people viewing and maybe hundreds clicking on your links to view what you have to offer.

Knowing where to send your article

Any website or blog that reports, writes, or covers your topic is a candidate for your articles, even if the site isn't obvious about accepting articles. As a leading negotiation expert remarked, everything in life is negotiable (well, almost). It is even truer online. If you have valuable content (your article) and the site needs content, you have an opportunity.

Content is king on the Internet, which means more marketing potential for you. Here are some places to consider both to research for your articles and also to find places to post your article:

✔ **Specialized search engines:** Search for sites that can use your content with specialized search engines where possible or available. Many specialized search engines only search a particular topic. You can find them at places, such as Search Engine Guide (www.searchengineguide.com) and Search Engine Colossus (www.searchenginecolossus.com). You can also find more search engines and discover how to use them in your marketing plan in Chapter 15.

✔ **Meta-search engines:** *Meta-search engines* cast a wider net across many areas compared to the search engines in the previous bullet. A meta-search engine does a single search simultaneously across many search engines. A good example is Dog Pile (www.dogpile.com), which uses Google, Yahoo, and a batch of other search engines in a single search and gives you the results. You can find out more about meta-search engines in Chapter 15 as well.

✔ **Specialized directories:** A *specialized directory* is a website that has gathered an extensive database or collection of organizations, individuals, or other entities or resources in a particular way. Some directories simulate Yellow Pages and others list data according to industries or specific interests. To look for companies in any niche or geographic area, I suggest you use Super Pages (www.superpages.com). Plenty of others are scattered across the Internet. Investigate to see whether one covers your content. Just do a search for directories using the search engines earlier in this list. You can also find more in Chapter 15.

✔ **Similar sites:** This type of site (www.similarsites.com) will help you find sites that are similar in content. Say you wrote an article on wellness at a wellness site and you want to find similar sites. This site allows you do so. Another great site is More of It (www.moreofit.com) that does the same thing.

✔ **Article databases:** You can place your articles at these sites, also called *article databanks,* and have access to many sites that would run your articles in their blog or website. Some to consider include

 • **Article City** (www.article-city.com)

 • **Ezine Articles** (www.ezinearticles.com)

 • **Go Articles** (www.goarticles.com)

You can use the website www.similarsites.com to find more.

✔ **Technorati:** This site (www.technorati.com) is the most active database of blogs. Blogs constantly need content, so submit your article for them. Find the active ones and find out about getting your content there (in the form of guest blogging). Check out Chapter 16 for more about marketing with and at blogs.

✔ **Social media sites:** Sites such as Squidoo (www.squidoo.com) and Facebook (www.facebook.com) are perfect for posting your articles because they have lots of traffic, and a good article can generate a lot of attention. Chapter 17 has more information about how you can use social media for your business and marketing pursuits.

Pointing to profits

With article marketing, you provide the content to generate interest and traffic to your website or blog where prospective customers can then click on a link so they can view your services or products. If you're selling a low-cost item, the link can be to a direct sales page where they can buy immediately. If you're selling a higher-cost item or you provide a more complicated transaction (such as signing a membership or other continuity program), then the link can go to a page that provides more details.

No matter what you're selling, you can use links to dovetail with article marketing and increase your profits. Here are some ways you can make money with article marketing:

✔ You can provide links to what you directly profit from, such as your products and/or services.

✔ You can sell a Kindle book (or other book or product) at Amazon. Other vendors (such as Barnes & Noble) do similar offerings. Refer to Chapter 10 for how you can write a Kindle or other type of ebook.

✔ You can build your list of subscribers. They become prospects for what you're later selling.

✔ You can sell digital products (such as ebooks, reports, or audio programs) at places such as e-junkie (www.e-junkie.com) and Payloadz (www.payloadz.com).

✔ You can join affiliate products with places such as Clickbank and Commission Junction. (You can find out more about affiliate marketing in Chapter 11.)

✔ You can create videos and link to them at your YouTube channel. Refer to Chapter 10 for how to make videos.

✔ Be creative and research to see what else you can sell by having people click on a link.

Using Publicity and Press Releases

The main theme for this section that I want you to remember is actually just one word — newsworthy. This word can help you open up an entire world of free advertising for you and your business.

The media world needs news to inform its audience. In fact, a large variety of different media outlets need an ongoing, relentless supply of news to satisfy their large variety of audiences. This is where you come in.

No matter the specific media outlet (magazine, newspaper, website, and so on), content (news, commentary, and so forth) is their lifeblood. They need to hold (and hopefully grow) their audience, because a large and growing audience means (ideally) a large and growing advertising revenue. It is a simple equation:

> More readers or viewers = More advertising revenue

Media outlets want to inform and entertain their readership (viewership, listenership, or some other ships), and you want the exposure about your business. *Publicity* is zero-cost marketing at its best. You send the information (in a press release or other form of communication), and you have the potential to reach prospects that can lead to subsequent clients and/or sales.

If you don't look into getting free publicity, you're losing out on major opportunities. These sections can help you, first by explaining what newsworthiness means so you can give these media outlets what they want. I then walk you through the ins and outs of writing and distributing a press release so media sources choose to run the story. Finally, you can also use radio and TV appearances to promote your business. Read on for more information.

Knowing what newsworthy means

In order to get publicity for your service, product, or even business, the bottom line in the media outlet's eyes is that what you're announcing has to be newsworthy. *Newsworthy* means that the item has sufficient interest or importance to merit having a particular media source report on it.

Getting a handle on what is and isn't newsworthy is important, especially if you're a micro-entrepreneur seeking to grow your business. The problem is determining exactly what is newsworthy. What is newsworthy to you and me may not be newsworthy to someone else. Your customers need to know you're there, and you need to help them figure out who you are and the value of what you offer. Included in this mix is finding that *communications bridge* — that appropriate media venue that will connect the two of you (without charging you a toll).

Whatever product or service you offer, the chances are good that others are offering a similar product or service or are doing publicity in the same niche or category as you. To discover whether what you're currently doing is newsworthy, find out what those media outlets are already providing coverage to and see whether what you do has the same level of newsworthiness.

Searching for examples of newsworthiness

A huge chunk of what is reported stems directly (or indirectly) from publicity. That means that you (and I mean you!) are either doing something newsworthy right now or you can create newsworthy events that can benefit your business.

To help you see what media outlets consider newsworthy, scan the media outlets you're interested in. Look at newspapers, magazines, websites, and blogs that cover your topic and see whether you can tell the difference between news and publicity. Use your creativity for publicity by using the grid of possibilities here (I discuss it in Chapter 13).

When you're scanning the headlines, look at the story and see whether it has contact information for the main person or organization covered in the story. You can tell a lot from the types of stories.

- A straight news story won't have contact information; a news story is about a significant event that happened, such as a psychotic killer killed another victim or the city council approved the new human rights ordinance. The story won't have contact info (to contact Charles Manson, email him at `killer@killme.com`).

- A story based on publicity typically has a call to action (a *call to action* is a direction within the story to actually do something, such as contacting someone or visiting a website), which may be overt or subtle. An overt call to action may be the news story on a charity that implores readers to contact the charity with contributions. A subtle call to action may be another story on a charity, and it only mentions a website.

Here are a few examples:

- The local paper has a story about the neighborhood church that has a fund-raising event, such as a garage sale, a craft fair, or a white elephant auction. This story has information on the event details, such as when and where. The church probably sent a press release to the local paper for the coverage.

- The town's website has a story about an interesting speaker that will do a class for the board of education's adult school program. That adult education program director probably sent a press release about the class along with all relevant details to the website's editor.

✔ The 25th anniversary of the opening of the town's only dry cleaner is reported in the town's newspaper. The owner is the colorful octogenarian Biff Kowalski who is also a decorated war veteran. This story is a nice human interest story, but Biff's son (the new manager of Biff's Dry Cleaners) probably sent a press release to the town newspaper.

✔ A software company is launching a new app that helps people do scheduling. You find out about it when you read a report at a website that runs news and views on personal productivity. That website found out at a site that provides company announcements through press releases (see the later section, "Knowing where to send your press release" to find out more about these types of sites).

As you can see, lots of news stories are actually supplied by businesses and organizations. Many people have the idea that most news stories appear because the media's staff journalists were out, beating the bushes trying to dig up newsworthy information for the media's audience. Journalists only have so much time in their day, and they rely on any help they can get. Press releases can supply those stories in one way or another.

In some news venues, about 80 percent of articles may actually be news and 20 percent may come from press releases and similar communications. In fact, many of those news stories come from press releases or statements issued by the organizations being reported on. In some trade publications (and their accompanying websites) the news stories are nearly 100 percent by way of publicity! I know some publications that are entirely about products and services from the industry's companies.

Creating publicity ideas for your business

If you aren't doing anything newsworthy (that you know of; I hope you aren't doing anything criminal that would get you truly bad publicity), then you can do something to create publicity.

To uncover some publicity ideas for your micro-entrepreneurship, take time to read all of the media sources that cover your business topic. You can find them online or head over to your local library. Carefully go through each page and posting and ask yourself whether the story is an organic news story or a publicity-driven news story. Look for the dead-giveaway clue in the story, which is a call to action ("visit X" or "contact Z"). *Publicity-driven* means the story was generated because someone sent a press release or other type of message intended for the actual purpose of publicizing an organization or whatever it's offering or involved with.

Have a pencil and a piece of paper with you as you're scanning. Keep in mind that the best way to get publicity is to first see what has already worked for others in gaining publicity and utilizing some of the same techniques.

Consider these potential ideas when creating your press releases:

- ✔ **Hold an event.** Events are some of the easiest things to publicize, and they can be inexpensive (even free). Schools and libraries regularly do public events, such as book-signings, author lectures, adult workshops, and even how-to demonstrations (such as cooking, magic, or home security).

- ✔ **Have a charity tie-in.** Charities generally have an easier time gaining media exposure than businesses. Consider doing a promotion or event with fund-raising or raising consciousness over an issue or concern.

- ✔ **Commemorate a holiday or anniversary.** See whether you can do something tied to a special holiday or the anniversary of a historically significant event. Just don't get tacky. (I don't recommend boating lessons on the anniversary of the Titanic.)

For example, a friend of mine and publicity expert, Paul Hartunian (he's getting publicity right now), got big chunks of the old bridge when the Brooklyn Bridge was being redone many years ago. He broke them down into small pieces and created publicity by selling you the Brooklyn Bridge! He sold the smaller pieces as keepsakes via mail order. Doing so generated lots of publicity for his firm. He was even invited as guest on *The Tonight Show* with Johnny Carson.

Drafting a press release

Writing a press release isn't rocket science. You can follow a simple formula, and you can also find plenty of examples of press releases. The following sections take a closer look at the necessary elements to include in a press release and the style for writing them.

Using the third person

You have to write in the reporter's third-person style even though you're writing about your own company or your own activities. *Third person* means you're writing as if you were a reporter and you make no reference to yourself (as if you were narrating). With third person, use words such as "he," "her," "them," and "it".

Think about how journalists write. When you read a news story on the front page of a major newspaper or a major news website, look to see how it's written. The reporter writes about the event but isn't part of the story being written.

You write in third person for the benefit of the editor. The editor (really the publisher) doesn't have the resources or desire to provide a reporter for every event that comes along. You provide convenience; you write your story as if you were one of their reporters. You help them with some content and do so as a "substitute reporter," and in exchange you get the publicity that can boost your business. It is a nice-win.

Recognizing the components of the press release

Here are the basic elements of a press release:

- **Headline:** It should be catchy and attention grabbing.

- **Contact information:** This information includes who the media can contact, including email address, phone number, mailing address, and contact person.

- **Dateline:** The first line of the first paragraph lists the date of the press release, the city, and state.

- **Introduction paragraph:** This paragraph is the most important as far as the media is concerned. As in a typical news story, it succinctly tells the who, what, why, where, and when of the event or development.

- **The body of the story:** The body usually is several paragraphs that provide details and background information.

- **What readers can do about event:** This information includes what they can do if they want more information (for example, "for more details, call . . . ").

- **Final paragraph:** This paragraph offers extra or extraneous information that the media source's editor may cut, including background information about the company or historical data.

- **The close:** Press releases typically end with symbols such as "###" or the old " — 30 — " which signifies the end of the press release.

Read as many press releases from other organizations (especially small businesses and business associations) as you can and use the preceding as your press release checklist. Doing so can help you build the valuable skill of writing a press release (unless you want to pay a publicity professional, which may not be a bad idea until you get a handle on it).

To see an example of a press release or to get more information about publicity and free press releases, check out the following resources:

- Paul Hartunian's Free Publicity Information Center (www.prprofits.com)

- E Releases (www.ereleases.com)

✔ PRWeb (www.prweb.com)

✔ Marketing Profs (www.marketingprofs.com)

✔ American Marketing Association (www.marketingpower.com)

✔ Marketing Sherpa (www.marketingsherpa.com)

✔ About.com's Marketing section (www.marketing.about.com)

✔ The latest edition of *Public Relations For Dummies* by Eric Yaverbaum, Ilise Benun, and Richard Kirshebaum (John Wiley & Sons, Inc.)

✔ *Publicity Tactics: Insights on Creating Lucrative Media Buzz* by Marcia Yudkin (Creative Ways Publishing)

✔ *Guerilla Publicity* by Jay Conrad Levinson (Houghton Mifflin)

Knowing where to send your press release

After you complete your press release, you need to submit it where publications, news sites, and other media outlets can see and possibly run it. You can either submit it directly or to publicity sites:

✔ **Directly to a media outlet:** If you're doing a gardening event, then certainly submit your press release to that gardening publication or site. Before you do so, make sure that you get the specific name and position of the contact person at that organization. Call or email first and find out who to send the press release to. You may also be able to find a masthead on the website or in the publication that lists the editors.

✔ **To publicity sites:** Many press release distribution sites are online. They can distribute your press release to media outlets that subscribe to it. Here are a few:

  • **PR Newswire** (www.prnewswire.com)

  • **PR.com** (www.pr.com)

  • **24-7 PressRelease** (www.24-7pressrelease.com)

  • **1-888-Press Release** (www.1888pressrelease.com)

Do a search to see what you can find. Dozens of press release distribution sites are online.

Hiring a publicity professional

For new micro-entrepreneurs getting launched on a limited budget, hiring a public relations person may be an expensive proposition. Using full-service public relations firms and the services of a true publicity professional can easily run into the thousands. However, if you're interested in what a professional has to offer, contact public relations firms and see samples of their work and what media they work with. If they reach the media that you feel will benefit you (and you can afford their fee), go ahead. If you do hire them, do a three- or six-month trial period so that you can evaluate them without obligating yourself to an expensive contract.

If you don't need full-service public relations, then determine what specific needs in publicity you may have and pay for only that. For example, if you only need good press releases to be produced and successfully placed or media interviews, then just seek those services.

For paid services in terms of writing a press release, consider places such as E Releases (www.ereleasesmedia.com), PR Web (www.prweb.com), and PR Leap (www.prleap.com). For media interviews, consider Help a Reporter Out (www.helpareporter.com), Radio-TV Interview Report (www.rtir.com), and Alex Carroll's Radio Publicity (www.radiopublicity.com).

Doing a radio or TV interview

One of the greatest forms of free publicity is to do a radio or TV interview. What better way to get positive exposure in front of your target market?

Doing a radio or TV interview is easier than you think. Some of the same principles that I discuss in the previous section "Using Publicity and Press Releases" also apply here. Radio and TV (and now many Internet-based programs) need content in the form of guests and experts so their hosts can provide a compelling and interesting reason for their viewers and listeners to tune in. These sections explain in a nutshell how to get radio and TV interviews.

Preparing before you're on the program

Before you contact any program and say, "Hello, I am available as a guest! When and where do I show up?" you need to do some preparation to maximize your approach and also do well on the interview. Make sure that you're the right guest and that the program reaches your target market. The best way to see whether a program thinks that you're a good guest is to see what guests the program already has found acceptable. If you have all the attributes that current guests have, then you have what it takes to be a future guest!

Focus on finding every show (TV, radio, and Internet) that covers your topic. Review their lineup of covered topics and find an angle for your story that works for the program. After you find them, listen carefully for several weeks (or even months), and take notes about what guests they have on and why. Answer the following questions as you listen:

- Who are these guests? Are they professionals like you?

- Why are they on? Did they write a book? Are they a consultant or a speaker? What is their expertise? Did a major event occur and they were the commentator called for insights on what happened?

- After they're on, what are they saying? How are they saying it?

- What do they offer? In other words, what products or services are they selling or offering?

- What are they offering as a call to action to attract passive listeners or viewers into taking the next step (such as contacting the interviewee in some way, shape, or form)?

As you compare your idea with what the programs are already running, make sure your story is also newsworthy. Being newsworthy is just as important with radio and TV as it is with other media outlets. If the program's director thinks you're just what the program's audience needs, you have a much easier chance getting on the program. (Refer to the earlier section, "Knowing what newsworthy means" for more information.)

Approaching the program

After you find the right show and have the right angle, make the inquiry. Contact the different executive producers (the main decision maker) for the shows you're interested in. Don't assume that the program's host is the one to contact (he or she may be, but usually it's the executive producer). Sometimes the host is the producer of the show too.

After you get their contact information, send an inquiry that has four elements to it:

- **The reason you're contacting them:** Are you contacting them because of a major event, controversial issue, a new book, upcoming conference, or something else? This reason is what should be newsworthy.

- **Your bio:** It includes your credentials, expertise, and so on that make you stand out as the person to appear on the program.

- **Questions to ask you:** This list includes 8 to 12 interesting and compelling questions they can ask you as a guest. These questions not only serve as marketing tools, but if they're interesting and compelling, it gives them more reason to have you on the program.

- **Background information:** This may include a copy of your book or a brochure of the event or conference.

Here are some resources to help you gain interviews:

- ✔ Alex Carroll (www.radiopublicity.com)
- ✔ Help a Reporter Out (HARO) (www.helpareporter.com)
- ✔ Bill and Steve Harrison's Reporter Connection (www.freepublicity.com)

Appearing on the program

After you've been selected to be on the show, remember that you aren't the star of the show. Not even the host is the show's star. The sponsors are the star of the show, so treat the advertisers with respect. Don't say things like "Can you hold off on the commercial? I have more to say!" Saying things like that will never get you called back again!

When you're being interviewed, follow the host's lead. Make sure that your answers are succinct and to the point. Keep it moving. Don't give any long answers or any laborious responses or tedious stories. Your responses need to be informative, entertaining, and brief. Also, don't do any heavy selling or high-pressure tactics. Don't worry; the program will inform the audience about who you are, what company you are from, and what your website is.

An effective way to get responses is to offer something of value that listeners or viewers can get for free at your site (or by mail from your company). Let them know if you have a free report or ebook for anyone that emails them. You want to be able to collect names for your list so that you can invite them afterwards to subscribe to your ezine, blog, or video channel.

After the program, email your appreciation to both the host and the producer of the program. Then, rinse and repeat! The more shows you are on, the more publicity you can generate for your business!

Focusing on Forum Marketing

Whatever product or service you offer, you can market where your target market is. A great place to do so is forums. A *forum* is basically an online gathering place of folks that have a common interest and seek others to discuss that interest and share news, views, and information on it. Forums can be general interest or very focused on a particular topic. You can find forums on topics ranging from sports and animation to dating and history trivia. The diversity is great; you can find a forum where your target market is dwelling right now.

To find forums that may be a good fit for you, check out these resources:

- **Search your favorite search engine for forums on your topic.** Find as many as you can. Use search phrases such as "topic X forum" or "forum + [topic]". Use all the ways and replacement words. If your market is home businesses, use phrases such as "home business forum" or "forum for home business". You can also use substitute words, such as "entrepreneur," "freelancer," and "home-based business". For "forum," also use words such as "board," "bulletin board," and "big board".

- **Big Boards:** This site (www.big-boards.com) tracks the most active message boards and forums on the Internet.

- **Board Reader:** This site (www.boardreader.com) is a search engine for message boards and forums.

- **Omgili:** This site (www.omgili.com) is a search engine for forums.

These sections walk you through the ins and outs of forums, including how forums can help you, how to behave appropriately in a forum, and how to actually make the sale in the forum.

Eyeing the benefits of a forum

After you find a forum where your target market is, sign on to a forum, and begin to get active. If you correctly use forums, they can be a boom to your business. However if you don't, they can be a flop in your marketing efforts.

Here are some other benefits to joining a forum:

- **Search engine potential:** Many forums tend to rank high on search engines.

- **Free market research:** You're within your niche; the value of consumer opinions will be valuable to you developing either a winning product or a winning sales approach.

- **Competition research:** You can discover valuable information about your competitors by asking open-ended questions that can give you insight. For example, find out which companies have the best products, who offers the best customer service, and so on. Just make sure you don't slam your competitors. (Refer to the next section, "Using forum etiquette" for more insight into what behavior is appropriate and not appropriate.)

✔ **Others' experiences:** You can read about other experienced business people's war stories and discover from what they did right and wrong. Experienced entrepreneurs can help you avoid common business mistakes and stay focused on the things that matter.

✔ **Marketing intelligence:** Some great Internet forums concentrate on Internet marketing (and others on sales, advertising, and other important topics). Keep up-to-date with Internet marketing practices from those people who daily do it.

✔ **Joint venture opportunities:** You may find potential partners for your business in a forum.

For more in-depth information about forums, mingle with those that do marketing on a daily basis. Here are forums that specialize in news, views, products, and services on Internet marketing:

✔ Internet Marketing Forum (www.ewealth.com)

✔ Online Marketing Forum (www.onlinemarketingforum.org)

✔ Warrior Forum (www.warriorforum.com)

✔ Wicked Fire (www.wickedfire.com)

Using forum etiquette

Until you know how the forum works (and the forum knows you), you want to be a good member in the forum. Avoid doing the following, which can potentially annoy any active and long-term forum participants:

✔ **Overt overselling:** If you've just joined, stay away from giving sales-pitch mode. Marketing and sales are a process, and a forum is a warmer sales environment when you first want to establish relationships.

✔ **Avoid bad-mouthing anyone:** You may cause some bad feelings if you attack a respected company or organization or maybe someone in the forum itself.

Conflict, criticism, and complaining are very delicate things to do, and they can backfire. Your ultimate goal is to build your (and your company's) reputation, not to do and say things that could result in self-sabotage. Also keep in mind that forum operators monitor forums. They decide whether you continue in the forum or shut you out.

In the early days of participating in the forum, avidly read everyone's comments and make no attempt at communicating (yet). Get to know a bit about the others. Discover how the forum works and its ways first before you attempt to sell.

Selling on forums: The how-to

When you're ready to participate in a forum, you can begin by asking questions or offering positive feedback and suggestions. Do what it takes to build your reputation within the forum community.

You can slowly work into your conversations and comments some points about your website or blog. If you do what you think is a great article at your blog about a topic that is relevant to the forum, consider inviting the forum participants to read your article and give some constructive feedback. People will eventually see you as a reliable person, and in due course you'll be able to confidently post about your business activities. It will take time and effort, but it should be worth it.

Watch carefully how others are selling on a forum. Look to see what they do and don't do. Examine to see how long they've been on the forum. Many forums provide public profiles, so you can see how long they've been members. Ask yourself whether their approach is a one-step sales approach or a two-step approach.

- ✔ A *one-step* approach means they make a sales pitch on the spot.
- ✔ The *two-step* approach means that there is an intermediary step before the sales pitch occurs.

Maybe the first step for you in the forum is to get participants to "click here to see the article on topic X." The sales pitch is the secondary step with links in the article that take them to the sales page. The odds are high that the approach that works in forums is the two-step approach.

These sections can help you select the forum that fits your needs and what you can do to make the sale.

Figuring out which forums are right for you

Many forums exist online, so focus your attention on forums that are

- ✔ The most targeted to your market
- ✔ The largest

The psychology of online forums

Even though a forum is an online community, many people are still skeptical about anyone or anything new because of the anonymity. Some of this stems from the functionality of the Internet experience; it's not a face-to-face conference or cocktail party that gives you more than one way to size up a person or group.

In addition, the Internet has been the home of plenty of high-profile scams. You probably have received an email from some abandoned traveler in Nigeria who needs money to get home to England, and all you need to do is submit your credit card information to help. As a result of these types of scams, you need to build trust and a comfort level for people who interact with you as a businessperson in online forums.

You have no idea what has happened to the folks you're dealing with that are on the other side of that faceless post. Maybe they were burned. Remember that your integrity isn't just some slogan or selling point; it's a foundational point for doing current and future business.

 If you have to choose between a large forum that is vaguely close to your market or a smaller one that is closer to your target market, choose the smaller forum that is closer to your target market. Of course, if you have the time, do both and track the results.

 As you're evaluating which forum is right for you, ask yourself these questions as you evaluate different forums (or decide to start to participate in one):

- ✔ Is this the right forum? I know. This question sounds basic, but you should be choosy. Joining and marketing in a forum isn't fun time; it's time to find your target market and make money (Don't get me wrong: If you find a forum that has your target market in it and you're making money, then it's fun time!)

- ✔ Does the forum have regular discussion about your niche or topic?

- ✔ If this forum yields good results (such as generating traffic, leads, and sales for you), are there others just like this one that you can add to your forum marketing activities?

- ✔ Is the forum active? In other words, do you see daily activity such as posting, commenting, and so on?

- ✔ What are the forum's posting guidelines? What are you *not* allowed to post?

- ✔ What are you allowed to put in your profile? Can you place links in your posts and/or profile?

- ✔ Are you allowed to directly promote anything you're offering?

- ✔ Can you use marketing messages in your signature when you post?

- ✔ Do new users have special requirements?

Use the resources in this chapter to find forums that are the most likely places for your type of business. Because access to a basic forum is usually free, it's worth some time and effort to participate and explore the forum. If you find it is worthwhile (such as you're finding good contacts and opportunities), then stick around and continue. If not, look elsewhere.

Upping your selling in forums

Beyond building trust and making folks comfortable about you, keep the awareness going about the value of what you offer and making it easy to contact you. You can do some effective, yet low-key things such as:

- ✔ **Always have a link to your blog or website present in your forum signature if possible.** In other words, end your posts with something like "Regards, Betty Johnson, debt counselor at XYZdebt.com" or "Regards, Paul Smith, podiatrist at FootAchesRus.com".

- ✔ **Answer or respond completely and make sure your post has keywords connected to your specialty.** Making sure that you have keywords in your site helps people find your post if they're doing a keyword search.

Part IV
Considering Taxes and Legal Issues

Five Tax Deductions That Can Offer Savings on Your Tax Bill

✔ **Business meals:** A business meal can be tax-deductible (with some limitations). To make it a business meal, you need to conduct business during the meal (such as talking with potential clients). You also must document it (with a receipt, details about who you had the meal with, what business was conducted, and so on).

✔ **Auto expenses:** Whether you're traveling to a business conference on the other side of the state or doing a business errand on the other side of town, the business usage (parking, tolls, wear and tear on the vehicle, and so on) is tax-deductible. If you use mass transit (bus, taxi, or train), you can also deduct the business usage portion of that cost.

✔ **Home office expense:** If you regularly and exclusively use a portion of your home for a home office for your business, then you can deduct those business-related expenses, which can include a portion of your mortgage interest, real estate taxes, and property insurance (or your rent, if you're a renter), along with a portion of utilities.

✔ **Health-related expenses:** You can utilize a health savings account (HSA), which has the potential to make more healthcare and medical expenses easier to deduct and can save you on your tax bill.

✔ **Retirement accounts:** You can open tax-advantaged accounts that allow you to deduct greater amounts than a regular individual retirement account (IRA). Operating a small business gives you several types of plans available to you, such as a simplified employee pension plan (SEP-IRA) or a 401k plan, among others.

Building wealth through your business isn't just about making money; it's also about keeping it. Chapter 21 has more information to help you save on your tax bill.

Head to www.dummies.com/extras/microentrepreneur for important forms and advice to help you file your taxes as a small business owner.

In this part . . .

✔ Make your business more successful by paying outsourced workers to help you with different tasks.

✔ Hire micro-tasking sites to help you with administrative or technological requirements so you can focus your attention on doing what you need to do to make your business successful.

✔ If your business continues to grow, see how you can take your business to a macro level by hiring permanent employees.

✔ Know how to handle and file the unique tax forms and schedules relevant to micro-entrepreneurs.

Chapter 19

Outsourcing: Getting Others to Help You

....

In This Chapter

▶ Understanding what outsourcing is

▶ Recognizing the advantages and disadvantages of outsourcing work

▶ Knowing what to do when you outsource

▶ Locating qualified workers

....

Ringo Starr got a little help from his friends. In fact, everyone needs a little help once in a while. Even stout-hearted micro-entrepreneurs like you and me can use a little help — if not from actual friends, then maybe friendly, helpful strangers.

When you run a business, especially in the beginning, you end up wearing a lot of hats. After you do the main work — be it product creation or some badly needed marketing — you still have a batch of other tasks to do, such as filing, entering data, running errands, writing ad copy, and a myriad other tasks both big and small.

In order to juggle and keep track of these different tasks, you may seek to outsource some of those tasks. Larger enterprises often have the ability to hire employees, but when you launch and run a fledgling enterprise, hiring an employee can be cost prohibitive. Until you have the need and financial clout to be an employer, some form of outsourcing may by your best option. That's where this chapter comes into play.

Defining Outsourcing and How You Can Use It in Your Business

As far as you're concerned as a micro-entrepreneur, *outsourcing* is using workers that are technically independent contractors. (An *independent contractor* is a self-employed individual that provides services to businesses but isn't an employee. The independent contractor is responsible for his/her own taxes and tax reporting and receives a 1099. You can read more about taxes in Chapter 21.) That means you can outsource different tasks of your business, so you can focus your attention on what you need to do to maximize profitability.

If you expect to grow your enterprise to the next level, you'll need competent help. Explore outsourcing so that you can go from merely getting by (while doing everything yourself 24/7) to being a business leader and seeing your business grow while you're home with the family relaxing or doing whatever it is you want to do.

To better understand the different ways you can potentially outsource work, you need a decent grasp of the different types of outsourcing available to you. Here is a list, based on the kind of work for which you need help:

- **Administrative assistance:** You may regularly have this need, especially for those tasks and processes that aren't difficult to do (such as data entry or word processing), but bog you down and keep you from doing higher reward projects. *Virtual assistants* (an independent contractor that provides general administrative services for a business via the Internet and is physically off-site) can also help with these types of tasks.

- **Micro-tasks:** You may only need help with a *micro-task,* in other words a brief assignment (like put up a blog or do a marketing test with Twitter). You can hire someone to help you; you can find someone on sites like `fiverr.com` or `gigzon.com`. (Refer to the later section, "Finding Outsourced Workers" for more information on these and other sites.)

- **Technical assistance:** Every business has its technology needs. Some are more technical than others, depending on what product or service you're providing. If you're not an expert, for example, with a computer network, then you can outsource your technology needs to someone who is an expert in that field.

- **Work overload:** If you have a lot of work at a particular period, you need diligence and a get-it-done attitude. Agency sites or virtual assistants can help you with this need. (Check out the "Hiring an Outsourced Worker: The How-To" section later for more information about agencies and virtual assistants.)

Whatever work or assignment you may have, you need to figure out some of your needs and goals before you spend your first dollar on outside help. Figure out what you need help with. You have things you're good at doing, and other tasks that aren't your strength. You also enjoy doing certain tasks and dislike doing others.

Identifying the Pros and Cons of Hiring an Outsourced Worker

Hiring an outsourced worker can be a beautiful thing. Image someone else doing all the tasks you hate doing or you don't have time to do for a fraction of what it would cost to hire an employee. The following sections take a closer look at the advantages and disadvantages of using outsourced workers.

Seeing the upsides of using outsourced workers

Hiring and retaining employees (refer to Chapter 20 for more information) can be a daunting task for the micro-entrepreneur. But making the initial foray into hired help can be much easier with outsourcing. Here are the potential benefits to outsourcing:

- ✔ **Cost:** Hiring an employee can be expensive, especially for cost-conscious micro-entrepreneurs. Outsourcing can be a fraction of the cost compared to hiring an employee. The total labor cost per hour for an outsourced worker for a small business can easily be 25 to 50 percent lower than the total labor cost for a conventional employee (this savings is for using outsourced worker in the United States). Some of these workers may be overseas and have even lower labor costs.

- ✔ **Temporary needs versus permanent cost:** Hiring an employee can end up being a long-term arrangement (the whole point of hiring someone is to pay him or her for ongoing service for the foreseeable future). Outsourcing means that you only pay for what you need; temporary needs mean lower and/or limited labor costs.

- ✔ **Labor cost arbitrage:** *Arbitrage* is the act of buying something at a low cost in one market and simultaneously selling it at a higher cost in a different market and profiting from the net difference. In the case of outsourcing, you can easily get five or ten or even more hours of productivity from a worker in Asia, for example, for the same cost as one hour from a worker in the United States.

✔ **Profit increase:** Using outsourced workers for some relatively simple tasks frees your time so you can perform higher-profit potential activities in several ways.

- Outsourced workers can do low-priority tasks while you do high-priority tasks. If they do something worth $10 an hour, it frees you up to do something worth much more to you.

- If a particular task is valuable to you and adds revenue to your business, you can copy yourself with an outsourced worker, allowing you to do more and leverage human time and effort. Think of a process (like selling a product online with search engine optimization) that makes you a profit and have an outsourced worker do the task and net a profit. If the process, for example, makes you $75 when you do it, you can hire an outsourced worker, train him, and pay him $15 each time he replicates the task. If this approach succeeds, you can hire more outsourced workers to do the same and generate more total revenue for your business. You can essentially copy yourself and re-do that profitable task over and over again.

✔ **Different time zone:** When you hire outsourced workers that are in different time zones, you can coordinate the project or work to continue while you aren't personally working (like when you're catching up on some sleep) and keep the productivity humming along.

✔ **Peak workload accommodations:** Say your business gets busy around Groundhog Day. You can simply hire a temporarily outsourced worker just for a few days to help out at that time.

✔ **Different skill set:** Some projects in your business may require skills you don't have. You can choose from thousands of outsourced workers with different skills to do the job.

✔ **Efficiency:** When you outsource, you reduce the need for you to do everything and juggle so many tasks. You can then focus your time and energy on the more urgent tasks (For instance, you can have someone do data entry for an email marketing campaign while you write the email sales copy). Spending your time on what you do best and having someone else do the tasks you don't enjoy just makes sense.

Naming the downside of using outsourced workers

Before you hire an army of outsourced workers and decide to sip your piña colada poolside, hold on. You need to be aware of some potential pitfalls. When you're dealing with humanity, you'll have issues. People don't always come through when you need them to. So when dealing with your critical business projects, you have to be wary of whom you're dealing with. Here are some issues that can be problematic with outsourcing:

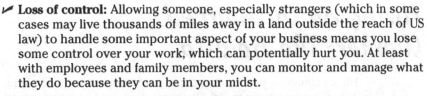

✔ **Loss of control:** Allowing someone, especially strangers (which in some cases may live thousands of miles away in a land outside the reach of US law) to handle some important aspect of your business means you lose some control over your work, which can potentially hurt you. At least with employees and family members, you can monitor and manage what they do because they can be in your midst.

Finishing work with someone in a remote town in Asia or some other faraway spot can be difficult. Although you can do your due diligence before you use these types of workers, it's still a justified concern. If being in total control is a primary concern, then you may want to re-think outsourcing. Of course, if you're outsourcing with someone you know (maybe an ex-coworker, for example), then some of these concerns may not be justified.

✔ **Quality of work:** The quality of work from outsourcers both foreign and domestic can be all over the place. Hiring a techie in Bratislava named Sergei for only $7 to create a full business website may seem like a deal, but remember the "you get what you pay for."

To reduce potential issues, get references and don't skimp when hiring an outsourced worker. Strive to get a better worker for a higher price because you're already saving by doing outsourcing in the first place.

✔ **Impact on customers:** Using outsourcing to service customers in any way may be a concern and something you should seriously monitor because you need to be aware of how the workers are interacting with your customers. Any worker acting on your behalf will have an impact on customer relations. You probably have heard the horror stories of how some major companies outsourced their customer service functions to lands where there was a real disconnect with their customers back in the States with language, culture, customer sensitivity, and so on.

As the micro-entrepreneur, you and/or people you trust or can easily oversee should primarily handle your customer service.

✔ **Time factor:** Sometimes the issue is timeliness of the work. If an out-sourced worker is late on deadlines regarding work that your customer needs as soon as possible, that tardiness can definitely be an issue even if quality is acceptable. Make sure that guidelines for timely work are in place.

✔ **Security and privacy:** When you're dealing with outsourced workers, be wary if the work to be done involves sensitive data, particularly customer data. This type of information can include customers' Social Security numbers, financial accounts, and so forth. This type of information is readily bought and sold in dark corners of the digital world. Be safety-conscious here and limit access where possible.

✔ **Language barrier:** When you hire an outsourced worker outside of your native language, you need to communicate clearly with him about the expected outcome of the project. Misunderstandings can lead to shoddy quality of work or delays in your timeline.

Hiring an Outsourced Worker: The How-To

Hiring someone you don't know to work for you may seem unusual, but it's actually very simple to do. Plenty of competent and enthusiastic workers are willing to work for you. You just need to do it the right way to prevent problems. These sections provide some helpful pointers for you to follow.

Establish clear goals, milestones, and requirements

Someone once said, "An ounce of prevention is worth a pound of cure." (I am probably giving away my age with that one). Outsourcing was made for that old saying. Too many projects run over budget or the allotted time or deadline.

To avoid overages, make sure you clearly do the following:

- **Define clear objectives for the work to be done from the start.** Don't leave anything to guesswork.

- **Be accurate and provide complete information.** Make sure you give clear steps from start to finish for the project.

- **Have the potential workers ask you questions about the work requirements both before the work starts and in the initial phase of work.** If they don't have any questions, ask them questions, such as do you have any questions about this requirement? Furthermore, ask the workers about their approach and methodology to work to get a better understanding of their knowledge and experience.

- **Where possible, provide milestones.** *Milestones* are definable points where work is progressing, such as 25 percent finished by a certain date, 50 percent completion by a subsequent date, and so on, until the project or task is 100 percent complete. For example, if the worker is writing a detailed, 50-page report, tell her that you want to see the work after 10 pages, at 20 pages, and so on, until you're confident that she is performing as you want.

Focus on qualified workers versus cheap workers

The levels of expertise and experience among workers can vary tremendously. Hence, you need to figure out what specific work you need to have done and limit your search to only those individuals that have a track record in that type of work. Furthermore, make sure you ask for credentials and references to support what the candidate is stating about his expertise.

If, for example, you need an advanced shopping cart system set up, ask to see what shopping carts he has completed with links to operational websites with the shopping carts. In this case, don't look for "ecommerce experience". Instead, look for "ecommerce experience and specialization in advanced shopping cart system set-up and maintenance" with work samples and references.

The more specific skills you look for, the better off you will be. Hiring someone who is more qualified may cost you a little more than a generalist, but in the end, doing so will be worth it. Over the long run, you'll also save on hassles and money. Choosing a worker solely because the quote was the lowest can be an expensive mistake.

Review portfolios and samples

Previous work can be a great indication of the skills that workers possesses and the quality of the work they're capable of performing.

Particularly if what you need for the workers to do isn't within your expertise, such as something technical, and you're still unsure about whom you should hire after reading and applying the above information, send the potential applicants an email detailing some of the problems you're looking to address by hiring them. Their responses to the issue can give you a feel for their knowledge on the subject as well as professionalism.

Tip toe in with any new workers and don't give them critical projects related to your business's success. Give some work that you need done that isn't particularly critical for your business so you can get a sense of how they perform. As they become more familiar with your business needs, your managerial style improves, and your confidence and familiarity with them increases, you can increase their workload.

Have an agreed payment plan before you hire

When working with outsourced workers, you usually have two options on how to pay them:

- **Hourly:** You pay by the total hours they need to finish the job. If you contracted with this outsourced worker through freelance sites such as www.elance.com and/or www.odesk.com, you'll have access to "screen shot function" so you can actually see the screens of the workers for the hours you're paying for. A *screen shot function* means they can send you an image of their work to show you a visual point of progress.

- **Fixed:** A set price for the specific task or project. You can pay a lump sum after the project is completed or you can set up project milestones where the worker will be paid after a specific milestone is completed.

The choice is yours. Using the hourly payment structure for less complicated projects, such as menial or administrative tasks, is typically better. However, for more complicated projects with set milestones and that require certain skills, such as AutoCAD or programming, a fixed payment is better, because these projects can have setbacks and quickly go over budget if you pay hourly.

Use an agency

Whether you're using outsource workers from across the street or across the globe, I highly recommended that you go through an agency, such as www.elance.com or other similar agencies. (Refer to the "Finding Outsourced Workers" section later in this chapter for a more comprehensive list.)

Agencies screen workers and protect safeguards to make sure that you're happy with the work. The agencies provide guidance from start to finish, which is very important, especially for those micro-entrepreneurs (or anyone else) just getting started with outsourcing.

Consider other potential issues

In addition, make sure you know about these other potential quirks in the world of outsourcing before you have problems:

- **Language barrier:** For jobs that require customer interaction, you need to be aware of the worker's English skill level. Many outsourced workers speak English as a second language.

- ✔ **Access:** Be aware that outsourced workers will sometimes need access to your website or your source code. Make sure you secure your data (such as backing-up your critical computer files).

- ✔ **Piracy:** Piracy (the unauthorized use of copyrighted material) hasn't happened to anyone that I know, but it's still a potential risk you must consider. Intellectual property theft does happen so make sure you sign *nondisclosure agreements* (a document two parties sign that protects confidential material). Usually agency sites have protection built into their agreements.

- ✔ **Distance from your workers and time zone:** You may not be able to visit your workers and chat with them, which may be difficult for you to get used to. If you need to have more interaction than an occasional email, I recommend talking with them on Skype once in a while.

Finding Outsourced Workers

If you decide to consider hiring outsourced workers, knowing where to locate the best ones for what you need can make your job so much easier. Although you may be able to find some workers through referrals, the best way to find them is online. The following sections identify different resources you can turn to, depending on the type of worker you need.

With the following resources and sites in these sections, visit them and review everything they have to offer because each one has its individual strengths and weaknesses. You can peruse how other micro-entrepreneurs use outsourcing, review resumes of experienced freelancers and other outsourced workers, or share advice with others that also do outsourcing.

Using general outsourcing websites

To discover all sorts of technical assistance on a wide variety of specialties, start your search and check out these websites:

- ✔ **Elance:** This site (www.elance.com) is the most active site for businesses and freelancers. This platform has more than 500,000 businesses and 2 million freelancers (stretched across nearly 150 countries).

- ✔ **Freelancer:** This site (www.freelancer.com) specializes on freelance services that are more affordable (projects start at $30 and most assignments are typically $200 or less) for entrepreneurs and small businesses.

- ✔ **Get a Coder:** This site (www.getacoder.com) specializes on technical freelancers, such as programmers, coders, and software developers. Hirers also get a free guide on successful outsourcing.

- ✔ **Guru:** This site (www.guru.com) is an extensive platform of freelancers with an emphasis on technical expertise, such as computer programmers and software developers.

- ✔ **Ifreelance:** This site (www.ifreelance.com) doesn't take out fees or get a percentage of the assignment. This site is run like a membership site where freelancers pay monthly membership fees.

- ✔ **Odesk:** This site (www.odesk.com) is one of the most active for outsourcing, and it contains experienced freelancers across many technical and nontechnical specialties.

- ✔ **Project4Hire:** This active site (www.project4hire.com) is essentially like Odesk and boasts a large database of local and international freelancers.

A micro-entrepreneur and freelancer: Sometimes one in the same

All freelancers are micro-entrepreneurs, but not all micro-entrepreneurs are freelancers. In this chapter, they tend to be one and the same. If you're a lone businessperson and your income is primarily generated by providing a service (writing, programming, and so on), then you're certainly a freelancer. The extent to which you do outsourcing is primarily in the realm of getting you work (sites like Odesk and Elance effectively get you contacts and help you gain work). When you get active with the sites listed here, you can refer to Chapter 8 for more insight about freelancing as your primary micro-entrepreneurial activity.)

If you want more knowledge about how the trends for the freelancing market are and what you can expect, look no further than online. Although these sites specialize on the written word (ranging from writing reports and brochures to website design), they do provide more information about freelancing:

- ✔ **Freelance Folder:** At this freelancer's site (www.freelancefolder.com), you can find everything from job posts and how-to articles to the latest freelancing news and views.

- ✔ **Freelance Switch:** Besides job and assignment pots, this site (www.freelanceswitch.com) also has an ezine along with a forum and blog for freelancers.

- ✔ **Freelancer Job:** This site (www.freelancer-job.com) has plenty of business advice and tips for freelancers.

- ✔ **Freelancer Life:** This site (www.freelancer-life.org) has plenty of how-to articles and guidance on running your business and life as a freelancer.

- ✔ **Job Stock Blog:** At this site (www.jobstock.com/blog), you can find lots of business and marketing articles and information for freelancers.

Trying virtual assistant resources

If your needs are more mundane or administrative (such as data entry, book-keeping, and so on) or you need someone fairly regular, then look into the world of virtual assistants. As I mention earlier in this chapter, virtual assistants are outsourced workers that provide administrative services and other business support services, but are off-site. (In other words, they work from home but serve you via telephone and Internet access). These resources can help you locate a virtual assistant:

- **Administrative Consultants Association:** This site (www.administrative consultantsassoc.com) provides professional support and guidance for virtual assistants and also helps hirers to find qualified outsourced workers.

- **Alliance for Virtual Business:** This site (www.allianceforvirtual biz.com) offers advice and assistance for small businesses that many need the services of virtual assistants.

- **Hire My Mom:** Moms are among the most capable assistants that an entrepreneur can find. This site (www.hiremymom.com) can help you find them (and helps them find you!).

- **International Virtual Assistants Association:** This place (www.ivaa. org) is great to find qualified virtual assistants. In addition to plenty of resources for virtual assistants, it also has good resources for hirers (the site has free reports such as "101 Ways to Use a Virtual Assistant").

- **Real Estate Virtual Network:** If your micro-entrepreneur business is in a real estate-related industry, you can find virtual assistants with that spe-cialty at this site (www.revanetwork.com).

- **Virtual Assistant Forums:** This site (www.virtualassistantforums. com) has lots of information about virtual assistants (and how to become one, too).

- **Virtual Assistants Network & Forum:** This site (www.vanetworking. com) has information and guidance for virtual assistants as well as arti-cles for how to hire a virtual assistant for hirers.

- **The Virtual Link:** This site (www.thevirtuallink.com) offers Internet marketing–related virtual assistant services.

Before you hire a virtual assistant, make sure you ask some questions and try to screen your choices. Here are some questions and points to keep in mind:

- **Can they offer references?** In other words, check to see if the person currently assists other small businesses and whether he can provide you with contact information.

- ✔ **What is the virtual assistant's experience?** Is it mostly word processing and data entry or does he have customer service skills?

- ✔ **What is the virtual assistant's availability?** Check to see if it's the standard 9-to-5 business hours, or ask if he is available during weekends, too. If you hire someone from overseas, you may be able to have him work while you're asleep.

While you're at it, go to some small business sites and do a search for articles and posts on hiring a virtual assistant. As more and more entrepreneurs use virtual assistants, more guidance and how-to-hire information at those business sites will be available. (You can go to sites, such as www.entrepreneur.com, www.inc.com, and www.allbusiness.com.)

Tapping into micro-task sites

If all you need is the occasional task or a small job to be done, then maybe you don't need full-blown assistance. You may just need someone to complete a micro-task for you. (A *micro-task* is any small or minor task that someone is willing to do for a relatively small sum). Some examples of micro-tasks include the following:

- ✔ You posted a new video at your video channel, and you want a boost to the viewership. You can pay $5 or $10 to get 1,000 viewers or have it announced to somebody's 5,000 Twitter followers.

- ✔ You need a blog set up.

- ✔ You need a 500-word article on a particular topic.

- ✔ You need a two-minute promotional video produced for your company.

I have some examples from my business. I paid $5 to add literally hundreds of new followers to my Twitter account. I also paid $15 for someone to send my advertisement to their list of 200,000 subscribers.

If you need micro-task help, you can check out these main sites:

- ✔ **Fiverr:** This site (www.fiverr.com) is the premier (or at least most well-known) site on micro-tasking. Although you use it for business and serious pursuits, you'll find some fun and off-the-wall stuff, too (like having someone wearing a gorilla suit sing "happy birthday" to your sweetheart).

- ✔ **Gigzon:** This site (www.gigzon.com) offers a platform for buyers and sellers of services (and products, too) for up to $100.

- ✔ **Mechanical Turk:** This is a micro-tasking site from Amazon (www. mturk.com). Here the gigs are called HITs (Human Intelligence Tasks).

- ✔ **Micro Workers:** This site (www.microworkers.com) competes with Fiverr with a similar business model, but it's more geared to work-related tasks and costs can be higher than just $5.

- ✔ **NetTradr:** This popular site (www.nettradr.com) focuses on general micro-tasking; it's most similar to Gigzon.

- ✔ **Ten Bux:** This site (www.tenbux.com) is similar in look and feel to Fiverr (in fact, the same company runs it), but the work assignments (referred to as Jobs) can run between $5 and $10.

Chapter 20

From Micro to Macro: Growing and Selling Your Business

*I*f you have done everything right (and sometimes even if you didn't), you can see your budding enterprise go from a one-person operation or home-based company to a sizable entity. In due course, you may decide to grow your business and become larger. If so, you'll inevitably encounter some growing pains. You may need permanent employees. You may need additional funding and other resources. You may consider expanding with dealerships and franchises. You may even consider selling your business. This chapter can help you with these concerns if you get to that point.

Hiring Permanent Employees

Hiring an employee isn't a light decision, so if you decide to add permanent people, I want you to tread carefully. In other chapters (such as Chapter 19), I discuss how you can outsource workers if you need certain tasks completed that you may not be able to do. But outsourcing is a temporary and limited solution for workload issues where the need is, well, temporary and limited. When your business grows and you need regular, daily assistance, you can consider hiring people.

Before you hire any permanent employee, however, you should consider the significant associated labor costs (even for a part-time employee). A permanent employee is an ongoing expense (the total labor cost), week in and week out, whether your business is generating revenue or not. In fact, the labor cost will probably be higher than you expect. For example, an employee's $50,000 salary isn't the same as labor costs.

A general rule is that the cost of an employee will be at least 30 percent higher than the gross pay. In some states (such as California), it may be higher. Make sure you do the math and see whether hiring an employee will benefit your enterprise and perform functions that either increase sales or decrease expenses (or a combination of both) to a greater extent than the labor cost of having an employee.

These sections briefly discuss the labor costs that go above and beyond the mere costs of a salary or hourly wage. When you hire permanent employees, you open some significant doors that you shouldn't take lightly. You should seriously consider the decision and hold off hiring employees until you absolutely need to.

Identifying payroll taxes

As an employer, you're responsible for paying the payroll taxes for each employee you have. Payroll taxes come in several different forms, including the following:

- **Federal taxes:** The single biggest cost, above and beyond the gross pay that the employer pays the employee, is the employer's share of federal statutory taxes, including FICA (Social Security), Medicare, and FUTA (unemployment) taxes.

    FICA and Medicare taxes for the employer mirror those of the employee; 7.65 percent of gross pay (up to the level of $113,700 in 2013). In other words if you pay $50,000 in gross pay for the employee, then the employer will pay $3,825 ($50,000 times 7.65 percent) on top of that pay (and you, as the employer, are responsible for submitting both your portion and the employee's portion to the IRS during the tax year).

- **State and local taxes:** Every state and local jurisdiction is a little different. Some have high payroll taxes and some don't. Check with both the state's tax department and your tax person. Some state unemployment taxes are paid fully by employers while others are shared by both the employee and the employer.

Recognizing other employee-related costs

The associated cost to having an employee goes further than you may expect. In addition to the payroll taxes that I mention in the previous section, here is a laundry list of the most common mandatory costs related to having an employee:

✔ **Worker's compensation insurance:** This cost differs in every industry and is more prevalent in those industries with a higher degree of risk for occupational injury.

✔ **Reports:** There are indirect costs of having employees. Many businesses need to file various government reports that are filed annually, quarterly, and/or monthly with appropriate government agencies. Filing these reports cost time and effort. Your accountant may also charge you for doing so.

Costs not mandatory but usually covered by the employer include

✔ **Paid vacation:** When you have an employee, providing two weeks of paid vacation is standard practice.

✔ **Benefits, such as health care insurance:** The employer may share these costs with the employee.

✔ **Access to retirement plans, such as 401k:** To get and keep good employees, it's important to provide them access to ways to save and invest for their future.

Avoid hiring an employee until it's necessary and you have the cash flow to pay for the cost. For more information, speak to your accountant or refer to the resources such as the following:

✔ Inc. magazine (www.inc.com)

✔ Service Corps of Retired Executives (www.score.org)

✔ Small Business Administration (www.sba.gov)

Getting Your Hands on Money to Finance Your Business

At some point, your business may need financing to help pay for things, such as expansion. Maybe you're a home-based business that does mail order and the operation has grown to the point that you need warehousing for your growing inventory. You'll likely need financing. These sections explain some of your financing options for your business.

Eyeing the debt financing route

Debt financing refers to loans and other types of financing where money is loaned to you and your company that requires repayment. Debt financing can mean taking out a business loan from your local bank or borrowing in other ways to get the funds you need. Many micro-entrepreneurs borrow money from sources, ranging from credit cards to getting a second mortgage on their house. Of course you want to be careful because carrying debt and paying back loans can be difficult if you have cash flow problems.

To gain funding, an existing and operating business has an easier time gaining financing than one that is a start-up situation. Think about it from the lender's point of view. If you were the lender, which type of business would you give a loan to: a business that is currently operating and has customers or a business that is brand new and untested and has no customers yet?

Therefore, to increase your chances of success at qualifying for a loan (if you're a start-up situation), start your business immediately no matter how modestly. Then, consider getting the financing you want six months later. At that point, you aren't seeking start-up or seed money. At that point, you're technically seeking expansion financing, which is easier to get.

Here are some resources to help you understand and navigate the lending process:

- ✔ *10K Right Away:* This self-published book written by Scott Jordan (www.10krightaway.com) is a must-read with great financing pointers.

- ✔ *Get Your Business Funded:* This book written by Steven Strauss (John Wiley & Sons, Inc.) (www.wiley.com) provides solid guidance on funding strategies for your business.

- ✔ **Lending Tree:** At www.lendingtree.com, you have the opportunity to submit your funding needs and have various lenders compete to provide you with lending programs to meet your needs.

- ✔ **LinkedIn:** Business lenders and investors (and advisers) have their own groups at www.linkedin.com. This site provides you with contacts to inquire and help you with your funding needs.

- ✔ **Small Business Administration:** This site (www.sba.gov) has an amazing amount of resources for businesses seeking funding.

Trying equity financing

Equity financing refers to who is investing in your business and receiving some type of *equity* (or partial ownership) in your business. Many firms (such as venture capital firms) get involved in this type of funding because it can be lucrative if the business does well.

You as the owner need to give this type of funding serious consideration, because it can mean that you relinquish control of your business to some degree. Speak to an experienced business attorney about all the ramifications before you do this type of financing.

Here are some resources for equity financing, Refer to the resources in the previous section for guidance as well:

- ✔ **Funded:** This site (www.funded.com) is a network of investors and lenders that work with small businesses that need funding.

- ✔ **Gust:** This site (www.gust.com) lists more than 40,000 accredited investors.

- ✔ **Microventures:** This site (www.microventures.com) helps small business owners connect with a network of investors and lenders that can provide financing of up to $30,000.

- ✔ **On Deck:** This site (www.ondeckcapital.com) has insights about small business loans and business credit.

Considering joint ventures

You can also go the joint venture route with other firms to leverage your activities. A *joint venture* is when two or more people or organizations agree to launch a cooperative effort to accomplish an objective for mutual gain.

Always be open to joint ventures because they can work better than getting loans or giving away too much equity. Many entrepreneurs team up with others to make great sales. Find affiliates for your business (Chapter 11 is all about affiliate marketing).

Some entrepreneurs were able to successfully sell their products with a joint venture with mass media, such as QVC (www.qvc.com) and the Home Shopping Network (www.hsn.com). You can even read a book on the subject — *Make Millions Selling On QVC* by Nick Romer and published by John Wiley & Sons, Inc. (www.wiley.com).

Several active groups of entrepreneurs and investors are on LinkedIn (www. linkedin.com). In addition, here are some active groups on LinkedIn to help you find creative ideas for financing your venture (or seeking joint ventures):

- ✔ Joint Venture Bank
- ✔ Second Bounce: Web Entrepreneurs and Investors
- ✔ On Start-Ups: Community of Entrepreneurs
- ✔ New groups form all the time on LinkedIn, so regularly do a group search.

Going public

You may even consider taking your micro-entrepreneurial enterprise and going public with it. *Going public* is the process of turning a private company into a public company that the investing public can buy shares to profit in the venture (like stocks that are purchased on Wall Street). It's also known as doing an *initial public offering (IPO)*.

How cool it would be for me to see your business jump from this book (on micro-entrepreneurship) to my other book (*Stock Investing For Dummies*)! Every major business that you can think of, from IBM, Amazon, Google, and Apple to General Electric, Proctor & Gamble, Exxon, and so many others all started as micro-entrepreneurial enterprises. Look at Hewlett Packard, for example. It literally started as two guys tinkering in their garage. As they created their technology products and grew their business from a two-man operation to becoming a larger enterprise with employees, they went public. An investment banking firm helped them create an IPO, and they became a public company where anyone could buy their stock.

Now, it doesn't just mean that you find an investment banker and a team of lawyers and accountants, get an IPO issued, sell stock, and become a millionaire (when you tally all of your shares at whatever the stock price is on the day it starts to trade in the stock market). Your potential wealth can come in a variety of ways. You can still run the enterprise as a Chief Executive Officer (CEO) and essentially become the top employee of the firm (but you would have to answer to a board of directors, which oversee the company's general management and have decision-making power over you and the company).

Maybe you don't want to be a CEO. Instead, you could do what other entrepreneurs do. They sell the company and aren't formally involved in the company. Instead, they negotiate (as part of the sale) to become a well-paid consultant to the company's new management team.

A real-life hot example

You never know what the fruits of your labor can produce. Think of this true story.

Does the email program called `hotmail.com` sound familiar? Two guys (Sabeer Bhatia and Jack Smith) originally launched this micro-entrepreneurial enterprise in 1996. They were slaving away programming this free web-based email program. They didn't generate much income from it (it was actually losing money). However, they did sell it to Microsoft in 1997 for $400 million (nice!). This story teaches every micro-entrepreneur some valuable lessons.

✔ If you build an enterprise that has value to others, you can make a great deal of money when it zooms from the micro level to the macro level.

✔ Even if you don't make a fortune from generating revenue directly from the sale of products and services, you can still generate value and make your fortune in other ways.

Hotmail didn't generate much in the way of revenue in the early years when it was a micro-entrepreneurial enterprise, but it became a valuable acquisition for Microsoft, and it resulted in great wealth for the two partners.

For more information on going public, check out these sites:

✔ Going Public Information (www.goingpublicinformation.com)

✔ NASDAQ (www.nasdaq.com)

✔ Securities and Exchange Commission (www.sec.gov)

For more information on IPOs and stocks of all stripes, check out the book the latest version of my book, *Stock Investing For Dummies* (John Wiley & Sons, Inc.). You can find it at www.dummies.com.

Looking At Franchising and Dealerships

If your business has done well and it's a business model that can be copied and sold, then you may want to consider franchising or creating dealerships. You can grow your business and make more money going this route in many ways. These sections give you a quick glance at each option.

Franchising

A *franchise* (or *franchise dealership*) is a type of license that someone (the *franchiser*) gives someone access to a business's proprietary processes, knowledge, and trademarks so the franchisee can sell products and services under the business name. In this arrangement, you would be the franchiser that grants these rights.

In the franchise, the franchiser exerts a great deal of control in how the business is run. Everything is virtually run according to the franchiser, ranging from the type of accounting system to uniforms, suppliers, advertising, and so on.

In the same way many other entrepreneurs will take a single-location business and grow it to a multiple-location business. A micro-entrepreneur can go big by utilizing the franchising model. When you create a successful methodology for running a business, other entrepreneurs pay you (probably a large amount) to be a franchisee.

To find out more about franchising, head to these resources:

- American Association of Franchisees and Dealerships (www.aafd.org)
- Franchise Associations Directory (www.franchiseassociations.org)
- Franchise Direct (www.franchisedirect.com)
- International Franchise Association (www.franchise.org)

Independent dealership and service marks

An *independent dealership* (also called a *distributorship*) is a different animal. This type of arrangement is typical in the automotive retail industry. The biggest difference between a dealership and a franchise is the level of control involved by the franchiser (or company that sold the dealership). In a dealership, the entrepreneur that bought the dealership maintains a lot of independence and personal control.

In the automotive industry, for example, you may have a Ford dealership called Bob's Fords. The Ford Motor Company doesn't exert any control over how the business is run except for how they represent their cars. The Ford doesn't mandate that the dealer has to wear uniforms or adhere to a particular methodology.

Another good example is when some businesses service marks (SM) their model. A *service mark* is similar to a trademark, but it applies to a service and not a product. Say that you do a successful business that is in seminars and training. You can brand your business and sell it to other entrepreneurs. They pay you and you do this particular program your way. The entrepreneur that paid to be able to do your program your way is really only buying permission to do your program and the rules and regulations only apply to that particular program and nothing further.

For more information on service marks, go to the US Patent and Trademark Office site at www.uspto.gov.

Selling Your Business

The business that you started, nurtured, grew, and managed all these years is ready to give you one last profit — hopefully a windfall! As I have told people for nearly three decades, when you start a business, remember a very important point from day one: Your business is a product in and of itself.

Businesses are bought and sold everyday. Some businesses are very cheap to buy, whereas some will cost a fortune. When you're ready to sell your business, I certainly hope you sell it for a fortune — how sweet that would be! The main draw for people getting into business is to generate *current income* (or revenue), but don't forget *capital gain* (in this instance, the idea that you create value to sell at a great place later on).

Sometimes the best way to make a fortune in business is to package your business the right way and sell it. Making another six or seven figure from the sale of your business is a nice kicker.

If you're seriously contemplating selling your business, you've come to the right place. These sections can help you with the important points.

Figuring out what makes a business sell

If you have a business with a customer base, you can get a lot of money for it. Businesses being sold generally fall into two basic categories:

- Those that have customers
- Those that don't

Imagine that two businesses are being sold: Business A has a list of customers, and Business B is functioning, but it has no customers. Which will be sold for a lot more money? This may qualify for the "duh!" question of the day, but it's important to emphasize. Businesses that don't have customers are sold for next to nothing; some can't even be given away! But businesses with customers can be sold for a fortune.

Say that you were going to buy a business and make believe that the business you want to get into is hamburgers. Some people will buy a McDonald's franchise whereas others will spend a fraction of the amount to buy a hamburger joint. They bought a business to sell hamburgers, but the McDonald's franchise will be sold for millions whereas the generic hamburger stand could probably be up and running for next to nothing (comparatively speaking). Why?

When people buy a major franchise, they're also buying a built-in customer base that didn't come with the hamburger stand. Customers are already familiar with the big name brand; they've been presold. Yes, the buyers paid a steep price, but when they bought the franchise, they bought the company's marketing and reputation, too. In a nutshell, they bought the customers as well as the company.

Sticking to the steps to sell your biz

When the time comes to sell your business, here are the steps to keep in mind.

Step one: Put together your team

Selling a business (or buying one) can be a complex transaction that will need an accountant, an attorney, and maybe a broker (a business broker).

- **Accountant:** The accountant helps to prepare the financial data that your buyer will need to assess the financial condition of the business. The accountant prepares financial statements, such as a balance sheet (to show the assets and liabilities of the business), the income statement or profit and loss statement (P&L, for short) for the business, and any other necessary financial documents. In addition, the accountant helps you with any potential tax impact of the business (such as figuring out if you will have any tax on the gain from the sale of the business).

- **Attorney:** The attorney prepares all the legal documents for the transaction, such as the contract for the sale of the business.

- **Business broker:** A business broker can help you find a buyer. A business broker is similar to a real estate broker in that he or she can find a buyer and receive a commission, which is typically a percentage of the final purchase price of the business.

Step two: Determine why you're selling the business

If your decision is to sell your business, then any buyer will ask you why. Make sure you know. The most common reasons are as follows:

- ✔ Retirement
- ✔ Health reasons
- ✔ Partnership issues
- ✔ Moving on to new ventures.
- ✔ You simply don't have it in you to keep the enterprise running. Maybe you're tired of running it, bored, or are looking for a different routine.

If you're selling your business because it's no longer profitable, have a good explanation for the potential seller or take steps to make it profitable. After all, if the business can't show a profit, then it makes a sale more difficult. Confer with both your accountant and the business broker on strategies to make the business more attractive to buyers.

Step three: Time the sale

Selling your business isn't a decision that happens that morning after you have your breakfast. You should plan long before you actually put the "For Sale" sign on your front door. Some advisers tell you to plan at least a year before you decide to sell. This gives you enough lead time to prepare the business for an optimal sale. You can work on increasing the revenue, decreasing expenses, and preparing your business records for when you will need to show them to prospective buyers.

Step four: Determine the value of your business

Decide whether you will get paid for the full value of your business or whether the amount will fall short. Considering how long and hard you worked to build to your business, you should do what you can to figure out the full worth of your business (*business valuation*). Your accountant can help you with this step.

Step five: Prepare documents for the sale

Put together all the necessary documents (financial statements, tax returns, and so on). For income statements and tax returns, give three years' worth for the buyer to review with his or her advisers. Also provide information regarding any partners, suppliers, vendors, and such. You should provide a summary for business activities and your mission statement (refer to Chapter 2) so the buyer sees what kind of philosophy drove your business during that time.

The buyer of the business may also have documents. A buyer will commonly ask the seller to sign a *noncompete agreement* so that the seller doesn't re-enter the market with a new business in the same field as the buyer.

Step six: Market your business

If you're selling your business to a trusted buyer, such as a key employee or a family member, then selling or marketing your business isn't an issue. However, if you need to find a buyer, you can market your business your-self or get a business broker to help advertise that your business is for sale. In the same way a real estate broker can be of great assistance, a business broker is equally helpful (maybe more so because a business is more compli-cated than a house).

Although you only need a single buyer, keep in touch with all prospective buyers just in case a sale isn't consummated with the initial buyer. Find out if the buyer is qualified for financing or if you plan to help the buyer finance the transaction.

Sometimes you have a situation where the seller does financing and the buyer makes monthly payments to the seller. This arrangement can work out well if the seller is heading into retirement and needs that type of cash flow.

Step seven: Know what to do after the sale

After the sale is made, many entrepreneurs continue in a consulting capac-ity with the new owners to make sure the transition goes well. Find out if the buyer requests your assistance. In addition, discuss with your accountant how to handle the gain from the sale of the business in terms of federal, state, and local taxes. Some type of estimated tax payment may need to be done.

Looking for additional help for selling your business

These resources regularly cover the topic of selling (or buying a business) and related issues such as franchising, business succession, and so on:

- ✔ **All Business** (www.allbusiness.com)
- ✔ **Entrepreneur** (www.entrepreneur.com)
- ✔ **Inc. Magazine** (www.inc.com)
- ✔ **Small Business Administration** (www.sba.gov)

Looking at your enterprise's future when you can't continue

When you're no longer in a position to keep your business going, but you want it to continue, you need to make the necessary preparations. Look to see if you have people in your life (particularly family members) who can continue the business after you're out of the position, either due to retirement or even death.

For many businesses, the death of the entrepreneur means the death of the business, too. If your business becomes successful, make legal arrangements about who will succeed you so that your business can continue to operate for the benefit of your loved ones. For more information and guidance on business succession, speak to a business attorney who is experienced with business succession issues. The resources throughout this chapter (such as Inc. Magazine and the SBA for example) can also help you.

You may also want to check out *Business Succession Planning For Dummies* by Arnold Dahlke (John Wiley & Sons, Inc.). You can find it at www.dummies.com.

If you want specific sites on the Internet where businesses are bought and sold, check out these:

- **Biz Quest** (www.bizquest.com)
- **Biz Buy Sell** (www.bizbuysell.com)
- **Businesses for Sale** (www.businessesforsale.com)
- **BusinessBroker.Net** (www.businessbroker.net)
- **Business Opportunities Weblog** (www.business-opportunities.biz)

Chapter 21

Uncle Sam Comes Calling: Tax Issues for the Micro-Entrepreneur

In This Chapter

▶ Grasping the difference between profit and loss from a tax standpoint

▶ Knowing your tax obligations

▶ Getting tax benefits in your business

▶ Seeing how to set up your business

You just finished working hard to make your client happy, and getting paid sure feels great. Your family is proud of you, and one family member in particular is interested in your success — Uncle Sam.

Benjamin Franklin said that the only guarantees in life are "death and taxes"— and I choose to address the more complicated (and painful) one — taxes — in this chapter. In the event that you have a *net loss* (you don't have a profit) in your business, you generally don't have to deal with paying any taxes, at least on the federal level. If you have a net business loss, you generally don't pay state income taxes either, although some states exact a minimum tax regardless of any business net income or net loss. Therefore, check with your tax pro.

This chapter gives you a basic overview of taxes, including the different obligations and benefits you'll face as a micro-entrepreneur. In addition, I discuss how to set up your business so you'll know how to report your taxes.

Understanding Net Loss and Profit

To have a better grasp of what you pay (and don't pay) taxes on, you need to understand the concepts of net loss and net profit.

Take your total income and subtract your total expenses:

- ✔ **If you have a negative number, you have a net loss.** For example, if you have $10,000 in revenue (or sales or gross sales) and $12,000 in expenses (refer to the later section, "Recognizing the most common tax-deductible business expenses" for specifics), then you have a net loss of $2,000. This net loss usually goes against any other income you may be reporting (such as wages or bank interest) on your tax return and lowers your total gross income.

   Basically, this $2,000 loss becomes essentially tax deductible on your federal tax form because it acts to lower your overall total income. (You may have to pay a minimum state tax, depending on where you live; check with your tax professional.)

- ✔ **If you have a positive number, you have a net profit.** Every entrepreneur (micro or otherwise) needs to pay taxes on their net profits. For example, you have $10,000 in business revenue and expenses of $7,000. In this case, you have a net profit of $3,000, which is subject to income tax. In addition, other taxes, such as self-employment tax and (very likely) state income tax, may kick in. Consult with your tax professional about your particular situation.

Keeping Good Records

Being organized and keeping detailed records may sound simple, but doing so is important. Come time to report your business activity on your taxes, your record-keeping system will be invaluable. Maintaining good records can make tax preparation (or giving all the relevant information to your tax professional, if you don't actually file your own taxes) less stressful. If you don't keep good records, you'll be scrambling around, trying to locate all the important documents. In a worst-case scenario, you may end up not being able to find important documents, which means you can't take any deduction related to that record.

To maintain good records so tax preparation is less of a hassle, do the following:

✔ **Prepare a filing system.** Filing your receipts and statements are better done on a regular basis so you aren't playing catch-up at year's end. Finding receipts later can be difficult if you don't immediately put them in their proper file. Get manila file folders and consider color-coding. For example, get green manila folders for income, consulting, product sales, and so on. Get yellow or beige folders for expenses and create specific folders for office expenses, auto expenses, and so on. I also like to break up the expenses based on how the payment was made. For example, if I have an expense folder for parking expenses, I try to have several expense subfolders, one for parking — cash receipts and one for parking — credit card receipts. That means you can more easily match up when you get your credit card statements and your checking accounts statements.

✔ **Do your data entry at least weekly.** Before you file that receipt, enter it either in a spreadsheet (with columns for each expense category with subtotals) or use accounting software (such as QuickBooks). Doing so also comes in handy when you need to incorporate data from your checking and credit card accounts.

✔ **Always ask for a receipt.** Because more and more transactions are taking place online, receipts are quickly becoming more digital than paper. Keeping receipts will soon go from being a batch of disheveled manila folders and shoe boxes to maybe something as simple as a data CD or a flash drive (or a file folder on your computer's hard disk).

For paper receipts, find a filing system that you keep updated weekly and monthly. I like to use a scanner and scan the receipt so that I can easily store a copy and find it later on my computer. Just remember to do regular backups of your main hard drive where you keep your vital data and have a secondary drive to archive those important tax documents, receipts, and other important data.

✔ **Get advice from your tax professional.** Ultimately, the people who have to compile and prepare your financial statements and tax returns will give you guidance on what types of records they need and recommendations on how to keep and record various documents, such as receipts and statements. Because each business is different, there are different requirements for recordkeeping, and your tax professional can tell you what and how to keep your documents and files.

✔ **Hire an office organizer if it helps.** Office organizers are professionals that can help you set up an efficient system that works well with your personal style and business needs.

✔ **Wrap it up at year-end.** Move all of your records to a separate location for the year ended. Put the past year's records into a second file drawer and create folders for the current year in a location where you can easily find the most current documents and records.

In any case, be aware of the Internal Revenue Service's (IRS) backup documentation requirements and record-keeping guidelines. For more details on these guidelines, consult IRS Publication 583, "Starting a Business and Keeping Records" (found at www.irs.gov).

Being Aware of Certain Tax Obligations

If you make a net profit in your business, plan on paying taxes. A profitable home business certainly has obligations to be aware of. These sections explain the tax obligations you can expect to pay.

Dishing out federal income taxes

Well, someone has to pay for the federal deficit, right? When you generate a net profit in your business, it becomes a taxable event, and you have to pay a certain amount of federal tax, depending on the tax rate in which you fall. (Check with your tax professional for specifics on how much you may owe.) Fortunately, if you had a small profit, the income tax won't break you. In addition, other tax benefits kick in, which can help to shield or offset or even wipe out the potential federal income tax. (Check out the later section, "Identifying General Tax Benefits for Micro-Entrepreneurs" for more specifics.)

Say, for example that your net profit in your business was $15,000; it was your only income and you're single. The standard deduction for 2012 is $5,950 and the personal exemption amount is $3,800 (per person). Given that, your taxable income is $5,250 ($15,000 less $5,950 and $3,800). Because this taxable income is less than $8,700, you'll pay a federal income tax rate of 10 percent or $525 (10 percent times $5,250). In addition, you'll pay 15.30 percent (self-employment or SE tax) of that net income or $803 (by the way, half of that SE tax is tax-deductible as an adjustment to your gross income, but it's a tad more complicated, so I leave it out for now to keep this example simple). After all that, your total federal taxes to be paid are $1,328 ($525 plus $803). Don't forget that you also have state and local taxes, which are typically much lower, although some states don't have income taxes.

As a self-employed person, you won't have any taxes withheld from your paychecks. As a result, during the course of the year, you're required to submit estimated payments. In this preceding example, you should have sent those taxes (the $1,328 paid) in four estimated payments on the four estimated tax dates of the year (usually April 15, July 15, Oct 15, and Jan. 15, about two weeks after the end of that tax year). Form 1040-ES can help you estimate your taxes and provide coupons and the mailing instructions for sending in those payments.

You don't have to be precise when you estimate the taxes; the IRS gives you some leeway. You can send any taxes due of $1,000 or less by April 15 of the following year. (April 15, 2013 is the deadline for any taxes due for the tax year 2012, for example.) The IRS expects that you would have sent in at least 90 percent of your taxes due during the four estimated tax dates and the remaining amounts (if any) by April 15.

Handing over state and local taxes

State and local taxes are a little trickier. Some states have no income tax, and most cities don't have a local income tax. Most states have an income tax whereas some cities do have a local income tax. Some places have a tax just because you're a business. Some places have low taxes whereas others have high taxes. Because each state and municipality is unique, I suggest you work with a tax professional who is familiar with your state and local tax law. State taxes usually aren't more complicated than federal taxes, but it's easy to miss something.

Most states have an economic development agency (or similar-sounding agency) that encourages business development and attempts to make it as easy as possible to conduct business and deal with various state and local bureaucracies. The website www.usa.gov has a directory with direct links to the 50 state government websites plus the territories. In turn, these websites usually have links or contact information to counties and municipalities.

Submitting sales tax on products sold

Depending on what you offer and where your business is located, you may be liable for the collection and submission of sales taxes. Allow me to clarify: You (your business) don't pay the sales tax, but you're required to collect it and send it in to the sales tax authorities. Basically you become an unpaid sales tax collection agent, working on behalf of that particular taxing authority.

What is subject to sales tax? Typically, sales tax needs to be collected at the point of sale on goods that meet requirements for such a tax by that state or local municipality. Some goods aren't subject to sales tax, whereas others are. Many states have a sales tax on new goods and not on used goods. The rules vary greatly and across literally thousands of tax jurisdictions. In other words, check with the sales tax authority that covers your area and also talk with your tax professional.

As complicated as the rules may be, some changes may be coming. As I write this book, federal and state officials are working on a new sales tax system that will also include a sales tax on Internet transactions. These new developments may be months or years away, but you should keep alert. To keep abreast of developments, check with the following:

- ✔ **Professional associations:** They're usually among the first to find out about pending rules and taxes that affect businesses. Two organizations that would be among the first to see such changes on their radar screens are the National Mail Order Association (www.nmoa.org) and the Direct Marketing Association (www.the-dma.org).

- ✔ **Your tax professional or accountant:** He or she should also be aware of any pending changes.

Identifying General Tax Benefits for Micro-Entrepreneurs

As a general rule, expenses incurred on behalf of your business are tax-deductible. The IRS makes the general point that in order for an expense to be deductible, it must be "ordinary and necessary" for your business. Although there is some gray area here, you know your business as well as anyone else. Deciding where an expense is ordinary and necessary in your business shouldn't be a tough decision. Of course, if you aren't sure, then ask your tax person. These definitions may help:

- ✔ An *ordinary* expense is any expense that is common in a particular type of business. An ordinary expense for a trucking business, for example, is gasoline or highway tolls.

- ✔ A *necessary* expense is any expense necessary to operate a particular business. A necessary expense for a dentist, for example, is a license to practice dentistry.

In some cases, entrepreneurs in extraordinary cases have even asked the IRS directly and requested a letter confirming in advance as to the validity of the deduction.

The following sections walk you through the common deductions you can take as well as other possible deductions that your business can take during tax time.

Recognizing the most common tax-deductible business expenses

The following list of deductions is generally tax-deductible as business expenses, whether you're home-based or a small business located at the neighborhood shopping center or the office building downtown:

- Advertising and promotional costs
- Business conferences and educational programs
- Business publications (online and offline)
- Business-related tolls and parking expenses
- Business travel
- Business use of telephone and other communication devices
- Business use of auto
- Computer software and business-related applications
- Costs related to preparing business taxes
- Internet connection costs and related Internet expenses
- Miscellaneous business-related expenses
- Office supplies
- Payments to affiliates and resellers
- Payments to independent contractors
- Postage and shipping costs
- Professional fees
- Salaries, wages, and other compensation to employees
- Small tools and office equipment used for your business
- Supplies for creating arts and and crafts for resale purposes

Of course talk to your tax person about other possible deductible expenses. For more details on business expenses, go to IRS publication 535 ("Business Expenses"). For more details on special deductions, read on! *Special deductions* are those expenses that may need more documentation and proof than just a simple receipt.

Deducting home-office expenses

One of the most attractive deductions for home-based entrepreneurs is the home office deduction. Basically the *home-office deduction* allows you to deduct a portion of your home (whether you rent or own a house or condo) if you regularly and exclusively use it for your home business.

This deduction is easily worth thousands of dollars, so take a close look at it to see whether you qualify for it. The greatest advantage is that it allows you to make some of your business income tax-free income. I used to prepare taxes, and I was always surprised how many folks didn't take the deduction, either because they didn't know they could take it or they were discouraged by an overly conservative tax preparer.

Keep in mind that literally millions of legitimate home businesses can claim the home office deduction. The IRS even tells you how to do it! The full details are in IRS Publication 587 (Business Use of Your Home).

Can deducting a home office increase your chances of being audited by the IRS? Not necessarily. Literally millions of home businesses legitimately deduct a home office with no issues or problems with the IRS. Keep in mind that the audit rate for small businesses is usually higher than for filers who are W-2 employees anyway because the self-employed have a greater opportunity or temptation to under-report income or over-report deductions. In the case of home office deductions, the IRS is only apt to audit if it suspects abuse or impropriety. If, for example, you're home-based and you're deducting a whopping 80 percent of your living area as a home office deduction, then it certainly increases your chances of an audit.

Your best bet is to be honest and realistic about what is actually the space you're using for business purposes and carefully document it (such as taking good measurements and taking photos of the office). Some tax professionals actually advise clients to send in a photo of the home office area in the first year they're reporting the home office deduction and attaching the photo with the tax return. Consult with your tax professional about your particular situation. Here's an example:

Say that you're a renter and you rent a four-room apartment with a monthly rent of $1,000. You use one of those rooms regularly and exclusively for your home business. Assume that you pay $150 per month in utilities. To complete this example and show you how the home office deduction works, I also assume that in this business your net income is $3,000 ($10,000 less $7,000 of regular, deductible business expenses). Keep in mind that for a home-based business, the home office deduction is calculated after regular income and expenses are calculated.

Follow these steps to see how the home office deduction works:

1. **Calculate the total annual rent.**

   In this example, the monthly rent is $1,000, so the total annual rent is $12,000 (12 × $1,000).

2. **Calculate the total annual utilities.**

   The monthly utility cost is $150, so the annual utilities cost $1,800.

3. **Combine the total annual rent and utilities expense.**

   Here the total for rent and utilities is $13,800 ($12,000 plus $1,800).

4. **Take the percentage of living space you use for your home office and multiply it with the total rent and utilities expense.**

   In this case, you use 25 percent of the living area for a home office (one room out of four rooms). Therefore your home office deduction is $3,450, which is $13,800 × 25 percent.

   In this example, assume that the rooms are generally equal. If the rooms aren't generally equal in size, you'll then have to measure the total square footage and deduct the business portion. Say that your total living area is 2,000 square feet and the portion that you use regularly and exclusively for your home-based business is 600 square feet. In that case, the deductible percentage is 30 percent. In other words, you can deduct 30 percent of the rent, utilities, and other expenses that affect the total living area.

5. **Subtract the home office deduction from the net income.**

   Here the net income was $3,000, so $3,000 – $3,450 offsets the business income. As a result, your net taxable income from your business is zero.

   Keep in mind that the $3,000 of business income is cash in your pocket, and the home office deduction of $3,450 made it tax-free. Whether or not you had the home business, you still had to pay the rent and utilities, but now that you have a home business, that home office deduction becomes a powerful tax benefit.

   You used only $3,000 of the total home office deduction of $3,450. Unfortunately you can't use that $450 portion to give you a tax loss. However, you can carry it forward to be used in a later year.

Keep in mind that home office expenses fall into three basic categories:

✔ **Fully deductible:** If you have an expense that *only* benefits the home office, then you can deduct 100 percent of that expense. For example, say that you paid $150 to paint only the area that is used regularly and exclusively for your home business. In that case, the full $150 is deductible as a home office expense (on Form 8829 it's referred to as a *direct expense*).

✔ **Partially deductible:** This type of expense is when an expense benefits the entire living area and partially benefits your home office. Say that you're renting an apartment that is 3,000 square feet, the home office portion is 600 square feet, and you're painting the entire apartment with a painting bill of $1,000. In this case, only the portion of the painting bill that benefits the home office is deductible. Because 600 square feet is 20 percent of the total living area of 3,000 square feet, you can deduct 20 percent of the $1,000 painting bill or $200 (on Form 8829 it's referred to as an *indirect expense*).

✔ **Nondeductible expense:** This type of expense benefits your personal living area but doesn't benefit your home office. Say that your home office is in the basement, but you spend $900 to re-do the upstairs bathroom. In that case, none of the $900 is deductible as a home office expense. For more details, see IRS Publication 587.

Focusing on depreciation of assets

Now depreciation doesn't sound like an exciting word but when it comes to taxes, I am sure that you will appreciate it. Regular expenses (such as office supplies and business meals) are deducted (or written off) when they're paid or incurred. You spend $150 for, say, advertising during 2012, and then you write off the full $150. But what happens when you buy an asset for your business that costs $5,000 and can be used over a period of, say five years? How do you deduct that type of cost?

In this case, you write off the cost of the business asset over five years. The more technical term is *depreciation.* If you purchase something for $5,000, such as a used truck for delivery, you depreciate (or take a deduction for depreciation expense) the cost of the business asset and you deduct $1,000 per year over the five-year period. Think of it as deducting it on an installment plan where you write off a portion of it for five years until you deduct the full amount. Depreciation works this way because a business asset typically isn't used up in a single period (such as a year) — it is used up through wear and tear over multiple years.

Business assets are in different categories and can be deducted over these different periods of time:

✔ Three years, such as computer equipment

✔ Five years, such a cars and small trucks

✔ Longer periods of time, such as factory equipment or business real estate

Check out IRS Publication 946 for more information. I also suggest you discuss the topic in greater depth with your tax professional about what you can and can't depreciate and how you do so for the maximum tax benefit in your particular situation.

Dealing with inventory and goods for resale

When you're making creative things like arts and crafts or buying products for resale, you've entered the world of inventory. This type of expense is in its own category because it's also considered an asset that you own and has future value (when you sell it).

For example, you sell widgets (a perennial favorite). You bought 100 of them at $5 (wholesale price) per individual unit for a total cost of $500. Say that their retail price is $19 (hmmm, nice mark-up) and you sell half of them (50 units). You need to know how to handle this situation for tax reporting.

You basically have two options for reporting the sold items and the remaining inventory:

- ✔ You can write off half of your purchase. This amount would be $250 (half of your total items, 50 × $5), which is referred to as *cost of goods sold (COGS)*. COGS is treated like an expense in your profit and loss statement. It's also a deductible expense on your taxes.

- ✔ You enter the remaining half that didn't sell as inventory. *Inventory* is an asset that you have on hand.

For tax purposes, you can find some basic information on COGS in IRS Publication 334 **Tax Guide for Small Business.**

Eating and entertaining on the job

Business meals and entertainment are another special category of expenses. When you meet for a business purpose with folks like prospects, clients, vendors, and so on, the cost of that meal and/or entertainment is usually tax-deductible with a 50-percent limit on how much you can actually deduct on your taxes.

Say you're meeting with someone who is a potential client to discuss business during a meal. If that meal is $90, then the amount you can deduct is 50 percent, or $45.

Keep reading for more specific information you need to know before you can start deducting meals and entertainment.

Documenting a business meal

Just having a receipt isn't enough. A receipt by itself doesn't indicate that a meal is tax-deductible because everyone also has personal meals that aren't deductible. A receipt simply proves that a meal took place. To make it a business meal, you should attach more information to each receipt, such as:

- ✔ With whom did you meet and what was that individual's status at the time of the meal? (For example, was the person a sales prospect, client, partner, vendor, supplier, and so on?)

- ✔ What business did you discuss? (For example, did you discuss marketing your product or service, meeting an existing client, and so on?)

You can read more details on business meals and entertainment and how to document them in IRS Publication 463 **Travel and Entertainment Expenses.**

Looking at local meals versus travel meals

You also need to know a bit more about the business meals when looking to deduct them on your taxes. Business meals fall into one of two basic categories:

- ✔ **Local meals:** They're business meals you have in your local area and vicinity. Hence, you follow the documentation guidelines that I discuss in the prior section. After all, the IRS needs to know that the meal is a legitimate meal and not a birthday bash for your Uncle Serge from Bratislava.

- ✔ **Travel meals:** When you're on a business trip, the IRS considers meals in a slightly different manner. If you're on a business trip (meaning you're far from home to the extent that you need lodging or rest; you're too far away to conduct business in a single day), then the IRS accepts just a receipt, because the documentation for the entire trip should indicate the business purpose.

In fact, the IRS can allow the deduction even without a receipt if you opt to use what is referred to as the per diem method (*per diem* is Latin for "per day" or "each day"). In terms of deductible business travel expenses, per diem expenses refer to expenses you may take during each day of business travel. The IRS assumes that, for example, you'll have three meals while you're traveling on business trips. The IRS actually has a schedule for how much meals are estimated to cost at major cities across the country. You can also find more details on this method in Publication 463.

Putting money into a pension plan

No matter the type of business you're running from home, whether it's an arts-and-crafts business from your kitchen table or a multinational corporation stretching across the globe from your home office, you have real power to build wealth with your business. Even as a home-based business, you can set up a pension plan that has more power than a garden-variety Individual Retirement Account (IRA).

You can consider creating a Simplified Employee Pension Individual Retirement Arrangement (SEP-IRA). A small business can set this up and have the ability to sock away up to $50,000 (the 2012 limit) per year. You can have a SEP-IRA in addition to your own 401k. You may also want to look into other options, such as a Keogh plan and other pension plans.

This topic is very advanced for this book, but if you're interested in pursuing it to reduce your taxable income, I suggest you talk with your tax professional. I simply mention this option here to pique your curiosity and help you realize that even you, as a micro-entrepreneur, have things you can take advantage of either now or in the near future that can help build long-term wealth — all triggered by the positive decision to start your own business.

You can find out more about small business pension plans from the IRS by getting Publication 560 **Retirement Plans for Small Business** at www.irs.gov. The IRS also has a site on small business retirement plans called the IRS Retirement Plans Navigator, located at www.retirementplans.irs.gov.

Setting Up Your Business

How you set up your business will matter to you in terms of taxes, liability, and other legal and business issues. As I discuss in these sections, the type has different benefits and responsibilities, and tax laws can affect the net income and expenses. Therefore, discuss this topic thoroughly with a tax professional who is familiar with business entities and explore the pros and cons of each type of business set-up.

The simplest business structure . . . you!

Many people think that to go into business you'll need lots of paperwork and that you must register yourself as a corporation and jump through lots of hoops just to hang an "open for business" sign on your shingle. Not really!

As far as the IRS is concerned, you can be in business as long as you have a legal name, a tax ID number (like your Social Security number), and a serious desire — you're in like flint! (Just don't forget to pay the IRS its share when you start making some good profits; refer to the earlier section, "Being Aware of Certain Tax Obligations" for specifics.) Keep in mind that your name is a legal business title and your Social Security number is acceptable as a tax ID number for tax reporting purposes.

Under this status, you're a *sole proprietorship*, and you report this activity on Schedule C, which is attached to your Form 1040. Check out the later section, "Reporting Your Business Activities" for the different forms and schedules you may need to use.

The second-simplest business structure: Sole proprietorship (the DBA)

You may find that it makes a lot of sense to register a business name. At this point, you're still a sole proprietor. But with a business name, you can do more. *Registering a business name* is also called *registering a DBA*, which stands for *doing business as*. (It's also referred to as *filing a fictitious name certificate or registration*.) You can use the DBA designation to claim a name for your business so that you can conduct your entrepreneurial activities.

Some micro-entrepreneurs choose to go the DBA route for a few reasons:

- **Some state or local jurisdictions may require it.** It just depends on the kind of business it is.

- **Some micro-entrepreneurs choose it because it's a marketing choice.** A DBA can help you in selling what you offer. For instance, using a DBA of "Gift Basket Ideas" when you're selling gift baskets ideally can bring you more customers (and make marketing easier) than if you go by your name of Irv Shlabotsky.

In addition, when you formalize your business name as a DBA, you can take that registration form to your bank and get a bank account so that you can accept payment (deposit checks and so on) with your business name.

You can do DBA registration at either the county level or the state level. You can call, go online, or visit in person the county government main office building or your state capital about registering. Of course doing a search on your search engine can also help.

If your state registers DBAs at the county level, then contact the county clerk's office. If DBAs are filed at the state level in your state, then contact the Secretary of State. Keep in mind that DBAs are kept in easily searchable databases either in their office or online at their website, so you can find out whether a business name is available.

The Small Business Administration (SBA) keeps track of all the states and their DBA filing requirements. You can find out more at www.sba.gov. In addition, if you get a DBA and then need a bank account, I recommend that you consider opening your new business checking account at a credit union because they usually charge less, yet still have some of the basic services a small business needs.

After you get your DBA, you should get a separate tax ID number for it as well. A *Tax ID number* is also referred to as a Taxpayer Identification Number (TIN) or Federal Employer Identification Number (FEIN). The Tax ID number is for businesses and other organizations, and it's effectively the same for organizations as the Social Security number is for individuals. The IRS issues tax ID numbers. You can get one with Form SS4 (you can download it and other forms at www.irs.gov).

LLCs, corporations, and partnerships

If you choose, you can also go with other more complex business structures in the form of Limited Liability Company (LLC), corporation, or partnership. Each can be great for a variety of factors, such as personal considerations, tax laws, liability concerns, and so on. However because doing these structures as a start-up individual working from home in your spare time may be too much of a deal for a micro-entrepreneur, I don't cover them at great depth.

The costs, paperwork, and filing requirements are extensive. In other words, the benefits at that point in your home-business career don't justify the costs and burdens you would have to undertake. You don't even know yet if your fledgling enterprise will be a long-term success yet.

If you have a few years under your belt as a micro-entrepreneur, you may want to talk to others, such as an accountant, business attorney, or other business adviser, about the pros and cons of incorporating (or going with an LLC). At that stage in your business, going one of these routes may be a better option when you see your business growing and showing sales profits. In other words, these business structures become valuable when you see a clear path to becoming a macro-entrepreneur.

If you want additional information, you can check out Service Corps of Retired Executives' website (www.score.org) to find thousands of business folks who can act as a mentor for your budding start-up. Consider contacting the organization and asking to speak in person (or chatting online) with a retired CPA or business attorney. The people you talk with won't give you tax or legal advice, but they can answer questions about the pros and cons of various types of business structures.

Reporting Your Business Activities

After you have done your business all year round and have done a good job of record-keeping (refer to the earlier section, "Keeping Good Records" for more information), you have to actually do your taxes. I suggest that you do so long before the April 15 deadline to give you plenty of time.

Basically, you report your business activities (income, expenses, and the net gain/loss) on Schedule C, which you then attach to your personal Form 1040 for that tax year. (Taxpayers who need to file a Schedule C must use the long Form 1040.) If you're unable to meet the April 15 deadline, you can file an extension (file Form 4868 by April 15) to get an additional six months of time to prepare and send your taxes (the extended deadline would be October 15).

On Schedule C, you generally report the following:

✔ Your income

✔ Your business expenses

✔ The net income (or loss)

The net income (or loss) number carries over to page 1 of Form 1040. You combine that amount with any other net income (or loss) listed on your 1040, such as employee W-2 income, interest, dividends, and so on.

If you report a business net loss on your Schedule C, that loss isn't taxable on the federal level, and it would ultimately lower your total income and subsequently lower your taxes.

The amount you paid during the year in tax payments (or payroll tax withholding amounts) would either mean a lower tax or a greater refund. Your tax professional can help you figure out the specifics.

As the year progresses and you see that you'll have a profit, check to see whether you need to make estimated payments of your federal and state taxes. Consult with your tax professional about doing so. If, for example, you see that your total federal taxes will be $4,000 for the year and your state taxes will be $600, then you may need to send in quarterly amounts during the course of the tax year.

For the federal taxes (in this example, $4,000), you may need to send in four payments of $1,000 during the four estimated tax payment dates (usually April 15, July 15, October 15, and January 15, which is about two weeks after the end of the tax year). For the state taxes, you may need to send in $150 four times and typically on the same dates. For more details on estimated taxes, see the IRS form 1040-ES and also consult with your tax professional (the earlier the better, so you can estimate and plan your payment amounts properly).

In addition to Form 1040 and Schedule C, you may need to include one or more of these other forms with your 1040, depending on what happened in your business:

- **Schedule SE:** In the event that you have net business income, you may need to submit Social Security taxes. This form reports that tax; the amount due would need to be paid with your Form 1040.

- **Form 8829:** If you run a home-based business and you have legitimate home business expenses, you can report them on this form. The total amount then carries over to Schedule C and is included with your tax return.

- **Form 4562:** If you have claimed any depreciation (and/or amortization; check with your tax professional), then include this form. The net amount you're taking for that particular year carries over to Schedule C, and the form is included with your tax return.

You may need other forms, depending on your tax situation. Review Form 1040 and Schedule C to see whether you need any other forms, based on a particular line item.

To get professional assistance in preparing your taxes without the higher fees of a CPA, consider using an enrolled agent. An enrolled agent (EA) is a federally licensed tax practitioner who specializes in taxes and has the right to represent taxpayers before the IRS. You can find out more at www.naea.org.

Additional resources to help you with your taxes

This chapter only scratches the surface with tax issues, but it gives you the basics you need to know. If you want additional information, you can check out the following resources. Don't try to cram it all in; taxes have been known to cause mental breakdowns and alcoholic binges, so take your time. You have all year to get familiar with the topic.

Here are some IRS tax resources that can help you that you can easily download at www.irs.gov:

✔ **Publication 17**: It gives you a nice overview of Form 1040 and includes references to Schedule C as well.

✔ **Publication 334**: It's the IRS small business tax guide.

✔ **Publication 583**: This publication is for taxpayers starting a business. It also includes information on record-keeping and getting a Tax ID number.

✔ **Publication 587**: It guides you in how to set up your home office and how to take the home office deduction. It also includes information on Form 8829.

✔ **Publication 463**: It helps you understand travel and entertainment deductions as well as auto expenses and business gifts.

✔ **Publication 535**: It covers the general world of business expenses.

✔ **Publication 946**: This publication is all about depreciation and amortization. (Gee, can I wait for the movie?)

In addition, these websites provide more valuable information about tax issues:

✔ Tax Mama (www.taxmama.com)

✔ J.K. Lasser (www.jklasser.com)

✔ Top Tax Sites (www.toptaxsites.com)

Part V

the
part of
tens

In this part . . .

- ✔ Identify and avoid ten pitfalls that beginning micro-entrepreneurs often face.

- ✔ Make money quickly.

- ✔ Know how to market what you have to offer.

- ✔ Enjoy an additional Micro-Entrepreneurship Part of Tens chapter online at www.dummies.com.

Chapter 22

Ten Beginning Micro-Entrepreneur Pitfalls (and How to Avoid 'em)

In This Chapter

▶ Taking steps to reduce your risk

▶ Balancing risk against return

When you're starting a micro-entrepreneur enterprise, inexperience can be a stumbling block. It's sort of like cooking — you can't create a great meal until you cook, but if you don't know how to cook, you have to try. Fortunately for beginners, you can draw from the deep well of experience from those individuals who have been there, done that. This chapter includes ten pitfalls that beginners often make that can diminish your success and ways to avoid them.

Failing to Understand Yourself

Before you spend time, money, effort, and energy on launching a business, you first need to spend some quality time on figuring out who you are. I have seen individuals start a business and then stop doing it — and then repeat the process. They tried one business idea after another and subsequently abandoned the same idea they were previously excited about. They may end up blaming "bad luck" or some other factor.

If they had just taken the time to discover the businessperson in them, before trying to figure out their business, they may have been more successful. Check out Chapter 3 for how you find out exactly who you are before you start any business.

Listening to the Marketplace

Before you begin your career as a micro-entrepreneur, make sure that the size and scope of your marketplace and the profit opportunities within it aren't micro. In other words, you need to make sure that the market you're looking to succeed in is large enough to give you the income that you seek. Some markets are tiny and there are too few buyers, whereas some are large and have many buyers.

Even if you choose to do something that you like to do (the enjoyment point I make throughout this book), what completes the picture is how readily the marketplace accepts what you offer (product, service, and so on). In other words, you want to also check to see whether your market will enjoy what you're offering.

 Don't just investigate the quality of the market; you also need to consider its size. If you plan to offer a product or service and envision that your enterprise will grow enough to give you a full-time income, you want to ensure that your market is big enough to sustain such an income. To find out more about how to do market research, check out Chapter 13.

Checking What Others Do

Keep an eye open on what other micro-entrepreneurs are already doing when you're considering your plans. If you want to set up a blog as your enterprise, for example, I highly recommend that you visit many successful blogs to see how they do what they do.

 Ask yourself such questions as what they do, how they do it, how they pitch their offering, whether they make it interactive for visitors and guests, and whether you can pick up any marketing tips simply by watching their efforts to make money. For home businesses and micro-entrepreneurs, you live in a time when you don't have to re-invent the wheel. Other people have done much of the grunt work and guesswork if you just notice.

Acting without Planning

Every management book dating back to the Peloponnesian War (maybe earlier) has made this point. In my early days of being in my own business (circa 1981), which I started in my spare time, I made mistakes like every other start-up home-based business. To avoid those mistakes, do some planning before you act or make an important decision, which can save you some money and some aggravation.

Fortunately, you and I live in the Information Age. You can find loads of information to help you plan in the following locations:

- **The Internet:** You can find plenty of great websites for advice and information if you're starting your own business. Check out *Entrepreneur* magazine (www.entrepreneur.com), *Inc.* magazine (www.inc.com), and Small Biz Trends (www.smallbiztrends.com) for starters. I provide lots of websites throughout this book on both general and specific business issues and information.

- **The library:** Ask the reference librarian about business start-up resources and guidebooks. I regularly refer my readers and students to several resources, including the Encyclopedia of Associations by Gale Research (www.gale.cengage.com). Virtually every industry and business niche has an association, and most of them are listed there. You can find this extensive directory in the reference section of most well-stocked libraries.

- **Small Business Administration** (www.sba.gov): Whether you visit the SBA in person or on its website, the SBA has multiple resources for better planning for your small business. The SBA also works with the Service Corps of Retired Executives (SCORE; www.score.org), which has many retired business folks that give free advice to startup businesses.

The SBA also has business start-up kits that include checklists and sample business plans. These kits usually include full information on what licenses and permits you may need. Find out more about business plans in Chapter 2.

Getting Educated

Being in the Information Age gives you a great advantage compared to your predecessors. Accessing free or low-cost education for almost any business task or function has never been easier. Type "how to start a business" (or any variation of that phrase) into your favorite search engine, and you may be surprised what pops up.

Take any simple function (such as "create a webpage," "do a cold call," or "how to do a press release") and put the description into YouTube or at active tutorial sites such as www.good-tutorials.com and/or www.videojug.com. You can also use great "how-to" articles at places such as www.about.com and www.ehow.com.

Sometimes you can easily find the things you need to know from the preceding resources (and so many found through the book — and this book itself!). You don't have to know everything, but it's good to be familiar or as proficient as possible at those tasks necessary for your business success. In addition, it's good to know what tasks you can't do or prefer not to do and get others to help you if needed (you can outsource these tasks; refer to Chapter 19 for more information).

Spending Too Much Money

Too many times beginning micro-entrepreneurs spend money on needless services and products when they could have gotten by on so much less. Keep in mind that every dollar you spend means that you have to make back that dollar by putting the pressure on yourself to sell. Many beginners (and even some people who have been around for a while) spend to the point that they have little left for what really matters, such as advertising and technical support. Tracking your expenses and managing your cash flow should be a primary concern in the beginning because you don't yet have the budget of a Fortune 500 company. Get some good accounting software, perhaps even the services of a bookkeeper or accountant.

In the beginning of any enterprise (especially if it's home-based), keep down your costs. The more you do with *sweat equity* (putting in the time and effort to build value in your business) and other ways to conserve money, the more *working capital* (the amount of money you have after you have paid current bills, which is available for business use) you'll have and the better off you'll be.

Sticking to One Specialty

Because hopping from one thing to another is easy, you may be tempted to try to do many things or sell many different things to hopefully increase the chance of success. Unfortunately, doing so is more harmful, especially in the early going. When I think of all the successful small businesses that I have worked with — even down to those one-person operations that worked from their kitchen table — they all had one thing in common: They specialized.

Making sure you know everything about one product, service, or theme has been the ongoing of success for home businesses. For instance, if you're selling books, then stick to books until you make the venture profitable. You can expand later (as long as what you expand into has a logical connection to your original specialty). Keep focused on what you're good at and what will be the most profitable use of your time. For other tasks and those things that you may not be that good at, you can always get assistance from others. If you don't have people that you trust to help you, consider outsourcing (see Chapter 19 for details).

Failing to Rinse and Repeat

Success is oftentimes difficult to achieve and maintain. So after you have a successful moment in your business — your first sale or gaining your first client — think of the process that you undertook to realize that small (and very significant!) successful step. Try to repeat the process and gain the second sale and/or gain another client.

Sometimes hopeful micro-entrepreneurs don't see the success in an approach because it seemed small, so they don't build on that initial success — either by accident or on purpose. Make sure you don't make this same mistake. Look at each success as a breakthrough event to build on. The most successful entrepreneurs learn from their successes and keep repeating and building on them while others give up too soon. Don't get discouraged if you don't have huge success in the beginning . . . keep persevering.

Paying Attention to What Your Customers Tell You

Making your first sale or getting your first customer is indeed a great feat. Getting someone to voluntarily part with his money and give it to you for something that you're offering is significant, especially if it's your first time. I have been in business, either part-time or full-time, since 1981, but I still get a thrill when someone buys something that I offer. No matter how long you've been in business, make sure you pay attention to your customers and what they directly or indirectly tell you and figure out the reason why they bought something from you in the first place.

 Don't be bashful about asking after the sale why your customer made the purchase. You want to find out from actual buyers why they decided to buy something from you. Sometimes a single reason or buyer insight can help tremendously in your succeeding again. Maybe the buyer decided that he bought because the color was good or that the money back guarantee you offered gave him the confidence to buy. You can then highlight these selling points in your next ads. Sometimes buyers may give you reasons or points that you may not have even considered. The only way to find out is to ask.

In addition, those individuals that don't buy from you can offer valuable insights. If they didn't buy because the product was only one size or if the service you offered was too expensive, then you can adapt as you change and improve your approach. In this instance, having more than one size or different levels of service to provide buyers with choices that take into account affordability can help boost sales.

Anticipating Legal Issues

I recall a budding entrepreneur many years ago doing something that sounded quite interesting. Being a nimble fellow, he bought and registered domain names of major companies and then proceeded to contact them to offer the domain name for sale. He was hoping to make some big bucks, but he was not aware of intellectual property law when he did. He came to the United States from India and just wasn't aware, and he acted in a manner that he thought was not improper.

The companies sued, and he was in hot water. You can take an important lesson here: Make sure you check out the legality of what you plan to do. It may not be as profound a mistake, but it can be something else, such as not having a license when you need one or failing to get legal advice on an agreement. Today's world has lots of rules, regulations, and protocol. Always double-check issues of legality before you act on your plans.

For legal issues and concerns, seek an attorney (websites such as www.find law.com and www.attorneyfind.com can help). If your issue is something simple, such as whether you need a license or a permit, contact the Secretary of State in your state (the Small Business Administration can also help you find the government offices that issue licenses and permits in you state). On tax issues, find out more in Chapter 21.

Chapter 23

Ten (Plus One) Ways to Make Money Quickly

Sometimes you need some cash in a hurry or as soon as you can get it. Where do you start? I can show you dozens of different ways to make money, but to help you keep focused, this chapter identifies ten (okay, actually 11) proven ways to make money without going nuts.

Although I mention these sites, I remind you that these websites are only examples, and you can find many similar sites to duplicate or multiply your success. Just know that these sites are the ones I consider the best.

Use this chapter to truly grow your income using your time, effort, and creativity. If you use one or more of the following sites in this chapter to make money, such as eBay, then don't stop there. Go to a site like More of It (www.moreofit.com) or Similar Sites (www.similarsites.com) and type in the site's search field the website name in question (in this example, type www.ebay.com). Then hit "click," and the site will bring up lots of sites that are similar to what you entered. If you entered www.ebay.com, then many sites just like eBay will come up. You can then head to those similar sites and make more money. You can find more sites in the other chapters too, so that you can continue to locate opportunities to make more money, market your business, or research your customers.

eBay

I may as well start with the obvious. eBay (www.ebay.com) is still a selling powerhouse and the first place to turn when you want to get rid of stuff and get cash for it. It's indeed the "world's biggest garage sale" so you may as well take your first look there.

As you peruse eBay, let it give you an idea of what you can sell. Your creativity can also help. As you look, ask yourself what you have that people are willing to pay for on eBay. The possibilities are endless. For instance, I saw one person selling advertising space . . . on his forehead! No, I don't recommend you do that, but it can help you open up to the possibilities. More importantly, check in your attic, closet, basement, garage, or under your bed behind the dust bunnies. Something must be collecting dust that instead could be collecting you cash.

To find out more, check out www.pages.ebay.com where you can find great tutorials on selling your stuff. You can find more details on auctions and other selling venues in Chapter 7.

Elance

If you can type, write good copy, design a webpage, or even sing opera while standing on your head (okay, maybe not the last skill), then you have services you can provide others and make some money at the same time. One of the most active sites for you to consider is Elance (www.elance.com).

Plenty of companies (big and small) need services. They may not have the money for regular employees or they just have a temporary need. Either way, you, as an independent contractor, can meet those needs. You can make money by helping them.

Plenty of folks use Elance for some part-time cash or even into full-time income. For more information on selling services sites, such as Elance and others, check out Chapter 8.

Clickbank

Clickbank (www.clickbank.com) may very well be the most successful digital mall on the Internet. Thousands of people sell digital products such as ebooks, audio programs, and other products that are typically informational in nature and downloadable. Clickbank is also the largest affiliate site. In other words, you can sign up on the site and be able to sell anything and get paid a commission from that particular vendor. (I'm an affiliate.)

For instance, I recall a moment when I wanted to make some affiliate money. I registered on the site and found a great product (it was a digital product that buyers could instantly download after they purchased it), and I sent off an email to my list of subscribers along with the link.

Some of the subscribers did click on the link, read the vendor's landing page, and bought the offering. About two weeks later I received a check for $178.19 (my first check from Clickbank). I received more checks later . . . all from the same campaign. How long did I work to get that money? About 15 minutes to set up and send the email.

Making money as an affiliate isn't difficult. Refer to Chapter 11 for more information.

Fiverr

At Fiverr (www.fiverr.com), you can make decent money . . . five bucks at a time. In fact, thousands of people are already doing so. Fiverr is considered a *small services mall,* which means it's an active marketplace of buyers and sellers of low-cost assignments or *micro jobs.* Fiverr also allows you to make money by offering *bulk gigs* (simultaneously offering multiple gigs). You will find even more ideas on making money with Fiverr at its official blog (http://blog.fiverr.com).

At Fiver, you'll be amazed what folks will do for $5 (actually $4 after Fiverr takes its portion). For example, they make a YouTube video, send a tweet to their 5,000 followers, or sing a song in a gorilla suit for a business. You don't have to do any of that (unless you really want to); search for something worth your while to make a few bucks.

Some folks have arranged the offerings they accept in such a way as to make it financially feasible to do these micro assignments. For example, one person automated his approach so that he could easily do hundreds of assignments and earn nearly $1,000 within a month (not bad!).

Don't just look at Fiverr for how you can make some money. Maybe Fiverr is more profitable to you to find folks to help you for those same few bucks. Maybe you need a task done in your business, such as writing an article or setting up a blog. For five bucks, why not? For more information on Fiverr (and similar sites), go to Chapter 19.

Etsy

If you're creative and can make something unique, then you need to check out Etsy (www.etsy.com). This site refers to itself as "the world's handmade marketplace."

Many people are very talented (you may be), and they can create some very nice things, ranging from making ornaments and jewelry to knitting hats and sweaters. If you can craft something of quality — something that is one of a kind — then you can sell it, and Etsy is the place for you. For more information on Etsy (and similar sites), go to Chapter 6.

About.com

You probably know something inside and out. Think about what you're an expert in and then consider writing about it and getting paid, such as on a site like about.com (www.about.com). Lots of places both online and offline will pay you for your writing. The site pays for well-written articles done by experts and others who know a subject in depth.

 You may not know much about writing, but you can locate lots of resources to help break into writing. Even if you don't have a computer, you can go to your local library and look at books on writing or read the latest issue of Writer's Digest for great tips and resources on the world of writing.

 Before you submit any articles for payment, head over to the website and read what articles have been published on your chosen topic. What better way to find out about what the site will accept than to see what it actually accepted from someone else. (You can find more about making money with writing in Chapter 9.)

Amazon

The quintessential Internet retailer, Amazon (www.amazon.com), is a great place for you to make money. You can earn some bucks in several ways on the site, including the following:

✔ **Reselling your items:** The most accessible way for beginners to utilize Amazon is to resell some of their items (that are in marketable condition). Books and DVDs are good items to sell because they've been sold successfully on Amazon for many years. They're generally easy to pack and ship, and Amazon even gives you a shipping credit. When the item is sold, the proceeds are submitted to your chosen bank account.

Amazon sells lots of stuff in many different categories so check out what you can sell. Find out more about selling your stuff in Chapter 7.

✔ **Being an affiliate:** Becoming an affiliate at Amazon is easy and free (at Amazon, an affiliate is called an *associate*). Go to `https://affiliate-program.amazon.com` for more details. Yes, I have also done activity as an Amazon associate. Check out Chapter 11 for more about affiliate programs.

✔ **Doing your own Kindle book:** You literally can write and upload a Kindle book for resale in less than a week. I authored the book *Job Hunter's Encyclopedia* and as a Kindle version and uploaded it to Amazon's Kindle category. Chapter 10 discusses self-publishing (using Kindle and other publishing strategies).

Gazelle

If you have some unused or unwanted electronics grazing, you can sell them for cash at Gazelle (`www.Gazelle.com`). Search for your item on Gazelle. If you find it there, that means Gazelle is interested in buying it.

You can answer a few questions on the site to inform Gazelle of the condition of your items. You also can report any accessories you have (such as a power cord and so on). After providing the information, the site will make you an offer. If you like the offer, you then click "checkout" and either see about another item to sell or proceed to ship the item (in most cases Gazelle pays the shipping cost). Using the site is super easy. If the item is above a certain price, Gazelle will even send you a free prepaid box for even easier shipping, so start hunting.

Items Wanted Classifieds

You probably remember the newspaper classifieds and how people scanned the help wanted section. The Internet has turned old-fashioned classifieds into a fertile venue for opportunities without getting all that newspaper ink on your fingers.

Many people and businesses either need help or a particular item. You may be the one to provide that service or to sell them that item. Consider sites such as Craigslist (`www.craigslist.com`) and Classified Ads (`www.classifiedads.com`). Refer to Chapter 7 for more information.

Cash in on the Real You

You may be surprised (or not) by the ways parts of you can make some bucks. Some folks are making some cash selling . . . themselves. That's right. With the Internet, making some money selling your hair, blood, sperm, or other parts of you is easier than ever. Just keep in mind that some things are illegal to sell in the United States (such as kidneys) but are legal elsewhere.

For instance, some types of human hair fetch up to $400. To find out more, check out sites, such as www.hairsite.com, www.spermbanker.com, and www.bloodbanker.com. Just don't sell yourself short.

Gigwalk

If you have a smart phone (or a similar electronic device with Internet access), and who doesn't these days, consider Gigwalk (www.gigwalk.com). Gigwalk is a service that connects businesses that need some simple work done with folks that have smart phones and can do the assignment (can you?). The assignments can be simple surveys or some consumer research. Some folks have made as much as $60 to 100 per day.

As smart phones (and devices such as tablets) grow in popularity and usage, you'll probably have more ways to make money. Another example is iPoll (www.ipoll.com) where you get paid to do some polls and surveys.

Index

Apple & Mac

iPad For Dummies,
5th Edition
978-1-118-49823-1

iPhone 5 For Dummies,
6th Edition
978-1-118-35201-4

MacBook For Dummies,
4th Edition
978-1-118-20920-2

OS X Mountain Lion
For Dummies
978-1-118-39418-2

Blogging & Social Media

Facebook For Dummies,
4th Edition
978-1-118-09562-1

Mom Blogging
For Dummies
978-1-118-03843-7

Pinterest For Dummies
978-1-118-32800-2

WordPress For Dummies,
5th Edition
978-1-118-38318-6

Business

Commodities For Dummies,
2nd Edition
978-1-118-01687-9

Investing For Dummies,
6th Edition
978-0-470-90545-6

Personal Finance
For Dummies,
7th Edition
978-1-118-11785-9

QuickBooks 2013
For Dummies
978-1-118-35641-8

Small Business Marketing Kit
For Dummies,
3rd Edition
978-1-118-31183-7

Careers

Job Interviews
For Dummies,
4th Edition
978-1-118-11290-8

Job Searching with
Social Media
For Dummies
978-0-470-93072-4

Personal Branding
For Dummies
978-1-118-11792-7

Resumes For Dummies,
6th Edition
978-0-470-87361-8

Success as a Mediator
For Dummies
978-1-118-07862-4

Diet & Nutrition

Belly Fat Diet For Dummies
978-1-118-34585-6

Eating Clean For Dummies
978-1-118-00013-7

Nutrition For Dummies,
5th Edition
978-0-470-93231-5

Digital Photography

Digital Photography
For Dummies,
7th Edition
978-1-118-09203-3

Digital SLR Cameras &
Photography For Dummies,
4th Edition
978-1-118-14489-3

Photoshop Elements 11
For Dummies
978-1-118-40821-6

Gardening

Herb Gardening
For Dummies,
2nd Edition
978-0-470-61778-6

Vegetable Gardening
For Dummies,
2nd Edition
978-0-470-49870-5

Health

Anti-Inflammation Diet
For Dummies
978-1-118-02381-5

Diabetes For Dummies,
3rd Edition
978-0-470-27086-8

Living Paleo For Dummies
978-1-118-29405-5

Hobbies

Beekeeping
For Dummies
978-0-470-43065-1

eBay For Dummies,
7th Edition
978-1-118-09806-6

Raising Chickens
For Dummies
978-0-470-46544-8

Wine For Dummies,
5th Edition
978-1-118-28872-6

Writing Young Adult Fiction
For Dummies
978-0-470-94954-2

Language &
Foreign Language

500 Spanish Verbs
For Dummies
978-1-118-02382-2

English Grammar
For Dummies,
2nd Edition
978-0-470-54664-2

French All-in One
For Dummies
978-1-118-22815-9

German Essentials
For Dummies
978-1-118-18422-6

Italian For Dummies
2nd Edition
978-1-118-00465-4

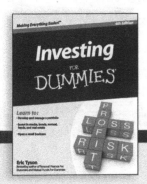
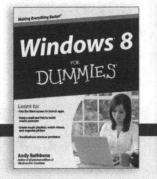

e Available in print and e-book formats.

Math & Science

Algebra I For Dummies,
2nd Edition
978-0-470-55964-2

Anatomy and Physiology
For Dummies,
2nd Edition
978-0-470-92326-9

Astronomy For Dummies,
3rd Edition
978-1-118-37697-3

Biology For Dummies,
2nd Edition
978-0-470-59875-7

Chemistry For Dummies,
2nd Edition
978-1-1180-0730-3

Pre-Algebra Essentials
For Dummies
978-0-470-61838-7

Microsoft Office

Excel 2013 For Dummies
978-1-118-51012-4

Office 2013 All-in-One
For Dummies
978-1-118-51636-2

PowerPoint 2013
For Dummies
978-1-118-50253-2

Word 2013 For Dummies
978-1-118-49123-2

Music

Blues Harmonica
For Dummies
978-1-118-25269-7

Guitar For Dummies,
3rd Edition
978-1-118-11554-1

iPod & iTunes
For Dummies,
10th Edition
978-1-118-50864-0

Programming

Android Application
Development For
Dummies, 2nd Edition
978-1-118-38710-8

iOS 6 Application
Development For Dummies
978-1-118-50880-0

Java For Dummies,
5th Edition
978-0-470-37173-2

Religion & Inspiration

The Bible For Dummies
978-0-7645-5296-0

Buddhism For Dummies,
2nd Edition
978-1-118-02379-2

Catholicism For Dummies,
2nd Edition
978-1-118-07778-8

Self-Help & Relationships

Bipolar Disorder
For Dummies,
2nd Edition
978-1-118-33882-7

Meditation For Dummies,
3rd Edition
978-1-118-29144-3

Seniors

Computers For Seniors
For Dummies,
3rd Edition
978-1-118-11553-4

iPad For Seniors
For Dummies,
5th Edition
978-1-118-49708-1

Social Security
For Dummies
978-1-118-20573-0

Smartphones & Tablets

Android Phones
For Dummies
978-1-118-16952-0

Kindle Fire HD
For Dummies
978-1-118-42223-6

NOOK HD For Dummies,
Portable Edition
978-1-118-39498-4

Surface For Dummies
978-1-118-49634-3

Test Prep

ACT For Dummies,
5th Edition
978-1-118-01259-8

ASVAB For Dummies,
3rd Edition
978-0-470-63760-9

GRE For Dummies,
7th Edition
978-0-470-88921-3

Officer Candidate Tests,
For Dummies
978-0-470-59876-4

Physician's Assistant Exam
For Dummies
978-1-118-11556-5

Series 7 Exam
For Dummies
978-0-470-09932-2

Windows 8

Windows 8 For Dummies
978-1-118-13461-0

Windows 8 For Dummies,
Book + DVD Bundle
978-1-118-27167-4

Windows 8 All-in-One
For Dummies
978-1-118-11920-4

e Available in print and e-book formats.

Printed in the USA
K060276SCI080817   01S29053000000002100